These Are Our Freedoms

NEW EDITION

By
Sister M. Perpetua, R.S.M.
Mary Synon, LL.D. and
Katherine Rankin

GINN AND COMPANY

BOSTON · NEW YORK · CHICAGO · ATLANTA

DALLAS · PALO ALTO · TORONTO · LONDON

Acknowledgments

Grateful acknowledgment is made to the following authors, publishers, and other holders of copyright for permission to use the following copyrighted materials:

Brandt & Brandt for "Western Wagons" and "Nancy Hanks," from *A Book of Americans*, published by Rinehart & Company, Inc., copyright 1933, by Rosemary and Stephen Vincent Benet; for "Listen to the People," from *Selected Works of Stephen Vincent Benet*, published by Rinehart & Company, Inc., copyright 1941, by Stephen Vincent Benet; and for "Renascence," from *Renascence and Other Poems*, published by Harper & Brothers, copyright 1912, 1940, by Edna St. Vincent Millay.

Doubleday & Company, Inc., for "To Two Little Sisters of the Poor," from *Candles That Burn*, by Aline Kilmer, copyright 1919, by Doubleday & Company, Inc.; for "Main Street," from *Main Street and Other Poems*, by Joyce Kilmer, copyright 1917, by Doubleday & Company, Inc.; and for "A Mystery of the Sea," adapted from *Master of the Girl Pat*, by Capt. Dod Orsborne, copyright 1949, by Dod Orsborne and Joe McCarthy, reprinted by permission of Doubleday & Company, Inc.

E. P. Dutton & Co., Inc., for "Kit Carson" and "Tall Men," from the book *I Sing the Pioneer*, by Arthur Guiterman, copyright 1926, by E. P. Dutton & Co., Inc., renewal, 1954, by Vida Linda Guiterman. Reprinted by permission of the publishers.

Harper & Brothers for "Treasure," from *The Adventures of Tom Sawyer*, by Mark Twain.

Little, Brown and Company for "Every Day Is Monday," from *I'm a Stranger Here Myself*, by Ogden Nash, copyright 1938, by Ogden Nash.

The Macmillan Company for "Emergency," from *All Over Town*, by Carol Ryrie Brink; and for "Adventure On," from *Poems, Complete Edition*, by John Masefield. The Macmillan Company and The Macmillan Company of Canada, Ltd., for "The Shell," from *Collected Poems*, by James Stephens.

Oxford University Press, Inc., for "Comanche," from the story of the same name in *Each in His Way*, by Alice Gall and Fleming Crew, copyright 1937, by Oxford University Press, Inc. Reprinted by permission.

The Viking Press, Inc., for "The Boy with the Bass Drum," from *The Bells of Bleecker Street*, by Valenti Angelo, copyright 1949, by Valenti Angelo; for "As Long as We Can," from *Blue Willow*, by Doris Gates, copyright 1940, by Doris Gates; for "The Doughnuts," from *Homer Price*, by Robert McCloskey, copyright 1943, by Robert McCloskey; and for "Love Letter to an Institution," from *The Love Letters of Phyllis McGinley*, copyright 1953, by Phyllis McGinley; originally published in *The New Yorker*. All reprinted by permission of The Viking Press, Inc., New York.

America for "Pioneer Sister," from *Mint by Night*, by Alfred Barrett, S. J.

2

Beckley-Cardy Company for "American Hill," by Frances Frost, from *The World Is Wide*.

Benziger Brothers, Inc., for "A River for Mary Immaculate," from *Mississippi's Blackrobe*, by Rev. Neil Boyton, S. J.

George T. Bye for "Independence Day," from *Farmer Boy*, by Laura Ingalls Wilder, published by Harper & Brothers. copyright 1953.

Chapman & Grimes, Inc., for "The Plainsmen," from *Sun and Saddle Leather*, by Badger Clark, copyright 1936, by Chapman & Grimes, Inc., Boston.

Curtis Brown, Ltd., and the author for "Skywriting," by Mary Maxtone, copyright 1947, by Janet Maxtone-Graham.

The Devin-Adair Company for "Epiphany," by Eileen Shanahan, from *New Irish Poets*, edited by Devin A. Garrity, published in 1948 by The Devin-Adair Company, New York, copyright 1948, by Devin-Adair.

Ginn and Company for "A Messenger for Liberty," from *Young Americans*, by Cornelia Meigs.

Harcourt, Brace and Company, Inc., for "Point Barrow," from *North to the Orient*, by Anne Morrow Lindbergh, copyright 1935, by Anne Morrow Lindbergh; for "Buffalo Dusk," from *Early Moon*, by Carl Sandburg, copyright 1930, by Harcourt, Brace and Company, Inc.; and for "A Child Looks Back," slightly abridged and adapted from *Abe Lincoln Grows Up*, by Carl Sandburg, copyright 1926, 1928, by Harcourt, Brace and Company, Inc., renewed by Carl Sandburg. All reprinted by permission of the publishers, Harcourt, Brace and Company, Inc. Harcourt, Brace and Company, Inc., and Faber and Faber, Ltd., for "Prelude I," from *Collected Poems, 1909–1935* by T. S. Eliot, copyright 1936, by Harcourt, Brace and Company, Inc., and reprinted with their permission.

The Horn Book, Inc., and the author for "A Prayer in Time of Need," by Marjorie Medary; The Horn Book, Inc., and Ginn and Company for "A Story of the South Seas," based upon Armstrong Sperry's Newbery Medal Acceptance Speech, reprinted in *Newbery Medal Books: 1922–1955*, and on the article about him in the same volume.

Houghton Mifflin Company for "Trades," by Amy Lowell; and for "How Pecos Bill Became a Cowboy," from *Pecos Bill*, by Leigh Peck.

Longmans, Green and Co., Inc., for "The Capture of the *Robert E. Lee*," from *Blockade Runner*, by Harold J. Heagney, copyright 1939.

G. P. Putnam's Sons for "Caught in a Blizzard," from *Boy Scout with Byrd*, by Paul Siple, copyright 1931.

Story Parade, Inc., for "Storm Flight," by Rutherford G. Montgomery, copyright 1939, by Story Parade, Inc. Reprinted by permission.

Sister M. Catharine Joseph, I.H.M., for "The Story of Margaret Haughery, the Bread Woman of New Orleans," based on the records of *The American Catholic Historical Society;* Betty Elise Davis for "The Doors That Tell a Story," originally published in *Child Life*, October, 1946; Louise Driscoll for her poem, "Hold Fast Your Dreams"; Daniel Henderson for "Hymn for a Household"; Isabel Garland Lord for "My Prairies," by Hamlin Garland; Mrs. Denis McCarthy for "The Land Where Hate Should Die," by Denis A. McCarthy; Sister Maryanna, O.P., for her poem, "To Mary Immaculate"; Hope Newell for "Steppin's First Public Appearance," from *Steppin and Family;* Kenneth Robinson for his poem, "American Laughter"; Dorothy Brown Thompson for her poem, "The City and the Trucks."

The pictures in this book are by Merrill Bent, Carlyle Browning, Cheslie D'Andrea, Bruce Howson, Will Huntington, Charles Kerins, Joel King, C. A. Murphy, Dale Nichols, Forrest Orr, Armstrong Sperry, and Cleveland Woodward.

3

Faith and Freedom

NIHIL OBSTAT: JAMES J. KORTENDICK, M.A., S.T.B., *Censor Deputatus*

IMPRIMATUR: † PATRICK A. O'BOYLE, D.D., *Archbishop of Washington*
Washington, November 2, 1958

COMMISSION ON

AMERICAN

CITIZENSHIP

THE CATHOLIC

UNIVERSITY

OF AMERICA

Rt. Rev. Msgr. William J. McDonald, *President of the Commission*

Rt. Rev. Msgr. Joseph A. Gorham, *Director*

Mary Synon, LL.D., *Editorial Consultant*

Sister Mary Lenore, O.P., *Curriculum Consultant*

Published for The Catholic University of America Press

Contents

1. Listen to the People

Freedom!

What does that word mean?

A ball game after dark? A ride to a hamburger stand? A summer at a camp?

Is that all?

It should mean more, a great deal more. Freedom is one of God's great gifts. Without freedom we could not have our American way of life.

The Constitution of the United States provides security for the American home. Even before the Constitution became the law of our nation men and women came from the old lands of Europe to build their homes in the New World. In these homes fathers and mothers and children lived in unity, loving one another, helping one another, growing with one another into noble standards of virtuous living. With their neighbors they shared the hope of a happy home in a free country. By their words and their work they made that hope come true. It was the American dream three hundred years ago. It is the American dream today.

SISTER MARYANNA, O.P.

To Mary Immaculate

PATRONESS of our loved land,
  Maiden Mother pure,
Guard thine own America
  From all harm secure.
Radiant with sanctity,
  Be thyself our light,
Guide our nation's destinies;
  Thou wilt lead aright.
By thy mystic crown of stars,
  By thy mantle's hue,
Keep our starry banner high,
  Help us to be true.
Let thy smile rest tenderly
  On our country's youth.
School their hearts in honor, faith,
  Purity, and truth.
Thou by God's foreshadowing
  Kept from sin-stain free,
Pray for us who have recourse,
  Virgin fair, to thee!

VALENTI ANGELO

The Boy with the Bass Drum

The war was over. The chimes from the Church of Our Lady of Pompeii echoed above Bleecker Street. Blackout sirens and automobile horns and factory whistles sent out shrill blasts. Shouts and cheers mingled with the sounds of the bells, whistles, and horns. Storekeepers on Bleecker Street were already placing the American flag over entryways to their shops. Men, women, and children hurried about, talking and gesticulating. Some wept. In front of the Church of Our Lady of Pompeii people were kneeling on the sidewalk and were praying. They cried aloud, "Thank God! Thank God! It's over. The war is over!"

No one on Bleecker Street was happier than Joey Enrico. Just yesterday a letter had come from his father, a sergeant with the United States Army in Italy. It was a sad letter. Joey's father was homesick, and he was saddened by the sight of hungry people and by the destruction of the beautiful Italian villages he had known when he was a boy. Now, with bells and whistles sounding news of peace, Joey knew that his father would soon be home.

Again the days and nights on Bleecker Street would be gay with song and laughter, with the happy cries of street vendors, with church festivals, with the sound of traps and drums in the music teacher's newly organized orchestra. The boys on Bleecker Street, thanks to Professor Dante who spared neither time nor effort, could now play trombone and French horn, clarinet and accordion, bass drum and violin.

LATER on that afternoon Professor Dante called a special meeting of the boys' orchestra. Assembled in his music studio, the boys listened to his plans.

"Father Bennino needs our help," he said. "There is to be a parade, starting from the Church of Our Lady of Pompeii, at eight o'clock tonight."

11

"A parade?" The boys perked up. They looked at one another, then waited with attention.

"The parade, as you probably know, is in honor of this memorable day. Father Bennino spoke to me about it early this afternoon. He thought it would be a splendid idea if all of you could take part. That is, sort of lead the parade with the orchestra. What do you think about it?"

"We think it's a swell idea! It's grand! It's wonderful! We'll be glad to do it," they chorused.

"It's sensational!" added Pete. "But how am I going to manage with all my drums?"

The boys laughed. Professor Dante tried to control his mirth. He was glad the boys had whole-heartedly accepted Father Bennino's idea. He turned his attention to Pete.

"You need only to beat time with your bass drum," he said.

Pete revolted. "What! No snare drum?" He looked at Professor Dante, and his round, freckled face went blank. "You know one drum can't do without the other." He made a gesture with his hand. "We've got to have a snare drum!"

Professor Dante smiled. This was not his first encounter with Pete's baffling temperament. He urged, "You'll only need to do it this one time, Peter."

"Ah, nuts!" said Pete.

Michael glared at his brother. "All right. Take it easy. You know well enough you can't play both your drums and walk at the same time."

But Pete hadn't heard a word his brother said. His mind was already busily engaged on a very, very brilliant idea all of his own.

At seven o'clock the street facing the Church of Our Lady of Pompeii was crowded with men, women, and children. Joey Enrico was so filled with excitement that he had hardly touched his dinner. Instead, he had gone to his room to practice on his violin. As he stood waiting for Pete, who had not yet arrived on the scene, he felt a slight disturbance in the region of his stomach. "I'll eat something after the parade is over," he thought.

Father Bennino hustled about assembling the boys and girls of his catechism classes four abreast. "Keep together as much as you can," he told them. Some of the older boys and girls carried banners, each bearing the picture of a saint. Many of the children held candles. Others carried flags.

Professor Dante arranged the boys of his orchestra two abreast. He placed David, who played the accordion, next to Larry, who played the clarinet. Chub and his trombone he placed beside Tony, who played the French horn. His eyes searched the crowd. "Where is Peter?"

"He isn't here yet," answered Michael. "My brother didn't even show up for dinner." He looked up and down the street. "Oh, he'll come. He said he would."

"Tell him to take his place at the rear of the orchestra," said Professor Dante. "And Michael?"

"Yes, Professor Dante?"

"You'd better march beside your brother."

"I'll be glad to do that."

"Joey? Where's Joey Enrico?"

"Here I am, Professor Dante."

"Father Bennino and his altar boys will lead the parade. You are to follow close behind them. It is important in this particular case that the violin lead the orchestra. Understand?"

"Oh, Professor Dante," said Joey, "I—I couldn't!"

"Never mind about that. We'll discuss the matter later." He looked over his orchestra, made sure each instrument was properly

tuned, and smiled. "Well, we're nearly ready to start."

Joey wondered what detained Pete. He looked up and down the line of participants. "Gee, it's a block long already." He saw Father Bennino, dressed in his black cassock. The priest carried a shiny silver staff. On its end a golden cross glittered against the glow of the street lamps.

The children were anxious for the parade to start. Their voices grew louder and louder.

Exactly at five minutes to eight the sound of a bass drum, accompanied by the rattle of a snare drum, was heard. The sound grew louder as it neared the Church of Our Lady of Pompeii.

"Here he comes," said Joey to Michael.

"Well, it's about time!" Michael replied with great relief. He looked and listened. When he saw his brother coming up the street, he gasped. Pete was standing behind two drums on a homemade platform, mounted on an old coaster wagon which was being pulled by two small boys.

For a time Joey was speechless. Then he burst into laughter at the sight of Pete. He laughed so hard he couldn't stop.

Professor Dante rushed forward. For a moment he was both amused and dumfounded at the sight before him. But he soon recovered and turned his head away.

Pete ceased beating his drums. He said, "Well, we finally got here." He laughed. "We had a heck of a time with this coaster. It wasn't wide enough. But after I found some boards to make this platform with, everything came out okay." He turned to the two companions who had pulled him along. Isn't that right?"

14

The two boys nodded their heads sheepishly. "That's right," they said, and swallowed hard.

Professor Dante had disappeared somewhere in the crowd. Joey thought, "He didn't look mad." Then he thought again, "Maybe he couldn't help laughing." He turned to Michael. "Your brother sure takes the cake!"

Michael was frantic. He called his brother aside. "What's the matter with you?" he said. "Whoever gave you the idea this parade was going to be a circus parade, huh?" He gritted his teeth angrily and made a pass at Pete. "Why'd you have to wear an outfit like that? Aren't you ashamed?"

"What's the matter with this outfit?" Pete retorted, challenge in his high-pitched voice. "It's all right. Just the thing. Aren't we celebrating the end of the war?" He pulled up the sleeves of his oversized Army coat. And while he brushed imaginary dust off the numerous medals pinned to it, he smiled and considered the matter ended.

The parade started, accompanied by the chimes of Our Lady of Pompeii and the music of the orchestra. Father Bennino, carrying the gold cross before him, led the procession. He led them across the Avenue of the Americas and down East Bleecker Street. Spectators lined the sidewalks. Men and boys took off their hats. Some bowed their heads. Some of the women knelt and crossed themselves. Boys and girls joined the parade. The orchestra played "America the Beautiful." Some of the children sang. The sound echoed and re-echoed over Greenwich Village.

At the start of the parade Joey had found it a little difficult to play his violin. But as he walked along it was no time at all before he fell into step with the slow movements of the marchers.

There were times when the music carried on without the aid of the drums, and Joey thought, "I guess Pete is having more than his share of trouble." Once during an intermission in the music Joey heard a very loud commotion. He turned to see Pete hurriedly gathering up his drums. Michael was so disturbed and angry he could hardly blow his trumpet. He promised himself revenge for his brother's latest stunt. "Seems to me the older he grows the less sense he gets," he muttered to himself.

The procession soon turned off Bleecker into Mott Street and

15

marched toward Old Saint Patrick's Church without further mishap. Joey knew this church to be one of the oldest in New York. He was not surprised to find a throng of people standing before it. He turned to Michael, who now seemed happier since he had securely tied his brother's bass drum to the coaster, in order to avoid further embarrassment. "Oh, gee, they're having a parade too," Joey said.

"They're all lined up and ready. Why don't they start? And look at Father Branigan. He's all dressed up in altar clothes."

Father Bennino steered his procession to one side of the street. When he reached the Irish priest, he stopped. The parade behind him stopped. He greeted Father Branigan with the sign of blessing.

Father Branigan's deep, mellow voice greeted the other. "Ah, dear Father Bennino! 'Tis a blessed day indeed. A blessed day to remember. A thankful day." He looked up at the figure on the crucifix, which he held in both his hands. Then his bright eyes searched those of Father Bennino.

"A day to give thanks indeed," Father Bennino replied. "And it is a fine parade you have there."

"And 'tis a grand parade you are leading," replied Father Branigan.

The two priests went on talking. The children waited. Father Branigan's parade consisted mostly of Irish boys and girls, but among them Joey could see the faces of many Chinese. He thought it a little strange at first. Then he recalled the words Father Bennino had once spoken in catechism class. "Protestant, Catholic, and Jew are praying and fighting, each for the same ideal." And that ideal, Joey knew, meant the road to freedom. His thoughts were interrupted by the voice of the Irish priest.

"But, Father Bennino," Father Branigan was saying, "it would give me great pleasure if you would lead both parades."

Father Bennino would have none of it. He objected firmly, "No, Father Branigan, it will give me great honor if you would be so kind as to lead the parade."

Joey listened, all ears. Much whispering went on among the boys and girls. The news spread quickly. "We're going to join parades," they said.

Pete, who stood waiting on the platform nailed to his coaster, stepped down and came forward. "Hey, what's holdin' up the parade? Why aren't we movin'? What's happened?" and he hitched up a pair of Army trousers twice his size.

"The two parades are going to march together," replied Joey. "Won't that be something!"

"Boy, I'll say!" Pete rushed back to his coaster. He mounted its platform and grabbed his drumsticks. With one foot on the bass-drum pedal, he waited anxiously for the parade to start. "I'll show those kids a thing or two," he said.

The loud, clanking sound of Saint Patrick's bells suddenly brought the crowd to attention. It was not until after the chimes from the Church of Our Lady of Pompeii joined the bells of Saint Patrick that the parade got under way.

Both Father Branigan and Father Bennino had reached the same conclusion. They had agreed to lead the procession together. As they walked slowly up Mott Street toward Bleecker, to the Church of Our Lady of Pompeii, their faces were bright with pious understanding. Joey thought of his father, Sergeant John Enrico of the United States Army in Italy. "Gee, I wish that Dad was here," he said.

Professor Dante, who walked beside the orchestra, was overcome with joy. Once or twice, when they passed over a stretch of cobblestones, he saved Pete from tumbling off his coaster. He spoke kindly. "Peter, my boy, the orchestra is playing 'Onward, Christian Soldiers.' Please do not beat your drums so fast. Remember, go slow, go slow."

That night as Joey lay in his bed he thought of the day's events. "It's been a wonderful day. The war is ended." He jumped out of bed. He took a letter he had received from his father out of the box where he kept all his father's letters. Sitting up in his bed, he reread a description of war-torn Italy. He thought, "Gee, it must be awful to be hungry. To have your house blown to pieces. To be

17

without a home and clothes." He looked around his room and at his numerous possessions. "I've got a radio all my own. I've got a violin, and a bed, and I've got a sister and mother and father." He gazed at a little plaster saint over his bed and thought further. "It must be terrible not to have a bed or a home, and no sister or mother or father." He folded up the letter. "I guess I'm very, very lucky. Those poor kids in Europe."

He sprang out of bed and knelt beside it. He prayed, "Dear Saint John, please don't let there ever be another war. Please don't. Maybe you already know about those kids over in Europe, the kids my father wrote to me about. They're hungry, and they haven't any clothes. It's awful. It must be terrible to be without clothes to wear. Please, don't let it happen again. The gang and I promised to send clothes to the boys and girls who need them."

His mother opened the door to his bedroom gently and peeked in. She said, "Joey, it's eleven o'clock. Please turn out your light and go to bed."

Joey finished his prayer with a hurried amen. He stood up. "All right, Ma," he said, and turned out the light over his cot. But he didn't go to sleep. He couldn't. He lay in his warm bed and listened. From the floor above him he heard Professor Dante playing softly on his piano. Joey whispered to himself, "He's playing Handel. It's the *Messiah*."

Understanding the Mood of a Story

1. What mood is established in the three introductory paragraphs of the story?

2. As the story concludes, what mood do we experience as we find Joey alone in his room?

3. In what ways are Joey and Pete alike and in what ways do they differ from each other?

4. Which of the two boys (Joey and Pete) did you like better? Why?

5. Did you ever march in a parade? How did you feel as you marched along in time with the music?

STEPHEN VINCENT BENÉT

Listen to the People

THIS is Independence Day,
Fourth of July, the day we mean to keep,
Whatever happens and whatever falls
Out of a sky grown strange;
This is firecracker day for sunburnt kids,
The day of the parade,
Slambanging down the street.
Listen to the parade!

There's J. K. Burney's float,
Red-white-and-blue crêpe paper on the wheels,
The Fire Department and the local Grange,
There are the pretty girls with their hair curled
Who represent the Thirteen Colonies,
The Spirit of East Greenwich, Betsy Ross,
Democracy, or just some pretty girls.
There are the veterans and the Legion Post
(Their feet are going to hurt when they get home),
The band, the flag, the band, the usual crowd,
Good-humored, watching, hot,
Silent a second as the flag goes by,
Kidding the local cop and eating popsicles,
Jack Brown and Rosie Shapiro and Dan Shay,
Paul Bunchick and the Greek who runs the Greek's,
The black-eyed children out of Sicily,
The girls who giggle and the boys who push,
All of them there and all of them a nation.
And, afterwards,
There'll be ice cream and fireworks and a speech,
And Tessie Jones, our honor graduate,

19

Will read the Declaration.
That's how it is. It's always been that way.
That's our Fourth of July, through war and peace,
That's our Fourth of July.

Frances Frost

American Hill

On the Fourth of July, we always go
Up to the hill where the brook runs slow,

Where Buffy and I can wade in the cool
And hemlock-shadowed speckled pool.

We picnic on the summer grass
And watch the slow cloud shadows pass

Like white majestic ships-of-line
Above the dark headlands of pine

While mother and dad tell us stories of
This great, strong country that we love.

And when at dusk we go back down
To the elm-shaded streets of town,

We all sing Yankee Doodle's song,
For we've been happy the whole day long

On our American hill reared high
Against our own American sky!

20

Independence Day

It was summer in northern New York State nearly one hundred years ago. Almanzo was eating breakfast before he remembered that this was the Fourth of July. He felt more cheerful.

It was like Sunday morning. After breakfast he scrubbed his face with soft soap till it shone, and he parted his wet hair and combed it sleekly down. He put on his gray woolen trousers and his shirt of French calico, and his vest and his short round coat.

Mother had made his new suit in the new style. The coat fastened at the throat with a little flap of the cloth, then the two sides slanted back to show his vest, and they rounded off just over his trousers' pockets.

He put on his round straw hat, which Mother had made of braided oat-straws, and he was all dressed up for Independence Day. He felt very fine.

Father's shining horses were hitched to the shining, red-wheeled buggy, and they all drove away in the warm sunshine. All the country had a holiday air. Nobody was working in the fields, and along the road the people in their Sunday clothes were driving to town.

Father's swift horses passed them all. They passed by wagons and carts and buggies. They passed gray horses and black horses and some dappled-gray horses. Almanzo waved his hat whenever he sailed past anyone he knew, and he would have been perfectly happy if only he had been driving that swift, beautiful team.

21

At the church sheds in Malone he helped Father unhitch. Mother and the girls hurried away. But Almanzo would rather help with the horses than do anything else. He couldn't drive them, but he could tie their halters and buckle on their blankets, and stroke their soft noses and give them hay.

Then he went out with Father and they walked on the crowded sidewalks. All the stores were closed, but ladies and gentlemen were walking up and down and talking. Little girls carried parasols, and all the boys were dressed up, like Almanzo. Flags were everywhere, and in the Square the band was playing "Yankee Doodle." The fifes tooted and the flutes shrilled and the drums came in with a rub-a-dub-dub.

Yankee Doodle went to town,
    Riding on a pony,
He stuck a feather in his hat,
    And called it macaroni!

Even grown-ups had to keep time to it. And there, in the corner of the Square, were the two brass cannons!

The Square was not really square. The railroad made it three-cornered. But everybody called it the Square, anyway. It was fenced, and grass grew there. Benches stood in rows on the grass, and people were filing between the benches and sitting down as they did in church.

Almanzo went with Father to one of the best front seats. All the important men stopped to shake hands with Father. The crowd kept coming till all the seats were full, and still there were people outside the fence.

The band stopped playing. Then the band tuned up again and everybody rose. Men and boys took off their hats. The band played, and everybody sang.

Oh, say can you see by the dawn's early light,
    What so proudly we hailed at the twilight's last gleaming,
Whose broad stripes and bright stars through the perilous night,
    O'er the ramparts we watched were so gallantly streaming?

From the top of the flagpole, up against the blue sky, the Stars and Stripes were fluttering. Everybody looked at the American flag, and Almanzo sang with all his might.

Then everyone sat down, and a Congressman stood up on the platform. Slowly and solemnly he read the Declaration of Independence.

"When in the course of human events it becomes necessary for one

22

people . . . to assume among the Powers of the earth, the separate and equal station. . . . We hold these truths to be self-evident, that all men are created equal. . . ."

Almanzo felt solemn and very proud.

Then two men made long political speeches. All the grown-ups listened hard, but Almanzo did not understand the speeches very well and he began to be hungry. He was glad when the band played again.

The music was so gay; the bandsmen in their blue and red and their brass buttons tootled merrily, and the fat drummer beat rat-a-tat-tat on the drum. All the flags were fluttering, and everybody was happy because they were free and independent and this was Independence Day. And it was time to eat dinner.

Almanzo helped Father feed the horses while Mother and the girls spread the picnic lunch on the grass in the churchyard. Many others were picnicking there, too, and after he had eaten all he could Almanzo went back to the Square.

There was a lemonade-stand by the hitching-posts. A man sold pink lemonade, a nickel a glass, and a crowd of the town boys were standing around him. Cousin Frank was there. Almanzo had a drink at the town pump, but Frank said he was going to buy lemonade. He had a nickel. He walked up to the stand and bought a glass of the pink lemonade and drank it slowly. He smacked his lips and rubbed his stomach and said, "Mmmm! Why don't you buy some?"

"Where'd you get the nickel?" Almanzo asked. He had never had a nickel. Father gave him a penny every Sunday to put in the collection-box in church; he had never had any other money.

"My father gave it to me," Frank bragged. "My father gives me a nickel every time I ask him."

"Well, so would my father if I asked him," said Almanzo.

"Well, why don't you ask him?" Frank did not believe that Father would give Almanzo a nickel. Almanzo did not know whether Father would, or not.

"Because I don't want to," he said.

"He wouldn't give you a nickel," Frank said.

"He would, too."

"I dare you to ask him," Frank said. The other boys were listening. Almanzo put his hands in his pockets and said, "I'd just as soon ask him if I wanted to."

"Yah, you're scared!" Frank jeered. "Double dare! Double dare!"

Father was a little way down the street, talking to Mr. Paddock, the wagon-maker. Almanzo walked slowly toward them. He was faint-hearted, but he had to go. The nearer he got to Father, the more he dreaded asking for a nickel. He had never before thought of doing such a thing. He was sure Father would not give it to him.

He waited till Father stopped talking and looked at him.

"What is it, son?" Father asked.

Almanzo was scared. "Father," he said.

"Well, son?"

"Father," Almanzo said, "would you—would you give me a nickel?"

He stood there while Father and Mr. Paddock looked at him, and he wished he could get away. Finally Father asked: "What for?"

Almanzo looked down at his moccasins and muttered: "Frank had a nickel. He bought pink lemonade."

"Well," Father said slowly, "if Frank treated you, it's only right you should treat him." Father put his hand in his pocket. Then he stopped and asked, "Did Frank treat you to lemonade?"

Almanzo wanted so badly to get the nickel that he nodded. Then he squirmed and said, "No, Father."

Father looked at him a long time. Then he took out his wallet and opened it, and slowly he took out a round, big, silver half-dollar. He asked: "Almanzo, do you know what this is?"

"Half a dollar," Almanzo answered.

"Yes. But do you know what half a dollar is?"

Almanzo didn't know it was anything but a half a dollar.

"It's work, son," Father said. "That's what money is; it's hard work."

Mr. Paddock chuckled. "The boy's too young, Wilder," he said. "You can't make a youngster understand that."

"Almanzo's smarter than you think," said Father.

Almanzo didn't understand at all. He wished he could get away, but Mr. Paddock was looking at Father just as Frank looked at Almanzo when he double-dared him. Father had said Almanzo was smart, so Almanzo tried to look like a smart boy. Father asked, "You know how to raise potatoes, Almanzo?"

"Yes," Almanzo said.

"Say you have a seed potato in the spring, what do you do with it?"

"You cut it up," Almanzo said.

"Go on, son."

"Then you harrow—first you manure the field, and plow it. Then you harrow, and mark the ground. And plant the potatoes, and plow them, and hoe them. You plow and hoe them twice."

"That's right, son. And then?"

"Then you dig them and put them down cellar."

"Yes. Then you pick them over all winter; you throw out all the little ones and the rotten ones. Come spring, you load them up and haul them here to Malone, and you sell them. And if you get a good price, son, how much do you get to show for all that work? How much do you get for half a bushel of potatoes?"

"Half a dollar," Almanzo said.

"Yes, Almanzo," said Father. "That's what's in this half-dollar. The work that raised half a bushel of potatoes is in it."

Almanzo looked at the round piece of money that Father held up. It looked small, compared with all that work.

"You can have it, Almanzo," Father said. Almanzo could hardly believe his ears. Father gave him the heavy half-dollar.

"It's yours," said Father. "You could buy a little pig with it, if you want to. You could raise it and it would raise a litter of pigs, worth four, five dollars apiece. Or you can trade that half-dollar for lemonade, and drink it up. You do as you want, it's your money."

Almanzo forgot to say thank you. He held the half-dollar a minute, then he put his hand in his pocket and went back to the boys by the lemonade-stand. The man was calling out, "Step this way, step this way! Ice-cold lemonade, pink lemonade, only five cents a glass!

Only half a dime, ice-cold pink lemonade! The twentieth part of a dollar!"

Frank asked Almanzo, "Where's the nickel?"

"He didn't give me a nickel," said Almanzo, and Frank yelled, "Yah, yah! I told you he wouldn't! I told you so!"

"He gave me a half a dollar," said Almanzo.

The boys wouldn't believe it till he showed them. Then they crowded around, waiting for him to spend it. He showed it to them all, and put it back in his pocket.

"I'm going to look around," he said, "and buy me a good little pig."

The band came marching down the street, and they all ran along beside it. The flag was gloriously waving in front, then came the buglers blowing and the fifers tootling and the drummer rattling the drumsticks on the drum. Up and down the street paraded the band, with all the boys following it, and then it stopped in the Square by the brass cannons.

Hundreds of people were there, crowding to watch.

The cannons rested on their haunches, pointing their long barrels upward. The band kept on playing. Two men kept shouting,

"Stand back! Stand back!" and other men were pouring black powder into the cannons' muzzles and pushing it down with wads of cloth on long rods. The iron rods had two handles, and two men pushed and pulled on them, driving the black powder down the brass barrels. Then all the boys ran to pull grass and weeds along the railroad tracks. They carried them by armfuls to the cannons, and the men crowded the weeds into the cannons' muzzles and drove them down with the long rods. A bonfire was burning by the railroad tracks, and long iron rods were heating in it. When all the weeds and grass had been packed tight against the powder in the cannons, a man took a little more powder in his hand and carefully filled two little touch-holes in the barrels. Now everybody was shouting, "Stand back! Stand back!"

Mother firmly took hold of Almanzo's arm and made him come away with her. He told her, "Aw, Mother, they're only loaded with powder and weeds. Honestly, I won't get hurt, Mother. I'll be very careful." But she made him come away from the cannons.

Two men took the long iron rods from the fire. Everybody was still,

watching. Standing as far behind the cannons as they could, the two men stretched out the rods and touched their red-hot tips to the touchholes. A little flame like a candle-flame flickered up from the powder. The little flames stood there burning; nobody breathed. Then—BOOM!

The cannons leaped backward, the air was full of flying grass and weeds. Almanzo ran with all the other boys to feel the warm muzzles of the cannons. Everybody was exclaiming about what a loud noise they had made.

"That's the noise that made the Redcoats run!" Mr. Paddock said to Father.

"Maybe," Father said, tugging his beard. "But it was muskets that won the Revolution. And don't forget it was axes and plows that made this country."

"That's so, come to think of it," Mr. Paddock said.

Independence Day was over. The cannons had been fired, and there was nothing more to do but hitch up the horses and drive home to do the chores.

That night when they were going to the house with the milk, Almanzo asked Father, "Father, how was it that axes and plows made this country? Didn't we fight England for it?"

"We fought for independence, son," Father said. "But all the land our forefathers had was a little strip of country, here between the mountains and the ocean. All the way from here west was Indian country, and Spanish and French and English country. It was farmers that took all that country and made it America."

"How?" Almanzo asked.

"We were farmers, son; we wanted the land. It was farmers that went over the mountains, and cleared the land, and settled it, and farmed it, and hung on to their farms. This country goes three thousand miles west, now. It goes 'way out beyond Kansas, and beyond the Great American Desert, over mountains bigger than these mountains, and down to the Pacific Ocean. It's the biggest country in the world, and it was farmers who took all that country and made it America, son. Don't you ever forget that."

Arranging Events in Order

This is an exercise to help you see how well you followed the author's plan in this story. The following statements list the events in the story, but not in the order in which they occurred. Read the statements and then write them on your paper in their proper order.

1. Father said that the farmer made America great.

2. The band played and everybody sang while the American flag fluttered against the blue sky.

3. Two men fired the cannons while everyone watched.

4. It was Independence Day more than one hundred years ago and Almanzo dressed in the new gray woolen suit his mother had made for him.

5. Mother and the girls spread the picnic lunch while Almanzo and his father fed the horses.

6. Father told Almanzo that he could buy a little pig with the half-dollar or use it as he wished.

7. Cousin Frank bought pink lemonade with the nickel his father had given him.

8. Almanzo was scared when he asked his father for a nickel.

MARY O'HARA

Taming the Colt[1]

Ken McLaughlin lived on a Wyoming ranch high up on a long hill called the Saddle Back. Looking west, he could see more than a hundred miles of green grass country. Looking south, he saw spread a great stretch of plateau land that ran down to Twin Peaks, and beyond that across crags and valleys and rocky headlands all the way to Colorado.

On the McLaughlin ranch, devoted to horse breeding, the boy Ken longed to have a colt of his own. At last his father, Rob McLaughlin, once a captain in the army, granted his wish. "Look them over and make your choice," Rob McLaughlin told him. On a day when a yearling filly cried out for help, Ken knew that he had come to the end of his search. He had not had to choose one after all: the filly he would now call Flicka had come to him. She would be his own, just his own. Later, on the day when the yearlings, including Flicka, were to be brought into the main corral, Ken McLaughlin was to prove the rightness of his choice.

WHEN Ken opened his eyes and looked out he saw that the house was wrapped in fog. There had been no rain at all since the day a week ago when the wind had torn the "sprinkling system" to pieces and blown all the tattered clouds away. That was the day he had found Flicka. And it had been ter- ribly hot since then. They had hardly been able to stand the sun. They had gone swimming in the pool every day. On the hills, the grass was turning to soft tan.

Now there were clouds and they had closed down. After a severe hot spell there often came a heavy fog, or hail, or even snow.

Standing at the window, Ken could hardly see the pines on the hill opposite. He wondered if his father would go after the yearlings

[1] From *My Friend Flicka*, by Mary O'Hara. Copyright, 1941, by Mary O'Hara. Published by J. B. Lippincott Company.

29

in such a fog as this—they wouldn't be able to see them; but at breakfast McLaughlin said there would be no change of plans. It was just a big cloud that had settled down over the ranch—it would lift and fall—perhaps up on Saddle Rock it would be clear.

They mounted and rode out.

The fog lay in the folds of the hills. Here and there a bare summit was in sunshine, then a little farther on came a smother of cottony white that soaked the four riders to the skin and hung rows of moonstones on the whiskers of the horses.

It was hard to keep track of each other. Suddenly Ken was lost—the others had vanished. He reined in Shorty and sat listening. The clouds and mist rolled around him. He felt as if he were alone in the world.

A bluebird, color of the deep blue wild delphinium that dots the plains, became interested in him, and perched on a bush near by; and as he started Shorty forward again, the bluebird followed along, hopping from bush to bush.

The boy rode slowly, not knowing in which direction to go. Then, hearing shouts, he touched heels to Shorty and cantered, and suddenly came out of the fog and saw his father. With him were Tim and Ross, two of the ranch hands.

"There they are!" said McLaughlin, pointing down over the curve of the hill. They rode forward and Ken could see the yearlings standing bunched at the bottom, looking up, wondering who was coming.

Then a huge coil of fog swirled over them and they were lost to sight again.

McLaughlin told them to circle around, spread out fanwise on the far side of the colts, and then gently bear down on them so they would start toward the ranch. If the colts once got running in this fog, he said, there'd be no chance of catching them.

The plan worked well; the yearlings were not so frisky as usual, and so allowed themselves to be driven in the right direction. It was only when they were on the County Road, and near the gate where his brother Howard was watching, that Ken, whose eyes had been scanning the bunch, as they appeared and disappeared in the fog, realized that Flicka was missing.

Rob McLaughlin noticed it at the same moment, and as Ken rode toward his father, McLaughlin turned to him and said, "She's not in the bunch."

They sat in silence a few moments while McLaughlin planned the next step. The yearlings, dispirited by the fog, nibbled languidly at the grass by the roadside. McLaughlin looked at the Saddle Back and Ken looked too, the passionate desire in his heart reaching out to pierce the fog and the hillside and see where Flicka had hidden herself away. Had she been with the bunch when they first were found? Had she stolen away through the fog? Or hadn't she been there in the beginning? Had she run away from the ranch entirely—and this thought made his heart drop sickeningly—had she perhaps died of the hurts she had received when she broke out of the corral and was lying stark and riddled with ants and crawling things on the breast of one of those hills?

McLaughlin looked grim. "Lone wolf—like her mother," he said. "Never with the gang. I might have known it."

Ken remembered what the ranch hands had said about the Lone Wolf type—it wasn't good to be that way.

"Well, we'll drive the yearlings back up," said Rob finally. "No chance of finding her alone. If they happen to pass anywhere near her, she's likely to join them."

They drove the yearlings back. Once over the first hill, the colts got running and soon were out of sight. The fog closed down again so that Ken pulled up, unable to see where he was going, unable to see his father, or Ross or Tim.

31

He sat listening, astonished that the sound of their hoofs had been wiped out so completely. Again he seemed alone in the world.

The fog lifted in front of him and showed him that he stood at the brink of a sharp drop, almost a precipice, though not very deep. It led down into a semicircular pocket on the hillside which was fed by a spring; there was a clump of young cottonwoods, and a great bank of clover dotted with small yellow blossoms.

In the midst of the clover stood Flicka, quietly feasting. She had seen him before he saw her and was watching him, her head up, clover sticking out of both sides of her mouth, her jaws going busily.

At sight of her, Ken was incapable of either thought or action.

Suddenly from behind him in the fog, he heard his father's low voice, "Don't move—"

"How'd she get in there?" said Tim.

"She scrambled down this bank. And she could scramble up again, if we weren't here. I think we've got her," said McLaughlin.

"Other side of that pocket the ground drops twenty feet sheer," said Tim. "She can't go down there."

Flicka had stopped chewing. There were still stalks of clover sticking out between her jaws, but her head was up and her ears pricked, listening, and there was a tautness and tension in her whole body.

Ken suddenly found himself trembling too.

"How're you going to catch her, Dad?" he asked in a low voice.

"I can snag her from here," said Ross, and in the same breath McLaughlin answered, "Ross can rope her. Might as well rope her here as in the corral. We'll spread out in a semicircle above this bank. She can't get up past us, and she can't get down."

They took their positions and Ross lifted his rope off the horn of his saddle.

Ahead of them, far down below the pocket, the yearlings were running. A whinny or two drifted up, and the sound of their hoofs, muffled by the fog.

Flicka heard them too. Suddenly she was aware of danger. She leaped out of the clover to the edge of the precipice which fell away down the mountainside toward where the yearlings were running. But it was too steep and too high. She came straight up on her hind legs with a neigh of terror, and whirled back toward the bank down which she had slid to reach the pocket. But on the crest of it, looming uncannily in the fog, were four black figures—she screamed, and ran around the base of the bank.

Ken heard Ross' rope sing. It snaked out just as Flicka dove into the bank of clover. Stumbling, she went down and for a moment was lost to view.

Ross hauled in his rope, while Flicka floundered up and again circled her small prison, hurling herself at every point, only to realize that there was no way out.

She stood over the precipice, poised in despair and frantic longing. There drifted up the sound of the colts running below. Flicka trembled and strained over the brink—a perfect target for Ross, and he whirled his lariat again. It made a vicious whine.

Ken longed for the filly to escape the noose—yet he longed for her capture. Flicka reared up, her delicate forefeet beat the air, then she leaped out; and Ross' rope fell short again as McLaughlin said, "I expected that. She's like all the rest of them."

Flicka went down like a diver. She hit the ground, her legs folded under her, then she rolled and bounced the rest of the way. It was exactly like a bronco that had

climbed over the side of the truck and rolled down the steep forty-foot bank; and in silence the four watchers sat in their saddles waiting to see what would happen when she hit bottom—Ken already thinking of the Winchester, and the way the crack of it had echoed back from the hills.

Flicka lit, it seemed, on four steel springs that tossed her up and sent her flying down the mountainside —perfection of speed and power and action. A hot sweat bathed Ken from head to foot, and he began to laugh, half choking—

The wind roared down and swept up the fog, and it went bounding away over the hills, leaving trailing streamers of white in the gullies, and coverlets of cotton around the bushes. 'Way below, they could see Flicka galloping toward the yearlings. In a moment she joined them, and then there was just a many-colored blur of moving shapes, with a fierce sun blazing down, striking sparks of light off their glossy coats.

"Get going!" shouted McLaughlin. "Get around behind them. They're on the run now, and it's cleared—keep them running, and we may get them all in together, before they stop. Tim, you take the short way back to the gate and help Howard turn them and get them through."

Tim shot off toward the County Road and the other three riders galloped down and around the mountain until they were at the back of the band of yearlings. Shouting and yelling and spurring their mounts, they kept the colts running, circling them around toward the ranch until they had them on the County Road.

'Way ahead, Ken could see Tim and Howard at the gate, blocking the road. The yearlings were bearing down on them. Now McLaughlin slowed up, and began to call, "Whoa, whoa—" and the pace decreased. Often enough the yearlings had swept down that road and through the gate and down to the corrals. It was the pathway to oats, and hay, and shelter from winter storms—would they take it now? Flicka was with them—right in the middle—if they went, would she go too?

It was all over almost before Ken could draw a breath. The yearlings turned at the gate, swept through, went down to the corrals on a dead run, and through the gates that Gus had opened.

Flicka was caught again.

34

Recalling Facts

From what you have learned in this story, write two sentences which give more information related to the main ideas contained in the sentences below.

1. The weather had been clear since the day Ken had found Flicka.
2. Ken possessed a great deal of courage.
3. Ken greatly loved the colt Flicka.
4. When the fog lifted and Ken saw Flicka, the colt was very unconcerned.
5. Ross was skilled with his lariat.
6. Ken at last breathed a sigh of relief.

Finding Word Meanings

Skim through the story and find the words listed below. Try to figure out their meanings from the way they are used in the sentence. Then write on your paper the letter of the phrase which defines the word correctly.

Words	Definitions
1. ____ yearling	a. discouraged, disheartened
2. ____ scanning	b. a pen for horses and cattle
3. ____ dispirited	c. a young animal
4. ____ languidly	d. weakly, without energy
5. ____ passionate	e. a very steep place
6. ____ corral	f. a noose, lasso
7. ____ precipice	g. a young mare; female colt
8. ____ floundered	h. showing strong feeling
9. ____ filly	i. plunged about; struggled without making much progress
10. ____ lariat	j. examining carefully

35

CARL SANDBURG

Buffalo Dusk

THE buffaloes are gone.
And those who saw the buffaloes are gone.
Those who saw the buffaloes by thousands and
    how they pawed the prairie sod into dust
    with their hoofs, their great heads down
    pawing on in a great pageant of dusk,
Those who saw the buffaloes are gone.
And the buffaloes are gone.

HAMLIN GARLAND

My Prairies

I LOVE my prairies, they are mine
From zenith to horizon line,
Clipping a world of sky and sod
Like the bended arm and wrist of God.

I love the hazel thickets; and the breeze,
The never resting prairie winds. The trees
That stand like spear points high
Against the dark blue sky.

I love my prairies, they are mine
From high sun to horizon line.
The mountains and the cold gray sea
Are not for me, are not for me.

Doris Gates

As Long as We Can

Janey Larkin was ten years old, and she had never known a real home. Once her family had lived in Texas—but then the drought and the dust storms had come. Now they were wanderers in California, following the crops, moving from place to place wherever her father could find work. It was a lonely life for Janey. There was never time to go to school or to make friends. Her only treasure was a lovely old willow plate, a bit of beauty saved from the happier days of the past. Camping for a time in an abandoned shack in the San Joaquin Valley, the family hoped for better times. Already Janey had become acquainted with Lupe Romero, a little Mexican girl, whose family lived in a house across the road. She hoped with all her heart that they could stay here a long time and that she and Lupe could be friends.

WHEN Janey Larkin returned from hanging out the washing, she found the boards of the cabin floor darkened with moisture and the smell of wet wood adding one more odor to those already filling the room. Mom was leaning a stubby broom against the wall.

"I couldn't do a proper job," she said, frowning down at the uneven boards, "the floor's too rough. But a broom and hot suds can do a lot with elbow grease mixed with them."

Janey looked at the floor without comment. It seemed all right to her, even if Mom wasn't satisfied. Why was she always fussing about dirt, Janey wondered, irritably. As a matter of fact, Mom fussed about a good many things. Lately nothing seemed to please her. The tired look hardly ever left her face. Of course Mom would be happier if they didn't have to move about from place to place. But there wasn't anything they could do about that. Dad had to look for work wherever work happened to be and it never lasted long in one spot. Janey could feel herself beginning to lose patience with Mom, then remembered in time that Mom had liked Lupe. Besides, she undoubtedly meant all right. Maybe it was better to prefer cleanliness to dirt, although it was a lot more trouble.

"I might as well stir up some corn dodgers while the oven's good and hot," Mrs. Larkin continued. While Janey watched, she wiped off the rickety table, produced a bowl and a small sack of yellow cornmeal and set to work. Janey eyed her speculatively. Would this be a good time for begging leave to return Lupe's call? She was nearly on the point of asking when Mom turned to her.

"As soon as I have this in the oven, we can start putting the place to rights. I can't seem to get used to living in a mess. Don't suppose I ever will, or I wouldn't mind it much by this time."

"I can untie the bedding and make up the bed," offered Janey in a small voice.

"No, it's too heavy for you. Wait till I'm through here."

Janey's neighborly inclinations strengthened.

Then, as if it were an afterthought, Mom said, "Have you done your Scripture reading yet today, Janey?"

"Not yet," admitted Janey. The two words seemed to put as many miles between herself and Lupe.

"Then you'd better be at it. You know what your father'd say if you let a day pass over your head without doing your stint."

Janey knew perfectly well what Dad would say if she neglected the two pages of Scripture which she was required to read daily. Dad believed there were some things second only to food and shelter in one's life. Reading was one of them.

So now Janey slid resignedly off her chair and dug to the bottom of the suitcase that held the willow plate. She lifted out a black leather-bound book, its back and edges worn.

It didn't seem strange to her that she should be using the Bible as a textbook. It was almost the only textbook Janey had ever known. Following the harvests from place to place had left her little time for schooling, even in the camp schools provided for the use of children like her. Sometimes, as now, she wished a little wistfully that she might some day go to a "regular" school where there were plenty of books, even new books, enough for every child. It occurred to her suddenly that probably Lupe went to such a school. She had lived here a whole year. Surely she belonged by this time. Janey walked slowly back to her chair, wondering what it would be like to belong—and go to school every day, a "regular" school, week after week, month after month.

She had seen a school like that once. It was over on the coast; she didn't remember just where. They had had to stop to change a tire right in front of the schoolhouse. It was a red brick schoolhouse, with white columns in front and a green lawn that stretched nearly to the road. Janey, feeling unusually daring that day, had crept up the walk until she could reach out and touch the smooth white columns. Glancing back at the car, she had made sure that her father and mother were still busy with the tire. And then she had edged along the building, her clothes brushing against the rough bricks until she was able to peep into a window. Inside was a room full of boys and girls. Some were sitting at desks, others were writing at the blackboard, and all of them looked as if they belonged. For a long time Janey stood there watching, until a shout from the car sent her speeding back along the way she had come. It is doubtful if any in the schoolroom had known they were being spied upon.

Yes, it would be nice to go to such a school. She wished she were there now. It would be lots more fun than sitting here in a stifling room, poring over tiny print full of "thee's" and "thou's" and words her tongue stumbled over when

39

she asked their meaning. Still, she had learned to read by this strange method, and she supposed it would be a very good thing to know how to read if she should suddenly find herself in a district school, though goodness only knew how that would ever come about. And then, besides that, there were good stories in the Bible. Very good stories indeed—Daniel in the lion's den, and Noah's Ark, for instance.

She decided she would read about the Ark and the Flood today. It was a good time to read about a rain that lasted forty days and forty nights. It might help as much as the blue plate to lift the weight of the heat.

Perching herself on the chair and hooking her bare heels over its rungs, she opened the worn, black book and began to read. Now and then she would put her fingers on a word to fasten it to the page until she had sounded it out. No matter how many times she read the chapter, those queer names always caused her to hesitate a little.

The oven door had slammed shut on the corn bread and Mrs. Larkin had gone outside for a breath of what might be considered cooler air before Janey came to the last verse.

"All the days of the earth, see
time and harvest, cold and hea
summer and winter, night and da
shall not cease."

She closed the book gent and squeezed it between the tw patches that covered her knee Her hands stroked the soft leath in a thoughtful way. There wa really nothing to be worried abou she decided, thinking of that la verse and of Mom's fussing. Go had promised that there would a ways be harvests, so Dad wou always have something to do. A the days of the earth. And even t hot weather couldn't last foreve Winter would have to come alor some day. And there was the blu plate. Now, if only Mom didr look quite so sad, and if only sh Janey, could go to a "regula school, the world wouldn't hav too much the matter with it, sh thought. And as if to prove it, sh

heard Mom say just at that moment: "You can run over to Lupe's for a while if you want."

It was sundown before Mr. Larkin came home. The shack had been settled for hours, the bed made, the suitcase shoved out of sight underneath it, while corn dodgers reposed in state in the middle of the table.

Once again, Janey was sitting on the top step to greet her father as soon as he should come into sight. Away off on the western edge of the world, a red and angry sun was being swallowed up in its own heat waves. It was nearly gone now, and the faintest hint of a breeze was beginning to stir a single hair here and there on Janey's tousled tow-head. If only the wind would really make up its mind to blow, to blow good and hard and send this dead hot air ahead of it out of the valley, or at least to some other part of it, she thought.

And then a battered car came into sight up the road, and Janey, with a cry over her shoulder, "It's Dad!" was off the step in a bound and down to the road. She trotted along beside the car as it bumped across the uneven ground to the house—the heat, Mom's tired face, and even Lupe were forgotten in this moment's joy. Dad was home again!

"Hi, young one," Mr. Larkin called as he slowly eased himself from behind the wheel. "Shouldn't run like that on a hot day. Your face's as red as a cock's comb."

Janey smiled happily and pressed close to him as he reached into the car and lifted out some parcels.

"Here," he said, "take these in to your mother while I lift out the cushion on the back seat."

Janey took the bundles into the house and presently her father appeared with the cushion to the back seat gripped awkwardly in his arms.

"Where do you want this?" he asked.

"Doesn't matter now," his wife answered. "When Janey goes to bed we'll put it across one of the doors. It'll be cooler."

For this was to be Janey's bed tonight as it had been for many, many nights before this one. In fact, Janey wouldn't have known how to sleep on anything else. It was all the bed she knew, and she found it entirely satisfactory in every way. Of course, now that she was ten, her feet stuck out over the end of it a little, but the suitcase, shoved across the end, solved this difficulty.

"Will the job last very long, Dad?" Janey wanted to know.

"Can't say exactly. More than likely, though. We'll keep on irrigating for a while, and when picking starts I can't see any reason why I shouldn't get in on that too. You never come to the end of work in a cotton patch, Janey."

"What's the pay?" Mrs. Larkin asked.

"Two bits an hour, and I worked eight hours. How much is that, daughter? Quick now."

He whirled on Janey and stood grinning while she turned over in her mind this problem in mental arithmetic. She fastened her eyes on his as if she thought she could read the answer there. And just when the grin was broadening accusingly, "Two dollars!" shouted Janey, as quick as that.

42

"Correct," said her father beaming. "That's a right pert child we're rearing under our roof."

"There are times when I'm glad it isn't our roof; like now," Mom returned, and walked heavily to the table where the parcels which held their supper lay alongside the corn dodgers.

"It isn't much to brag about and that's a fact," Mr. Larkin agreed, looking critically around him, "but it sure looks a sight better than it did this morning before you took it over."

Mom did smile at this, and Mr. Larkin, much encouraged, added in a teasing voice: "It must be awful to love to scrub as much as you do, Clara, and then never have a house worth scrubbing. Maybe it'll be different some day."

"Maybe," she returned briefly, the smile gone.

For a moment Mr. Larkin looked at her, his face suddenly sad and his shoulders drooping. Then he turned to Janey.

"Come on, young one. We'd better rustle up some more firewood before it gets dark."

Side by side, the two figures, one very tall, the other very short, both clad in faded blue overalls, moved slowly over the plain behind the shack. Each of them dragged a gunnysack and into these they poked whatever pieces of grease-wood branches or roots they could find. When the sacks were filled, Mr. Larkin took one in either hand and dragged them up to the back door. Then he and Janey took the water pail and went with it to the windmill in the neighboring field. It was necessary to open a gate strung with barbed wire in order to enter the field.

There were cattle in the field, red beasts that jogged away awkwardly and stood staring at the strangers as they opened the gate.

Janey hesitated.

"These steers won't bother us any—not like real range cattle," Dad said, and Janey, apparently reassured, walked boldly beside him. Secretly, however, she was still a little apprehensive and regarded the cattle with suspicion.

"Lupe Romero from across the road came over today," Janey said while they waited for the bucket to fill. "She says the house we're in belongs to the man who owns this windmill and these cattle."

"Yes, I know," returned Mr. Larkin. "Her father told me this morning when I went over there to see him."

"Does he know we're living in his house?" asked Janey.

"As far as I know he doesn't."

They were on the way back to the shack now. Janey closed the gate, then ran to catch up with her father, who had gone on ahead with the brimming bucket.

"Suppose he won't let us stay when he finds out; what will we do then?" she asked, a strange fear all at once seizing her. Suppose they should have to go away tomorrow or the next day? She might never see Lupe again!

Mr. Larkin stopped and looked over her head to the west and thought a moment before replying. Janey searched his face anxiously.

"He'd probably let us stay if we paid him something every month. I'd rather do that than move to the cotton camp. We'd have to pay rent there anyway, and we're better off by ourselves, Janey, even if we have to do without some things in order to stay that way."

Janey nodded her head in quick agreement.

"The Romeros have stayed in their house for a year. Do you think he'd let us stay that long?"

"If we paid up, he probably would."

Suddenly a strange tingling began to creep all over Janey, and her chest felt all at once too small for what was going on inside of it. Perhaps they wouldn't have to move on after a month or so! Perhaps Dad was going to stay put and she and Lupe could become real friends. She might even go to school wherever Lupe did—a "regular" school, not just a camp school for roving children.

Before she could gather her wits for a proper reply, her father was speaking again. "We'll have to call a halt somewhere pretty soon,

Janey. Mom isn't well, hasn't been for a long time. Maybe if she could stay long enough somewhere to get a real good rest, it would make a difference with her. It's hard to say, though."

"Then we'll stay as long as we can?" Janey asked.

"Yes, as long as we can."

Janey sighed and her bare toes dragged a little as she followed Dad to the house. It was the same old question and the same old answer. What wouldn't she give to be able to say just once: "We'll stay as long as we want to!"

When they got inside, they found supper ready for them. By moving the table over to the bed, there were seats enough for all three. After the dishes were washed, they sat on the front steps until bedtime. The little breeze had strengthened, and the moon was lighting earth and sky with a radiance that was like balm to eyes still smarting from too brilliant sunlight. From the top of a fence pole at the road's edge, a mocking bird dropped three notes as silvery as the moon's own light.

"All the days of the earth, seedtime and harvest, cold and heat, summer and winter, night and day, shall not cease," Janey remembered thankfully.

Across the road a light twinkled in the Romero house.

"And there's Lupe as long as we do stay," thought Janey with equal gratitude.

Relating Ideas

In the two columns below are listed ideas taken from the story. On your paper list the numbers from one to eight. Then read the statements carefully and write the letter of the statement in Column II which matches the idea presented in Column I.

Column I

1. _____ Janey Larkin never knew a real home.
2. _____ The Larkin family moved from place to place.
3. _____ Janey hoped that they could stay in the San Joaquin Valley for a long time.
4. _____ Mom looked sad and seemed to fuss about a good many things lately.
5. _____ Janey had never attended a "regular" school.
6. _____ Janey read two pages from the Bible every day.
7. _____ Mr. Larkin thought his new job would last.
8. _____ Janey was afraid that they would not be allowed to stay in their new home.

Column II

a. Janey wanted to attend a "regular" school and have Lupe for her friend.
b. Dad had to take work wherever he could get it.
c. There is never an end to work in a cotton patch.
d. The Larkin family lived in Texas, and now they were wandering in California.
e. Janey became acquainted with Lupe Romero, a little Mexican girl.
f. Wandering about was hard on Mom and she needed a good rest.
g. Moving about left little time for schooling for Janey.
h. Mr. Larkin thought reading was second only to food and shelter.

EILEEN SHANAHAN

Epiphany

A SMALL house with a pointed roof
A window kind with light
And overhead one watchful star
And all about the night.

A weary man who waits on God
A woman worn with tears—
On such as these the star has shone
Serenely through the years.

The cradle of a little child
The lamplight on the floor—
Three shadow Kings with shadow gifts
Come silent to the door.

The man, the woman, and the babe,
Toil, sacrifice, and pain—
The Kings kneel to the trinity
And Christ is come again.

BETTY ELISE DAVIS

The Doors That Tell a Story

THERE'S something magic about all doorways. Sometimes we stand for hours waiting for them to open, either to a land of make-believe, or just to see what is on the other side.

Once I had a little friend who collected doors. No, he did not go about removing them from their hinges. He was an invalid and had to spend many hours in bed. When Johnny grew tired of pretending that he could walk or run through the door of his bedroom, he asked his friends to bring him pictures or to draw sketches of doors that they had opened during the day. These he pasted in a large scrapbook.

His friend, Bennie, brought a drawing of the doorway to the large school which he attended. Johnny pasted it in the scrapbook carefully, and whenever Bennie came to call, he turned to this door and asked Bennie to open it for him. Then would follow an hour of fun in an imaginary trip through the school. Other friends brought their pictures and sketches of interesting doors. There were large white colonial doors, Dutch colonial doors, Spanish doors, and many others.

His friends hunted for old picture postcards of famous places in Europe, hoping that one might be a photo of some famous door. Someone found a picture of the bronze doors, covered with gold, that are in Florence. Someone else sent a lovely one of the cathedral doors in Milan, Italy. A friend found a picture of the heavy oaken doors of Toledo, Spain. They were studded with enormous nails, and

two huge knockers hung upon them, one to be used by pedestrians, and the other, much higher, to be used by horsemen.

All of this stirred Johnny's imagination so he began asking his friends this question: "Where are the most beautiful doors in the world?"

A neighbor who had visited Italy said that they must be in St. Peter's in Rome, and told the story of the beautiful inner sacred doors that were opened once every twenty years with a golden hammer in order to let the pilgrims through.

That same day Bennie came in with a picture and a magnifying glass.

"These are beautiful doors," he said. "The lady who gave me this picture said that in the building where these doors are found, there are five hundred and fifty doors."

Together they peered at the picture through the magnifying glass.

Johnny recognized the head of Columbus at the top of the door, but he looked carefully at all of the eight panels before he spoke. Then he called out excitedly, "These doors tell a story, Bennie, a story of Columbus. Tell me where they are."

Bennie's face fell. In his eagerness to bring the picture he had forgotten to ask, and all of the writing on the picture had been torn away.

"I'll go to see the lady tomorrow," he promised. "And I'll find out everything that I can."

"Now let's read the story that the doors tell," suggested Johnny.

The lowest panel on the left showed Columbus before the Council of Salamanca. There he stood, bravely presenting his plans to the six men.

"And they turned him down," commented the little invalid sadly.

"I know the story of the next panel," said Bennie. "Here Columbus is at the Convent of La Rabida, and his little son, Don Diego, is with him. The good friars let him stay there and rest."

"They looked at his maps and believed in him," added Johnny. "And through their aid an audience was secured with the King and Queen. See, Columbus is riding a donkey in this picture. He is leaving the monastery for the Court of Spain."

The next panel showed Columbus at the Court, appearing before Ferdinand and Isabella. The Queen was bending forward eagerly, the King looked doubtful.

Both boys exclaimed over the top left-hand panel, for in it again was the figure of the boy, Diego. Columbus was leaving him in the charge of the friars. In the background was a ship. He was ready to sail.

Moving their magnifying glass over to the right, the boys saw in the first panel Columbus' first encounter with the natives in the new world.

The next showed Columbus riding in triumph into Barcelona. The proud high-stepping horse was quite a contrast to the tired donkey in the second panel.

In the seventh panel Columbus was pleading vainly with lordly officials bearing orders for his arrest and return to Spain. The last panel showed the death of Columbus at Valladolid in his seventieth year.

Up above both panels of the doors was a half circle depicting the landing of the Spaniards in the New World.

The following afternoon Bennie came again to see Johnny. "I have the information," he announced. "The doors were made of solid bronze, by Randolph Rogers, and it is the only work of its kind in all America."

Bennie consulted a bit of paper. "The doors weigh two thousand pounds. The model for them was made in Rome and was taken by ox team from Rome to Munich where they were cast in the Royal Bavarian Foundry," he added.

"Any date?" asked Johnny.

"Oh, of course," replied Bennie. "The doors arrived in America in 1863."

"But where are they now?" demanded Johnny.

Bennie's eyes shone. "Well, they're in the most beautiful building in America. They are in our Capitol in Washington, D.C.!"

Fact or Opinion?

Copy the statements below on your paper and mark *F* before those which state a fact, and *O* before those which express an opinion.

_____ 1. Johnny was an invalid and had to spend much time in bed.

_____ 2. He had learned to use his time well.

_____ 3. Bennie was a true friend.

_____ 4. The sacred doors in St. Peter's, Rome, are opened every twenty years with a golden hammer.

_____ 5. In Toledo, Spain, the heavy doors are studded with nails and have two huge knockers.

_____ 6. Johnny's hobby of collecting pictures of doors was very educational.

_____ 7. Columbus left his son Diego in the care of the friars when he set out on his voyage.

_____ 8. People were very kind to Johnny.

_____ 9. The front doors of the Capital in Washington, D.C. were cast in the Royal Bavarian Foundry and sent to America in 1863.

_____ 10. There are many ways in which a person can use his leisure time profitably.

51

WEST POINT

1776

DALE NICHOLS

2. O Beautiful for Patriot Dream

PATRIOTISM means love of country. It is commanded by the law of Christ. It is part of the virtue of justice. It sets forth those duties which we owe to our fellow men because we share with them the same homeland, cherish the same ideals, and live under a government that protects our common interests.

The principles on which our democracy is founded spring from our heritage as Christians. They are rooted in the teachings of Jesus Christ. These teachings are not merely something to be remembered and talked about; they are something to be followed.

By Christian conduct in our daily lives we make a great and lasting contribution to American democracy. The truth will make us free if we live the truth.

Mr. John Nixon Reads a Paper

ELLEN BAXTER and Thomas Walsh,
Catherine Kenna and Henry Balch,
One of the Bryalds and two of the Careys
Came that morning from Mass at St. Mary's
Into the Philadelphia street,
Heavy already with July heat.

"Look at the crowd!" cried Thomas Walsh.
"Something has happened," said Henry Balch.
"Let's follow the others," yelled both the Careys,
And they all went pell-mell away from St. Mary's.

"Is it a battle?" asked Henry Balch.
"Washington's won it!" yelled Thomas Walsh.
"Three cheers for Liberty!" all of them cried,
As they rushed along, with the crowd for guide.

It wasn't a battle, they quickly found,
But they kept on going as they heard the sound
Of a bugle note rising, high and sweet,
From a balcony over Library Street.

"It's Mr. John Nixon," said Thomas Walsh;
"He has a paper," said Henry Balch.
"He's going to read it now aloud
To us and all the rest of the crowd."
"Listen!" said Ellen and both the Careys
And all the others who came from St. Mary's.

54

Mr. John Nixon wiped his brow,
Pulled down his glasses, and said, "And now
I have here a document, hardly dry,
Which the Congress passed on the Fourth of July."
He cleared his throat as a last command,
Then read from the paper in his hand:
"When, in the Course of human events, it becomes necessary
for one people to dissolve the political bands
which have connected them with another, and to assume
among the Powers of the earth, the separate and equal station
to which the Laws of Nature and of Nature's God entitle them,
a decent respect to the opinions of mankind
requires that they should declare the causes that impel them
to the separation.
We hold these truths to be self-evident:
—that all men are created equal;
that they are endowed by their Creator
with certain unalienable Rights;
that among these are Life, Liberty,
and the pursuit of Happiness."

Mr. John Nixon continued to read
To the final words of freedom's creed.
"And, for the support of this Declaration,
with a firm reliance on the Protection of Divine Providence,
we mutually pledge to each other our Lives, our Fortunes,
and our sacred Honor."

"Three cheers for Freedom!" cried Thomas Walsh.
"For the Continentals!" yelled Henry Balch.
"For God and for country," said both the Careys,
And all of the others who came from St. Mary's,
Then started home in procession gay,
Not knowing they had lived through their greatest day.

A Messenger for Liberty

HELPING Dick Anderson lift the heavy bag of bread and chickens to his shoulder, Farmer Hahn said somewhat anxiously, "It is beginning to snow. The flakes will be coming down like a blanket before you are a mile along the Gulph Road."

Dick only nodded in answer, but he did not turn. He knew, as good John Hahn did not, how many times he had begged his friend Colonel Timothy Allen to find something "that a boy could do" for General Washington's army, shivering and hungering in the camp at Valley Forge. Timothy Allen had shaken his head at first, as though he believed that fighting for liberty was a man's task and that the only share a boy might expect to have was tramping the hilly Gulph Road, day after day, carrying supplies from the neighboring farms to the half-starved soldiers. But after he had watched the boy's stubborn determination for some weeks, he had said at last in reply to Dick's begging: "Wait until the turn of the winter. Ask me again

when March is here, and I may have something for you which a boy can do better than a man. But it will mean going into great danger."

This, then, being the first day of March, was a moment when it would have needed more than a softly falling snow to make young Dick Anderson stay in comfort under Cousin Thomas Dermott's warm but unfriendly roof.

The boy's real home was in Vermont. His father, having joined General Stark to fight for the Revolution in the North, had sent his son to Pennsylvania to stay with a relative whom they had not seen for years. Cousin Thomas was old and cautious, and he was beginning to think—out loud—that perhaps there was no hope for the cause of liberty and that perhaps this General George Washington was not all they had expected.

Dick's cheeks burned as he listened to the talk around the supper table, evening after evening. He knew better; but it was not the part of a youngster to speak his mind among his elders. So he kept silent, and found his only real happiness in carrying supplies from all the farms round about to the camp among the wooded hills. He knew the way so well that although today the snow hid the campfires which usually guided him, he was certain, as he came up the last steep slope, that he would hear the clink of the hammers, busy night and day at the forge.

The leaping flames from the blacksmith's workshop, where guns and swords and stirrup irons were being mended, at last threw a faint glare through the cover of white. In the doorway, outlined against the light, stood a tall, thin figure.

Dick, blowing and breathless, recognized it at once. It was Colonel Allen, whom he had come to know on the very first day he had brought food to the camp. He wondered whether he would have to remind Allen of his promise and say that March had come, but the tall soldier's first words told him that Timothy Allen did not forget his promise when it was once given.

"I knew you would be here, and at this hour, in spite of the snow," he greeted the boy. "Dick, have you the heart for a great adventure?"

Had he? A glow of delight went through Dick, making him warm, even in the midst of that whirling cloud of snow. Allen, seeming to understand all that was meant as Dick stammered out his eager reply, swung about immediately and led the way down the lane toward the house of Mr. Isaac Potts, the owner of the blacksmith shop. It was this yellow stone dwelling which had been given over to the use of General Washington while his army was encamped at Valley Forge. The boy was seized by a spasm of shyness as he set down his heavy bag and waited on the white-banked step, but it was cut short by the opening of the door. At a word from Allen they were ushered into the little parlor, where a fire flickered on the hearth.

The man who stood looking into the flames had just come in, for the snow was not yet melted on the shoulders of his riding coat and his boots were wet and splashed with mud. He was so deep in thought that he did not hear them enter, nor did he turn until Allen spoke, "General Washington."

This was George Washington, the man whose name had now gone far and wide beyond the circle of friendly farming folk in the valley of the Potomac River where he used to live. In every corner of the American colonies men were talking about him, hoping in him, praying for him. Across the seas King George of England went uneasily to his sleep these nights and dreamed of George Washington. The great men of France consulted anxiously together over him and wondered whether it were best for their country to stand behind him and his cause of liberty. The small princes of Germany watched his military progress and hoped that he would not soon be defeated. They were lending troops for pay to the British government, and the longer this rebel Washington held out, the greater would be their gain. They would have taken heart if they could have known how long men would fight to be free.

Washington was now at the peak of his strength, at the very height of his manhood and power. Never was his tall figure more magnificently erect; never were his eyes, with their look of high honor and complete honesty, more clear and keen. The blind courage of youth had grown into the strong wisdom of middle life. He had need of all that power and wisdom this year, this day, this hour. As he moved across the room to sit down at the table, where he had set a lighted candle, Dick Anderson could see that he looked worn and anxious. Yet his face lighted up with a smile as he looked up to talk to the ever-gay Timothy Allen.

They were discussing, over a large map and some papers, a man named Oliver Pollock, who had grown up in Pennsylvania, but who was now a successful merchant in the Spanish city of New Orleans. More than once Pollock had bought supplies of powder and other necessary things for the American army and sent them North. Now it was time to send him an immediate request for further help. Since the British ships still guarded the coast, the message must be sent through the interior of the country.

"And the right men to carry it?" Washington asked. "You undertook to find them, Colonel Allen."

"Do you remember," answered Allen, "that there came to the camp, not so long ago, a Frenchman, a trapper and trader, named Jacques Perrin? He is not young, but he has come all the way from the Mississippi to be of what help he can to General Washington. He speaks some English and he knows the Western rivers."

"He is one," said the general; "but he cannot go alone."

"I have brought you the other today." Allen turned toward Dick, who had been standing quietly in his corner, wondering what all this could have to do with him. A wave of excitement broke over him, but he did not speak, even when General Washington turned to look at him.

"He has learned to paddle in the Northern woods," Allen went on. "He can swim and he can shoot. His father is with General Stark in New England. I suppose we must ask his cousin, Thomas Dermott, to give consent to his going. I will undertake to secure Dermott's permission."

Washington smiled as though he knew how few there were whom Timothy Allen could not persuade.

"To paddle down a river in spring flood does not take great strength," he said thoughtfully; "only skill and willingness. A boy is lighter in a boat than a man. And we can hardly spare anyone of the age and strength for bearing arms. Would you offer yourself for this service?" He turned to ask the question directly of Dick.

"I would." The boy's whole spirit was pressed into the two

59

words. Washington looked at him with a keen eye for a moment and then turned back to the table. He was already writing the letter to be carried to New Orleans.

He handed the finished paper to Timothy Allen, gave a few brief orders, and then rose and walked to the outer door with them. Standing bareheaded upon the step, with the snow coming down about him, he gave his hand to Dick Anderson and spoke a single sentence: "You know that my heart goes with you to success."

Because of their nearness to the British army camped in Philadelphia, Dick Anderson and Jacques Perrin had a guard of soldiers for the first few miles of their journey westward—Timothy Allen and two young friends of his, David Hale and Rolfe Turner. March frosts made the road as hard as iron under the horses' feet, although the March winds roared overhead, promising the rapid melting of drifted snowfields and icebound rivers.

Jacques Perrin, the lean, tanned old trader with dancing black eyes and hair streaked with white, had spent too much of his life in a canoe to make, as he put it, "any magnificent figure upon a horse." It seemed that years ago he had taught the two younger men to paddle a canoe, and now, with

laughter and jokes, they were making the most of this chance of teaching him to ride.

"If," said Perrin in a lively tone, "at the further end of our journey we meet any British soldiers who are said to be patrolling the Mississippi, I will have a boat under me and not a four-legged instrument of torture. Then Jacques Perrin will be his own man again and laugh at clumsy English soldiers."

As the friends said good-by to one another at the end of a day's journey, the talk was not of the long journey that lay ahead, but of that one man upon whom all their thoughts were fixed. "He is a great soldier," said Perrin, "and in spite of all his trouble, there is still the light of hope in his eyes."

"He is more than a soldier," said Timothy Allen soberly, "and it is not the light of hope that we see, but the light of victory."

At the little frontier town of Pittsburgh, surrounding Fort Pitt, which had once been Fort Duquesne, the name of Perrin seemed to carry magic power. Did he want a boat—supplies—blankets? He could have them all, and welcome, from his old trading friends. Even the river appeared to be trying to please him; for the ice was gone, and the muddy current of the Ohio, high with spring waters, was an open, waiting road into the West.

The skies were blue, and white clouds sailed overhead, although the woods were still bare and brown and the hillsides showed but a trace of green. The days of the journey passed as quickly as the river flowed. The two travelers reached the rapids and shot them easily, carried along by the great rush of water. In a surprisingly short time they reached a point where the river suddenly widened, carrying them into that greater stream toward which it had so long been hurrying them.

The Ohio is a big river, but the

61

Mississippi is a giant. At this hour the mists wrapped the shore opposite, so that there seemed nothing before them but that great flood of marching water. It was a silvery color in the evening light, with darker streaks where bars and low islands cut the smooth flow of the great current.

"It was so I wanted you to view it first," said Perrin, as their boat floated, a tiny speck on that broad surface. "As far as any man can say that he knows a river, I know this Mississippi and her sister, the Ohio, and yet they are always new to me."

A big cloud was rolling up over the last red of the sunset, and a drizzle of rain had begun to fall before the travelers made camp. They must take time now to lift their boat from the water and go over its seams, which had begun to leak. A long journey still lay before them. It rained steadily all the next day, so that they were forced to build a rude shelter of willow branches to make a dry spot where they could work.

"There is ice still lingering above in the Mississippi," said Perrin, pointing to some small patches of white which were moving down with the current. "It may be that this rain will bring whole drifts of ice upon us and delay us for some days." He set himself to scraping away the old pitch from the seams in order that the new could be placed there.

Toward afternoon a sharp wind began to rise, and Dick, looking upstream at the slightly greater number of drifting ice cakes, suddenly cried out, "See, Monsieur Perrin, a boat!"

It was not one boat, but two. A heavy flat-bottomed boat, on each side of which were eight or ten men at the oars and in whose bow was a small movable gun, was coming down the Mississippi, followed by a smaller craft. As the boats drew rapidly nearer, Perrin exclaimed anxiously, "A pest on our luck! Those men have seen us, and they wear red coats!"

Bad luck had indeed brought them within hail of one of those British patrols which tried, in that great wilderness, to cut off travel and messages between the seacoast colonies and the settlements of Louisiana. The larger boat drew in toward an island lying almost opposite where the two travelers were at work. Evidently the commander meant to make camp there for the night. The smaller boat, containing a young officer and two soldiers, swung toward the shore. There was no good place for so large a vessel to land, so with loud shouts they ordered Dick and Perrin to come over to the island and report to the British captain what their business was on the river.

"Certainly; but certainly." Perrin beamed across at the officer and bowed agreement. "Yet do you not see that our little boat is at present of no use? Therefore we cannot come to explain how an old French trader and a young boy are seeking their fortunes to the south." He pointed so that the Englishman could see the opened seams of the canoe. The other nodded unwillingly, agreeing that there must be some delay. He went away, leaving strict orders that they were to come over in the morning. He also took care to draw their attention to the fact that the larger British boat carried a gun. The moment he had rowed away, Perrin set to work with all his might.

"Build up the fire," he directed, "so that this pitch may dry. We shall have to slip downstream under protection of the darkness. Let us hope with all our hearts that the wind does not blow the clouds away and give us a moon."

But as they sat waiting for the pitch to harden they heard a strange noise that came, seemingly, from nowhere—a muttering and crackling and groaning. Then, in spite of all their wishes, the clouds broke and the moon sailed clear. It showed the island, like a black arrow, pointing downstream in the midst of the silver of the water; it showed great moving shapes rising and tumbling and marching down from the north in a mighty procession.

"See," Perrin almost whispered, "the ice—the real ice—is coming."

Great fields of white, grinding together with enormous power, were beginning to drift by. Smaller cakes dipped and floated between them. At the end of the point near by stood a single willow tree, its trunk as thick as Perrin's body. A great mass of ice piled against it, then rocked and crumbled and drifted away. When the space became clearer, Dick looked, and looked again, for the willow tree was no longer there. At that moment Perrin said quietly, "Our canoe is ready, my friend. No man will follow us now, for we are going down the river with the ice."

Dick gave a gasp of wonder, but he did not speak. As they pushed

their canoe into a bit of sheltered water, Perrin gave his orders: "Take the bow paddle; it lies within your younger powers to carry us safely. I have done this but once in my life before; it is a risk one does not take unless the need is very great."

All about them were the crowding, pushing monsters. Watching for a passageway to open between them, Dick would send the fragile canoe into the open lane with a quick stroke of his paddle. He could see how white and shining was the surface of the smooth tops, how dirty and yellow were the edges which touched the water. He could hear the smashing and splitting of ice on every hand; yet he thought nothing but of how to dart, now here, now there, always just clear of that giant grasp closing behind them.

A hail rang out from the island.

A soldier on the beach had caught sight of the canoe. There was running and shouting; then a pause and the dull boom of a gun. It sounded small and harmless in the midst of that great noise. Two enormous cakes of ice smashed together just in front of them, reared up on edge, and dropped with a great splash which almost swamped the canoe. Then they drifted apart and the canoe slipped between. It was threatened to the right and to the left. The minutes passed; half an hour, each second was a battle to live a second longer. Then, all at once, the river broadened in the moonlight, and the great, swimming beasts were beginning to land upon the shore. The cakes of ice could move no faster than the current, so that now it was only a

matter of hard paddling to leave them safely behind.

That one night's journey seemed so long that, by comparison, the rest of the voyage was short. Many days passed; the shores grew lower and more and more covered with green. Finally a veil of smoke which had hung before the travelers for miles began to show the roofs and spires of a great city. They had reached the seaport of New Orleans.

They landed on a crowded shore front. Perrin, looking about him at the fishermen whose boats were anchored next to theirs, firmly refused to leave the canoe and said that Dick should go up into the city alone "to look for Monsieur Pollock."

Such an errand was not to be carried out without long search. Dick asked the way many times, and was usually answered with politeness and understanding, for Oliver Pollock's name seemed to be known to everyone. But the directions given him were quite difficult to follow in a strange city. It was dark when he came to the end of long wandering through narrow streets, broad avenues, and leafy squares. Here at last was an iron gate opening on a flower-filled garden enclosed by walls. Three men were turning away from the gate and one of them was speaking the name of the man whom Dick had sought for so long.

The three were British, probably sailors from one of the ships in the harbor. Their visit to the gentleman within had evidently not been pleasant; for one of them, at least, was in an ugly mood. When Dick asked politely if this was the home of Oliver Pollock, the largest fellow laughed at him unpleasantly in reply. "Does Mr. Oliver Pollock live here?" he imitated Dick's words. "By your talk I take you for one of those rude rebels from yonder to the north, and I'll just undertake to find out what is your important business with Mr. Pollock." In answer to a good-natured objection from his comrade, he added, "This may be a neutral port where we're supposed to pocket our hate of our enemies; but there's one law practiced everywhere—that the biggest man gets his way. Now, what is your business here?"

Something suddenly broke inside Dick. Through many long days he had sat in the canoe, paddling steadily and patiently. He had not complained; he had been quiet and responsible, as is proper for a boy doing a man's task. Now all such control melted away, as did all wisdom and good judgment. In a burst of rage he sprang at the man. He heard himself shouting he did not know what, as the other staggered back, breathless from a hard blow somewhere near his broad white belt. Maddened with anger, the sailor swung a great blow which Dick avoided by ducking and dodging toward the wall. A second such blow would have knocked the boy over where he stood, for there was no space to dodge again. At this instant the door opened, letting out a flood of candlelight and showing a man in a velvet coat standing on its sill.

"Faith," said a warm Irish voice, "wherever there is a good fight Oliver Pollock wants to be near enough to take sides. But I would call it no fight at all. Be kind to the poor big fellow, young sir. Don't you see you've taken all the breath out of him?"

The sailor, with his companions, slipped away into the darkness, and the boy stepped forward, a rumpled travel-worn figure in the yellow light.

"I have brought you a message," he said with what grace he could gather, "a letter from General Washington." Then, as Pollock took the paper in haste and broke the seal, Dick sat down dizzily and rather suddenly upon a bench among the flowering magnolias. All at once he felt that he had come a long way from Valley Forge and that he was very tired.

Mr. Oliver Pollock was a generous, kindly man of great energy. He took Dick inside, questioned him about General Washington and his needs, and won the boy's immediate respect and friendship by his kindness and by his interest in that long river journey. He sent down to the waterside for Perrin and had them both stay with him. Before he slept that night he had begun making arrangements to gather the supplies which his friend General Washington needed so badly. Morning showed to Dick that the velvet coat was old and worn; that Oliver Pollock was stripping himself to help Washington.

In a very few days an armed boat was loading at Pollock's own wharf with gunpowder and medicines and other things of which the American armies stood in such great need. With this boat Perrin was to travel up the Mississippi and the Ohio as guide and pilot. But a boy of thirteen and a half is of no great use where heavy oars are to be pulled against a strong current; so, by Pollock's advice and arrangement, Dick Anderson was to go home by sea. A kindly French captain carried him north and slipped him ashore on the coast of Virginia.

Once landed, Dick began to hear exciting news on all sides. The French were now openly united with America. There had been battles and a victory for Washington at Monmouth. Dick, tramping the last few miles of his journey, stopped at a little roadside inn to inquire, "Where is the army now? Where is General Washington camped?"

"The troops are on the move," the landlord told him. "Sit down here beside the door for an hour and you cannot fail to see him pass."

He brought the boy food and drink and set the bench under the shade of the grapevines. Dick sat there for a long time, turning over and over in his mind all that he had been hearing and seeing in those crowded weeks since he had

67

walked to Valley Forge in the snow. Suddenly he raised his head. He had heard the sound of music up the road.

The advance guard was coming. The music was quiet now, but the drums were thumping to mark time for the marching feet. There was Timothy Allen, riding at the head of his men, the wind blowing, as it always seemed to be, through his bright hair. The lines of fighting men around him were thinner from their winter of hunger and from the battles which they had fought; but they were true soldiers every one, with one will, one purpose, and one leader.

The little group of people who had hurried out of the inn drew closer together as though something in all of them had tightened with expectation. There was no need for them to tell one another that General Washington was coming.

Here he was at last, sitting his tall gray horse with weary grace. Thin, and worn he was, like his men. How could he be otherwise? Dick could not speak to him now; later he would seek him in the camp and deliver Oliver Pollock's messages. Now he could only stand at attention, watching with shining eyes. Timothy Allen was right; here was a man who was more than a great soldier. It was truly the light not of hope, but of victory, that shone on the tired face as the commander of them all went by, with the drums beating before him.

Classifying Ideas

As you advance in your schooling, it will be of great help to you in all your studies if you are able to relate ideas and classify them under main topics. This is an exercise to give you practice in grouping minor ideas under major headings. Below is a list of happenings taken from the story. On your paper arrange them in proper time sequence. Then write the letter of the main topic to which it belongs before each item.

    A. Dick, a thirteen-year-old boy, a real American
    B. Victory through perseverance in trial and hardship
    C. Dangers encountered by Dick and Monsieur Perrin

1. _____ The British patrol ordered Dick and Perrin to report their business on the river.
2. _____ After giving the message to Oliver Pollock, Dick felt that he was very tired and had done a man's work.
3. _____ Dick learned that the Army was on the move after victory at Monmouth.
4. _____ Dick longed to help the American forces.
5. _____ Dick agreed to carry a message to New Orleans asking for supplies for Washington's men.
6. _____ Rain brought whole drifts of ice down the river.
7. _____ The adventurers outwitted the British patrol by escaping amidst the floating ice.
8. _____ Dick delivered the letter from General Washington.
9. _____ The men riding with Timothy Allen were real soldiers, looking tired and thin from the hard winter at Valley Forge.
10. _____ Dick went to the city of New Orleans to look for Oliver Pollock.
11. _____ Dick saw General Washington riding with his men.
12. _____ A British sailor attempted to discover Dick's business with Oliver Pollock.
13. _____ Pollock arranged for Dick's return home by sea.
14. _____ Because of his kindness and self-sacrifice, Pollock immediately won Dick's respect.

OLIVER WENDELL HOLMES

Old Ironsides

AY, TEAR her tattered ensign down!
　　Long has it waved on high,
And many an eye has danced to see
　　That banner in the sky;
Beneath it rung the battle shout,
　　And burst the cannon's roar;—
The meteor of the ocean air
　　Shall sweep the clouds no more.

Her deck, once red with heroes' blood,
　　Where knelt the vanquished foe,
When winds were hurrying o'er the flood
　　And waves were white below,
No more shall feel the victor's tread,
　　Or know the conquered knee:
The harpies of the shore shall pluck
　　The eagle of the sea!

Oh, better that her shattered hulk
　　Should sink beneath the wave;
Her thunders shook the mighty deep,
　　And there should be her grave;
Nail to the mast her holy flag,
　　Set every threadbare sail,
And give her to the god of storms,
　　The lightning and the gale!

Privates of the Army

We believe that our country's heroes were the instruments of the God of Nations in establishing this home of freedom.

—THIRD PLENARY COUNCIL OF BALTIMORE

I AM John Ames.
I fought at Lexington.
I stood there, in the dawn, behind the bridge,
With Jonas Parker and my other neighbors,
New England farmers, every one of us,
Ready to fight and die to save our homes.
We were all peaceful and peace-loving folk,
But there are times when men must go to battle,
And this was one of them,
And there we were,
Men of the blood of England, of that same blood
Which flowed within the veins of those redcoated soldiers
Who shouted at us, "Now, disperse, ye rebels!"
Our fathers and our fathers' fathers once had known
The quiet English countryside, and busy London,
The old cathedral towns, and the sea cities
Of the old England.
We stood, rough northern farmers,
Thinking of lands we should be plowing in April,
Thinking of orchards coming into blossom,
Thinking of cattle in the pleasant meadows,
But thinking, most of all, of liberty.

71

I am John Welch.
I fought at Bunker Hill.
With pick and spade I labored on the breastworks
Until the British guns came up the slope.
Then, with a musket, I stood waiting, watching
For first clear sight of white upon their eyeballs.
Below us roared the cannon. To our right
Charlestown began to burn. Our wooden houses,
Our only homes, dear to us in this new chosen land,
Burst into flame. I saw them blaze like tinder,
They all went up in smoke as we had seen
Our homes in Ireland blazing, long before,
Under the torches of the British soldiers.
Prescott called, "Fire!" We stood with muskets steady
Until, at last, we had no shots to fire.
They took the fort; but we had won the battle.
Gunless and homeless, but still undefeated,
We kept on fighting for our liberty.

I am John MacPherson.
I fought at Ticonderoga.
Back in the Hampshire Grants, among my people,
I had met Ethan Allen.
When he came, in April, asking for volunteers,
I joined his company. Through the wilderness
We went, just eighty of us. It was sunrise
When we came before the mighty fort.
"How shall we take it?" Matthew Lyon asked.
"By force," said Ethan Allen, and he led
Us forward through the open gate.
We struck down the guards. "Surrender!" Allen cried.
"By whose authority?" the British captain asked.
Then Allen roared, "Surrender in the name
Of the great Jehovah and the Continental Congress!"

We roared it after him.   The guns went down.
We had Ticonderoga.   How we laughed,
Thinking how daring might yet win our war,
Daring, and right, and faith in liberty!

I am John Collins.
I fought at Monmouth.
That day I saw one deed I shall long remember.
There was a gunner, Hayes, with the artillery.
His wife was with him.   She was Molly Pitcher,
Sturdy, and strong, and twenty-two years old.
While Hayes stood at his gun, she brought him water,
Though whistling balls and shrieking shells crashed through
The trees above her head.   Then Hayes went down.
"They've murdered him!" she cried, and, rushing back,
Knelt down to say with him his final prayer.

"Withdraw the gun," the captain said. "There is no man
Who can take over." Molly Pitcher stood.
"I can take over," quietly she said. She seized the rammer,
And swabbed the gun, then rammed home the charge.
Around her men began to fall, so close to her their blood
Spurted upon her gown; but still she stood
Beside the gun until the summer dark came down
Upon the field which helped to win our liberty.

I am Andrew Morgan.
I fought upon Kings Mountain.
My father was a North of Ireland man
Who'd come across the seas to make a home
Within the Carolinas. He had worked, early and late,
To clear our mountain farm.
Then, one day, the soldiers of Cornwallis
Came down upon us.
They killed my father and my elder brother.
I was just fifteen, too young, they thought, for fighting.
That night I took my horse and joined the Mountain Men.
I first went into battle at Kings Mountain.
We had not many orders. "Fire as you can.
Hold while you can. If you must retreat,
Come back and fire again." And that was all.
We fired; we held. We were driven back. We returned.
We fired again. Charge after charge burst on us.
Always we held. The last charge was a countercharge, our own.
Over the British ranks a white flag rose,
And Carolinians shouted, "Liberty!"

I am William Gauss.
I was at Valley Forge.
I had been in many battles,
Trenton and Brandywine and Germantown,
Since I had left my Pennsylvania farm

Near Goshenhoppen. Then we went to camp,
But what a camp!
The storms of winter fought us.
The winds of winter blew away the snow,
And left the ground in knobs that tore our feet
So that our blood left dark trail of our passing.
We stood guard, almost naked.
We lived in rude huts where we had to sleep
Upon the dirt floors. Blankets? We had none.
We starved. For days we had no flour, no meat.
What did we have?
We had our faith.
To me it was the faith I'd learned in childhood,
Far back in Father Schneider's little school,
A faith in God, a hope to win God's freedom;
And there were others who never saw the school but had the same.
There was the General, our George Washington.
I've seen him kneeling in the dark of night,
When all was worst. Once I saw Moylan with a little book,
Our Catholic prayer book. He handed it to me, and there I read,
"Grant us Thy peace within our day, O Lord."
"God grant us peace," said Moylan after me,
"When we have made our land forever free.
God grant us peace within our day, O Lord.
God grant us peace."

Something to Do

In your history or in the encyclopedia find the date of each historic event that is mentioned in this selection. Then make a map of the eastern United States. On it mark the location of the place mentioned in each stanza and beside the name write the date of the happening.

Liberty Bell of the West

CAST

In Virginia

PATRICK HENRY, *governor of Virginia*

THOMAS JEFFERSON

GEORGE MASON

GEORGE ROGERS CLARK

PEOPLE *of Williamsburg*

In Illinois

Members of Clark's expedition:

COLONEL GEORGE ROGERS CLARK

MAJOR JOSEPH BOWMAN

CAPTAIN LEONARD HELM

SIMON KENTON

JOHN SAUNDERS, *hunter*

OFFICERS *and* PRIVATES, HUNTERS *and* SCOUTS

People of Kaskaskia:

CHEVALIER DE ROCHEBLAVE, *commandant at the British post of Fort Gage (Kaskaskia)*

MADAME DE ROCHEBLAVE

DR. JEAN LAFFONT

FATHER PIERRE GIBAULT

FRENCH CITIZENS *of Kaskaskia,* MEN *and* WOMEN

MUSIC. *Roll of drums, built up to fifes and drums in "Yankee Doodle." After one chorus, music fades into soft background music for announcer*

ANNOUNCER. Here in Williamsburg, the capital of Virginia, it is the tenth of December, 1777. General Washington is about to take his ragged Continentals into winter quarters at Valley Forge. Benjamin Franklin is in France, but the French Treaty with our colonies has not yet been signed. Burgoyne has surrendered, but our War of Independence is not yet won. If England holds the forts of the West, our battles east of the Alleghenies will be shallow victories. There's trouble in the West now. The Indians are rising against us. The future of our nation, our own United States, depends upon the winning of the frontier.

FIRST VOICE. There have been bloody massacres in Kentucky.

SECOND VOICE. Who started them?

ANNOUNCER. Governor Henry

Hamilton, British commandant of the post at Detroit.

SEVERAL VOICES. Hamilton, Hamilton the Hair-Buyer! He gives the Indians knives and tomahawks. He pays the savages for every American scalp they bring him.

SOUND. *Angry murmur of voices*

FIRST VOICE. Who told you that?

SECOND VOICE. George Rogers Clark!

OTHER VOICES. Clark's a Virginian like ourselves. He's just back from Kentucky. He's here in Williamsburg to raise an army. For where? For what?

ANNOUNCER. George Rogers Clark has come to plead with Governor Patrick Henry for companies of militia. He'll take them down the Ohio River and into the Illinois country. He'll seize the British forts at Kaskaskia and Cahokia and Vincennes.

VOICES. We'll go with him! The Sons of Liberty will go with him! We'll win the West. God save the Commonwealth of Virginia!

SOUND. *Excited murmur of crowd*

MUSIC. *Fifes and drums, up and out, "Yankee Doodle." After a moment, fade out*

ANNOUNCER. The governor of Virginia, Patrick Henry, comes back to his house from the General Assembly. With him walk Thomas Jefferson and George Mason. Look! Here comes George Rogers Clark to join them.

FIRST VOICE. I'll follow his red head anywhere!

SECOND VOICE. How tall is he?

FIRST VOICE. Over six feet. He's young too. He doesn't look more than twenty-one.

SECOND VOICE. He's twenty-five.

SOUND. *Friendly murmur of crowd. Cheers*

VOICES. Clark! Clark! Huzzah for Liberty!

MUSIC. *Fifes and drums, "Yankee Doodle," under and out. After a moment, fades*

ANNOUNCER. Young. Hot-tempered. Brave. Ready to fight and ready to die for the freedom of the American frontier. Clark stands now before these three men, who will decide his fate and the future of the American nation. Three men. Patrick Henry. Thomas Jefferson. George Mason. They listen to George Rogers Clark.

CLARK. But I can do it, Governor Henry. Give me the troops, and I'll seize the British forts in the West.

HENRY. You may be right, young man. Perhaps we're losing a nation by our delay. What do you think, Jefferson?

JEFFERSON. France is about to make a treaty with us. Word may come now on any ship out of a French port. Why not wait for it? Then we'll have the good will of the French in the West.

CLARK. (*Passionately*) Our men on the frontiers will be dead by that time, sir. I've just come from Kentucky, and I've seen its burnt cabins and its dead men.

MASON. The Indians killed them?

CLARK. The Indians killed them, Mr. Mason, but it is Hamilton at Detroit who rouses the tribes to massacre. That's why we must take his forts. And here's the way to take them if you will give me authority to raise seven companies of militia in Virginia. I'll take them down the Ohio from Fort Pitt into the Illinois Country. I'll take Kaskaskia first, then—

MASON. Who is the British commandant at Kaskaskia now?

CLARK. A Frenchman named Rocheblave. He's held office under three flags, the French, the Spanish, the English.

JEFFERSON. (*Scornfully*) A multinational!

CLARK. We'll give him no chance to serve under the flag of Virginia, Mr. Jefferson.

JEFFERSON. Can you win the support of the people of the Northwest?

78

CLARK. If we could assure one of their leaders that our cause is their cause.

JEFFERSON. You might tell them of our Bill for Religious Freedom. Is there a priest out there?

CLARK. There is, sir. Father Gibault. He's been eight years at the Kaskaskia Mission. He may help us—if we can get into the fort. But to get there, we'll need boats and powder and—

HENRY. Boats and powder—and men! Where'll you get men, Colonel Clark? Even if I give you the authority to raise militia?

MUSIC. *"Yankee Doodle," fifes and drums, not too loud, up and under*

CLARK. Where shall I get the men, Governor Henry? They'll follow me to the wilderness from every county of Virginia. Men of the tidewater and men of the mountains. Virginians! Americans! Sons of Liberty, ready to fight for freedom, ready to win either glory or the grave!

MUSIC. *Not too loud*

HENRY. Glory it is! Gentlemen, he has won his first victory. George Rogers Clark, I hereby authorize you to proceed without loss of time to enlist seven companies of men to act as militia under your orders. You are to proceed to Kentucky at once.

CLARK. (*Excitedly*) And on to the British forts?

HENRY. (*Solemnly*) To the forts of the Illinois country.

MUSIC. *Up and out triumphantly. Through to finish of one chorus, with organ accompaniment, then under*

ANNOUNCER. It is St. John's Day, 1778. A total eclipse of the sun has darkened the Western world. In this gray dusk the Long Knives set out for the Illinois country, moccasins on their feet; flintlock rifles in their hands. They are a thousand miles from their source of supplies with no chance of help from behind them. The unknown wilderness lies ahead of them. Down the river to Fort Massac, only one hundred and fifty-three ragged men, they move bravely forward to victory or certain death. At the old fort they meet by chance a few hunters from Kaskaskia:

VOICES. John Saunders
    Thomas Dunn
    Samuel Moore
    John Duff

ANNOUNCER. It is a hundred

79

miles, as the crow flies, from Fort Massac to Kaskaskia. The road leads through swamps. Only a few dim, winding Indian trails mark the way. The success of the Clark expedition depends upon swiftness and secrecy. One of the hunters, John Saunders, offers to guide them. Three days out from Massac . . .

SAUNDERS. (*In a low, bewildered voice*) We can't be far from the trail. I must have made just one wrong turning. If you let me go ahead, I'll find the landmark.

VOICES. (*Excitedly*) We're lost! We're off the trail! I thought he knew the way! What are we going to do? We'll never see Kaskaskia! We'll never see Virginia again! God have mercy on us!

CLARK. (*In a rage*) Saunders, you cannot leave us wandering in a country where every nation of Indians could raise three or four times our number, where all is lost for us if our enemies find us!

SAUNDERS. (*Fearfully*) You and your men could return to Fort Massac. You could escape from here before it is too late!

CLARK. (*Raging*) Escape? Return to Massac? We'll not retrace one single step of our way! We've come too far! Our fate depends on you!

SAUNDERS. (*Frightened*) Give me time, sir! I'll find the path! (*Murmurs, as if to himself*) Down the buffalo trail, past the burnt grass, over a narrow stream, up a hill into timber. There was one tree taller than all the rest. A tree with a bloody mark. There was one tree—

VOICES. Watch him! He's going up the hill! Don't let him get away! Clark'll kill him if he doesn't find the trail. Look! Look! He's waving! He's shouting at us!

SAUNDERS. Here it is! I knew I'd find the path! Now we can go on! Follow me!

SOUND. *Murmur of excited voices*

MUSIC. *Up and out, "Yankee Doodle," fading after a moment*

ANNOUNCER. By day, in the blaze of the Illinois country; by night, with only the stars to guide them, they steal down into the Kaskaskia River valley. At last, on the evening of the Fourth of July, 1778, two years to the day after the signing of the Declaration of Independence, George Rogers Clark and his little company of brave men, a ragged, starving, dauntless band of Americans, come within the shadows of old Fort Kaskaskia, the British stronghold of the Mississippi Valley. They wait, quiet as wildcats, until a scout brings word to Clark.

SCOUT. (*Very low*) The enemy has gone off guard, Colonel. No one has seen us.

CLARK. (*Also low*) The company will divide into two parts. One will surround the town. The other will follow me into the fort. When you on the outside hear two sharp shots and a general shout, you will enter the town, run through the streets. Those of you who can speak French will proclaim to the people of the town what has happened. You will tell them to keep close to their houses, under pain of death. Are you ready?

VOICES. We're ready, sir!

CLARK. Let Simon Kenton lead the way. Forward!

VOICES. (*Speaking softly*) Kenton's leaped over the gate. He's opened it. Now we're in the stockade.

SENTRY. Who goes there?

VOICES. (*Lifting*) Virginians. The Long Knives of Virginia. The soldiers of George Rogers Clark. Americans.

SENTRY. How many of you are there?

VOICES. (*Loudly*) Five hundred of us—and an army coming from Fort Massac. (*Lower*) It's a good thing it's dark so that he can't see we're just a handful. Or that we're starving.

CLARK. I'm Clark. Where is your commandant, sentry?

SENTRY. I will not tell you.

CLARK. I'll find him!

VOICES. There isn't a light anywhere. Do you think he's here? Kenton'll soon know. He's got into the fort.

81

CLARK. (*Calling*) Kenton! Have you found the commandant?

KENTON. He's in bed.

CLARK. We'll wake him. Every man to his post. Guard the gate. Man the stockade. Fire the two shots. Give the shout. We're going in!

SOUND. *Two off-mike revolver shots. Shout. Wild cries*

VOICES. Hurrah for the Commonwealth of Virginia! Hurrah for the United States of America! You can't tread on us!

SOUND. *Thud of falling timber. Crash of glass*

VOICES. Here we go, men!

MUSIC. *Triumphantly, up and out, "Yankee Doodle." After a moment, fades*

CLARK. Are you the commandant?

ROCHEBLAVE. I am Chevalier de Rocheblave, British commandant of this fort.

CLARK. In the name of the Commonwealth of Virginia and the United Colonies I call on you to surrender it.

ROCHEBLAVE. The flag of Fort Gage will never come down to ragged rebels like you.

CLARK. It's ragged rebels who're fighting this war for independence. Ethan Allen's Green Mountain Boys are in rags. Washington's ragged army has just come out of Valley Forge. Marion's men lie in rags in the southern swamps. Yes, we're in rags, Chevalier, but our rags will one day be the liberty flag of the world. Get your things together. Give me all your official papers.

ROCHEBLAVE. I refuse. I will notify Governor Hamilton at Detroit. He will put you and your savages before a firing squad.

CLARK. He'll have to take us first. Seize this man, Kenton.

ROCHEBLAVE. You cannot do this to me. I am the representative of Great Britain.

CLARK. You are a prisoner of war.

SOUND. *Murmur of voices, then woman's shriek. Thud of feet on stairs*

FIRST MAN'S VOICE. We found this woman upstairs, Colonel Clark.

SECOND VOICE. She was packing official papers into a trunk.

ROCHEBLAVE. She has the right. She is my wife.

MADAME ROCHEBLAVE. Save me, save me from these barbarians!

CLARK. You are in no danger, madame. No soldier of my army will hurt. you. Go back to your room. Pack your clothes, but leave the papers.

MADAME ROCHEBLAVE. What are you doing with my husband?

CLARK. I am sending him to Virginia. You will make yourself ready to travel with him.

MADAME ROCHEBLAVE. It will do you no good to send us away. Kaskaskia will never submit to the Americans. Even if you surround us tonight, you cannot hold us.

ROCHEBLAVE. She is right. You cannot hold us. The French of Kaskaskia will decide which flag will fly over this fort.

CLARK. You've shifted your allegiance to every flag that's flown on the frontier, Rocheblave. You cannot speak for the French of Kaskaskia.

SOUND. *Murmur of voices, grows louder, then fades under*

FATHER GIBAULT. (*Fading in*) I can speak for the French of Kaskaskia, sir. They are my people. Their elders have come with me.

CLARK. Who are you?

FATHER GIBAULT. I am Pierre Gibault.

CLARK. The Catholic priest?

FATHER GIBAULT. The Catholic priest. I am pastor of the Mission Church of the Immaculate Conception. What have you come to do to us?

CLARK. I have taken the fort. You are now a conquered people.

FATHER GIBAULT. A captured people, perhaps, but not a conquered one. We French have long been in the Illinois country. La Salle passed this way. Father Marquette blessed this spot. Nearly one hundred years ago our people set up the Cross that still stands here. Through those years they have made this fort the outpost of civilization against the wilderness. We have been peaceful. We have been just. We have tried to live as Christians should. We have treated the Indians with honesty and with charity. We ask no more of you than we have given these Indians.

CLARK. What do you think we plan to do with you?

FATHER GIBAULT. Who knows? We have been told by the British that, if you should come, you Americans would burn our houses, seize our grain and our cattle, and take us all, men and women and children, into slavery. And from us all you would try to take our religion.

83

CLARK. Do you believe that?

FATHER GIBAULT. Why not? It is war. Governor Hamilton at Detroit buys scalps.

CLARK. We Americans don't make war that way. We come to make men free, not enslave them, as the British have told you.

FATHER GIBAULT. Free? What do you mean by freedom?

CLARK. I mean what the governor of Virginia means. I mean what Thomas Jefferson means in the bill he will bring before the Assembly of Virginia. That bill—he calls it A Declaration of Rights— provides that all men shall be free to profess, and by argument to maintain, their opinion in matters of religion, and that the same shall in no way diminish, enlarge, or affect their civil capacities.

FATHER GIBAULT. Will that bill become law if America wins?

CLARK. If we win this war, that bill will become part of the law of the whole United States.

FATHER GIBAULT. In the meanwhile, what proof have I that I may continue to say Mass in my church?

CLARK. I have nothing to do with churches other than to defend them from insult. By the laws of the state, your religion has as many privileges as any other.

FATHER GIBAULT. (Hesitantly) If I could believe that—

CLARK. The men of my army believe it. They wouldn't be with me if they didn't.

FATHER GIBAULT. How many Catholics are in your army?

CLARK. I don't know. Let them answer for themselves. Who are the Catholics here?

VOICES. Patrick Maher
John Murphy
Richard Luttrell
Patrick Kennedy
Samuel Moore
Henry Higgins
John Lyons
George McManus
Francis McDermott
Florence Mahoney
Daniel Murray
Edward Bulger
Hugh Lynch

FIRST VOICE. There are a dozen Catholics out in the town with Bowman's company.

SECOND VOICE. There are ten more in Montgomery's company.

FIRST VOICE. Captain Richard McCarty's a Catholic.

SECOND VOICE. So is Captain Quirk.

CLARK. Does that answer you, sir?

FATHER GIBAULT. The elders

84

have heard what I have heard. I shall question them directly. (*Pause*) Gentlemen, what is your will? Shall we trust the Americans?

DR. LAFFONT. If their own Catholics can trust them—

FRENCH VOICES. Yes, yes. We'll trust them. It is a cause we must join. Give us the opportunity to show our zeal. We should be the happiest people in the world to join the Americans. Freedom of religion. Your cause is our cause.

FATHER GIBAULT. Freedom of religion. If you had denied it to us, we would have died to defend it.

CLARK. Victory is the greater when it is without bloodshed.

FATHER GIBAULT. Kaskaskia is yours, Colonel Clark, but your cause is not won in the Illinois country unless you take the British fort at Vincennes. Have you men enough for that?

CLARK. More men will follow me.

FATHER GIBAULT. I am concerned with the fate of the people of Vincennes. If they understand, as I do, what the coming of the Americans means, they will join us. Let me go to them at once. They are my parishioners.

CLARK. It will be better to wait for more troops.

FATHER GIBAULT. No, no. As soon as the English learn of the loss of Kaskaskia, they will arouse the Indians. There will be massacres, many massacres. My people will be doomed. My people at Vincennes— I have baptized them. I have witnessed their marriages. I have heard their confessions and have given them Communion. When they are dying, I am near. When they are buried, I bless their

graves. Now I must prevent their destruction. Let me go—at once!

CLARK. But the dangers of the trail—

FATHER GIBAULT. I have ridden it.

VOICES. (*solemnly, as a chant*) A hundred and seventy-five miles. Wilderness.

Thunderstorms.

Fog along the Little Wabash.

Snakes at the Big Muddy River.

Buffaloes on the Four-Mile-Prairie.

Swamps of the Wabash.

Indians. Indians everywhere.

FATHER GIBAULT. God will guide me.

CLARK. You cannot go alone.

DR. LAFFONT. Let me go with him. I am Dr. Jean Laffont. I have long traveled the wilderness trails with Father Gibault.

CLARK. (*With some hesitancy*) If I could be more certain of the people's fidelity—will they take an oath of allegiance, Father Gibault?

FATHER GIBAULT. I will ask them. Will you, the people of Kaskaskia, take this oath?

VOICES. Yes, yes. We will take it.

FATHER GIBAULT. Summon them all. Let the church bell ring. The Liberty Bell of the West. We will take oath to be citizens of the new United Colonies. And now, Colonel Clark, may I be the first to take it?

MUSIC. *Organ plays "America," up and out triumphantly. Fades*

DR. LAFFONT. I, Jean Laffont, sign with you.

FRENCH VOICES. And I . . . and I . . . and I . . . and I . . . (*With a great shout*) Vive le Congress!

AMERICAN VOICES. God save the Commonwealth of Virginia!

FATHER GIBAULT. God save the new nation!

CLARK. Without you, Father Gibault, there might be no new nation.

MUSIC. *Organ, up and out, "America"*

FIRST VOICE. Look, the sun is rising. The sun of freedom.

SECOND VOICE. See, the flag is going up on the staff. The Stars and Stripes.

FIRST VOICE. Over there—beside the Mission Cross.

SOUND. *Church bell rings alone for a moment, then blends into orchestration of organ's "America." Fades under*

ANNOUNCER. The Cross and the Flag—may the sun of America never set upon them!

Recalling Characters and Dialogue

Below is a list of the names of some of the characters in this radio drama. Match the identification phrases with the names of the characters they identify. You are also given a series of quotations. Match the name of the character with something he said in this drama. Some names you will not use at all; others you will use more than once.

Characters	Identification
1. _____ Simon Kenton	*a.* Doctor at Kaskaskia
2. _____ Pierre Gibault	*b.* Hunter at Kaskaskia
3. _____ Colonel George Rogers Clark	*c.* British commandant of Fort Kaskaskia
4. _____ Patrick Henry	*d.* Governor of Virginia
5. _____ Thomas Jefferson	*e.* Pastor of the Mission Church of the Immaculate Conception
6. _____ John Saunders	*f.* Member of Clark's expedition
7. _____ Chevalier de Rocheblave	*g.* Leader of the expedition into the Illinois country
8. _____ Jean Laffont	*h.* Gentleman of Virginia

Quotations

I. _____ "France is about to make a treaty with us."

II. _____ "You could return to Fort Massac. You could escape from here before it is too late!"

III. _____ "The flag of Fort Gage will never come down to ragged rebels like you."

IV. _____ "But I could do it, Governor Henry. Give me the troops, and I'll seize the British forts in the West."

V. _____ "I can speak for the French of Kaskaskia."

VI. _____ "Kaskaskia will never submit to the Americans."

VII. _____ "I have traveled the wilderness trails with Father Gibault."

VIII. _____ "Victory is greater when it is without bloodshed."

IX. _____ "Freedom of religion. If you had denied it to us, we would have died to defend it."

ARTHUR GUITERMAN

Tall Men

Down the Chatterawha, the Ohio and the Green,
The Cumberland, the Licking and the waterways between,
They found the trail they wanted or they made it with the ax—
The Hunters of Kentucky with their rifles and their packs.

They built their lonely stations and the logs were cut and hewn
By the breed of Simon Kenton and the blood of Daniel Boone.
They stood behind the loopholes in their rugged palisades
Through hot and weary sieges, attacks and ambuscades.

They shot and made their sallies till the Shawnees broke and fled,
While the women charged the rifles and the women shaped the lead,
The women nursed the wounded and the women watched by night,
The women brought the water through the peril of the fight.

The mothers never faltered; and the sons that then were small
Grew as Hunters of Kentucky and were strong and brave and tall.

Jasmine and General Jackson

I. The Ursuline Academy

The night of January 8, 1815, was not like any other night I have known in New Orleans.

It began for me just as we came out from supper in the school refectory; I had known for days that a battle between the attacking British and the defending Americans was certain to come; but I was amazed when Sister Saint Angela called me out from the line and led me to the door which opened upon the garden. There, with gold hoops in his ears and with a bright bandanna covering his grizzled hair, stood old Michel, my father's servant.

"Your father sent me," the old man said. "He says that you are not to fear because he has come here with the pirate Lafitte."

"The Lafittes?" I cried. "Oh, no, Michel! My father would not have come with the Lafittes!"

"In time of war," the old man said, as if he spoke a lesson, "all men fight together for their country. Your father and the Lafittes are here to help General Jackson. Pray for him, for all of them."

"We will pray," said Sister Saint Angela, "Do you go back to Monsieur Louis, Elise's father?" she asked Michel.

"I go," he said proudly. "Tomorrow we fight."

"Tell him," Sister Saint Angela said, "that all of us here will be praying for him and for all the men who defend our city. We shall be praying to Our Lady of Prompt Succor."

He thanked her, and went out through the garden gate.

As he went, I spoke to Sister Saint Angela. "I am afraid, Sister," I said.

At last, this war, which had once seemed far away from us, had come close, too close. Tomorrow! Out on the plain of Chalmette my father would be fighting, perhaps dying. How would the battle end? For him? For all of us?

For days the city had been waiting for the British force of eight thousand soldiers to attack. General Jackson and his men were

89

camped on the Chalmette plantations. In all there were only four
thousand of them, soldiers from
Kentucky, soldiers from Tennessee,
Virginians, dragoons from Mississippi, and the militia of Louisiana.
Then the Lafittes and other men
from the Gulf islands joined them.
Oh, they were all brave, those soldiers who wore so many kinds of
uniforms and who stood ready to
follow General Jackson—but they
were only half the number of the
trained soldiers of the enemy.

For weeks New Orleans had
been a military camp. From the
windows of the academy we could
see and hear the soldiers, drilling,
marching, singing. Outside our
walls the town had been lively and
we had been merry. We had sung as
we sewed uniforms and prepared
an infirmary for the wounded who
would, we knew, be brought to us.
With all that, war had not quite
touched us. Then, with Michel's
message, its tightening hand
reached over the convent wall and
gripped our hearts. "I am afraid,"
I repeated.

Sister Saint Angela looked down
into my eyes. In the gathering
dusk I could see the fire in her own.
"Would you have your father know
that, Elise?" she asked me.

"Oh, no," I said.

"Then let no one else know,"
she bade me. She put her hand
upon my shoulder and led me
back into the long hall. "Call the
young ladies," she said to one of
the Sisters. "In fifteen minutes
we shall meet in the recreation
hall."

I went up to the dormitory to get
my veil, thinking that, after the
meeting, I should need it to wear
into chapel. I saw no one as I found
my way through the dusk to my
own alcove, that curtained space
which held a bed, and a chest of
drawers, and the few treasures I
had brought from home; but I
heard the sound of voices, and one
of them spoke my name.

"You should have seen him," a
girl was saying. I knew the voice
was Delphine's. "He was big, and
black, with a red scarf around his
head, and with gold hoops in his
ears. A pirate, one of her father's
friends, come with a message from
Jean Lafitte!"

"How do you know, Delphine?"
another voice asked.

"I heard him, Suzanne. I was at
the window just above the garden
door. He told her that her father
had come with the Lafittes to help
General Jackson win the battle. As

if the New Orleans militia needed the islanders!"

"The militia will probably be glad of any help they can get," I heard Adèle say.

"Not from the Lafittes or the friends of the Lafittes," Delphine said.

They went out from the dormitory without knowing I was there. For a moment I thought that I should cry, as I have so often cried because of their attitude toward me, an attitude which they managed to keep hidden from the Sisters, but which they showed me both by their words and by their actions. Long ago I had given up hope of making them know that my father was not even a privateer, as were the Lafittes. Everyone from the island called Barataria was, they thought, a pirate. Perhaps all New Orleans believed that. But what difference did it make when men from Barataria took their places beside men from New Orleans out upon the plain of Chalmette?

The bell rang, and I went to the recreation hall. It was already filled with Sisters and students. Sister Saint Angela was standing near the edge of the little platform. She began to speak. "All of you already know," she said, while her gaze moved over the rows of Sisters and students, "the danger which threatens our beloved city. The British have advanced almost to our lines. General Jackson expects the attack at daybreak."

"Daybreak!" the word ran like the rustle of leaves before a high wind. Every girl in the room was staring in fear at Sister Saint Angela, but her voice was steady as she went on. "The night before us is a fearful one. For all of us it will be a time of dread; but it must also be a time of preparation. I do not mean the work of making ready for the wounded who will come to us. That work is already done. I mean that we must prepare ourselves by prayer for what shall come. We must accept without complaint whatever is the outcome of this battle. To be able to do that, we must pray. Think of how great on this night is the need for prayer!"

I could see lips moving and hands groping for rosaries as Sister Saint Angela continued: "Some of you remember and others of you have heard of another time when we Ursulines of this convent faced a grave danger. That was ten years ago, just after our Louisiana had been sold by France to the United

States. Most of us are of French blood. We knew little of the Americans. We knew nothing of what they planned to do to our churches and schools. We feared; but we prayed.

"While we prayed, Mother Thérèse, our Superior at the time, wrote a letter to the President of the United States, President Thomas Jefferson. She asked him if our convent property right would be respected by the new government, as it had been respected by the French governors.

"President Jefferson answered that letter. All of you have seen that answer. All of you have read the lines he wrote. He told us that the principles of the Constitution and government of the United States are a sure guarantee that our freedom of education should be preserved, sacred and inviolate.

"That was his promise. The government, our government, has kept it. For we are all Americans now. We are now called upon to defend our new country—not with arms or men, but with nursing and with prayer."

Then, for the first time, Sister Saint Angela's voice broke a little. "Some of us have fathers and brothers on the plain of Chalmette.

For them, as for all who are in danger, let us pray tonight. In the morning, at eight o'clock, Father Dubourg is coming to offer the Holy Sacrifice of the Mass for the men who will be fighting, perhaps dying, on the plain. Perhaps, by then, we shall have news of the outcome of the battle. Whatever it may be, remember that it is the will of God!"

She came down from the little platform, but for a moment no one else moved. Sister Marie Madeleine arose. "In ten minutes," she said, "the chapel bell will ring."

I did not wait for the ringing of the bell, but hurried to the chapel. Within it the lights were dim. The sanctuary lamp, burning, as al-

92

ways, before the altar, cast shadows on the walls which seemed to tell of the terror of the night. There was a small light before the statue of Our Lady, that beloved statue which the Sisters had long ago brought from France; but the space around it seemed strangely bare. The day's flowers had been taken away, and fresh ones had not replaced them.

"There are no flowers for Our Lady, and yet we are asking her to help us," I thought, and hurried out from the chapel to the garden.

I hurried, for I knew that I must find Sister Marie Blanche before she went to chapel. Sister Marie Blanche is the custodian of the convent garden. She makes flowers grow where others cannot; but she always says that it is Saint Fiacre who helps the flowers to grow, and she has placed a little statue of the saint in a niche in the garden wall. She was near it when I found her and asked her for flowers for the altar of Our Lady.

She looked out over the dark garden. "Roses?" she asked as if she spoke to herself. "Lilies? No, not those." Suddenly the scent of a shrub must have come to her, as it came to me. "Ah, the jasmine," she said, "the night jasmine. It blooms for Our Lady when all the other flowers have gone to sleep. Take jasmine, Elise," she said, and handed me her gardener's shears.

I cut the bloom of the jasmine

until my arms were filled. Then, with Sister Marie Blanche beside me, I went back to the chapel. Just outside its door, I met Adèle. She gave me a puzzled look, then smiled. "I will get vases," she said.

It was the first time, since I had come to the school, that she had, of her own accord, offered to do anything with me. We arranged the fragrant jasmine in the vases that Adèle brought, then gave them to Sister Marie Blanche to take to the altar. When we went into the chapel, Adèle motioned to me to sit beside her in the pew. She gave me a little smile as she took out her rosary from the pocket of her dress. "My father too is at Chalmette," she whispered.

II. News of Battle

The chapel was already crowded. Many of the women who had come were mothers of the girls, fashionably dressed women from the lovely houses where the wealthy people lived; but there were others, probably from the poorer neighborhoods. Some of the women were weeping, and the Sisters went among them, comforting them. I saw Sister Saint Angela bending over a sobbing girl; and our Superior, Mother Marie Olivier, was holding the hand of an old woman, who was shabbily dressed.

Above them stood the statue of Our Lady, with the jasmine heaped below it. How many, many girls and women have knelt in that chapel, asking the intercession of the Mother of Christ, knowing that God sends many of His great gifts through her to us! The jasmine, I thought, was like our prayers, thousands of blossoms blending in one offering to Our Lady.

Some of the girls around me prayed, as did Adèle, calmly and steadily, but I could scarcely stay quiet. From the street beyond the walls rose the sound of voices and of horses' hoofs. What was happening? For hours I knelt there, listening and wondering. Then, at midnight, when the clang of the convent gate sounded like an alarm, I hurried out from the chapel.

The first messenger from the battlefield had come. He was standing at the door near the Superior and Sister Marie Madeleine. I moved near enough to hear him say that he had seen no action yet upon the field, which he had watched from a treetop on the Chalmette plantation.

"Will you ask him," I begged

Sister Marie Madeleine, "if he knows where Louis Rigaud, my father, is?"

She repeated my question.

"He is on Battery Four," the man said. "Just before I came here, I walked through the lines, and I saw General Jackson having a cup of coffee with them. He was saying, 'I wish I had fifty such guns on this line, with five hundred such fellows behind them!'" The messenger paused, and looked at me sharply. "You know Louis Rigaud?"

"He is my father," I said proudly.

Sister Saint Angela met me at the door of the chapel as I returned. I thought she would tell me that I must stay in the chapel, but instead she said, "Elise, you must watch for the messengers as they come. Stay at the door near Sister Marie Madeleine, and call me quickly if there is any news."

Sister Marie Madeleine knelt in the hall on a small *priedieu* below a painting of Christ in the Garden of Gethsemane. I knelt beside one of the windows, staring out on the deserted street while I tried to pray. From the chapel came the murmur of voices in rosary or litany and the strong, sweet smell of the jasmine. I am sure that, even if I live to be very old, older indeed than my father's grandmother, I shall always remember that odor of jasmine, which seemed to be going upward with our prayers to the kind Mother of God.

Just before daybreak, while I still knelt beside the window, I heard a huge explosion in the direction of Chalmette. The British had attacked! I could feel my heart pounding as I heard the roar of cannons and gunfire. I rushed toward the chapel; Sister Saint Angela was already coming out. "It has begun," she said and grasped my hand. "God help us, Elise! We must win; we must win!"

She went back into the chapel, motioning me to go back to my post at the window. There, in the spreading dawn light, I could see far down the street in the direction of the Chalmette plantations. Smoke began to show on the horizon. In a little while a rider, lashing his horse, galloped into view. He dismounted at our gate and Sister Marie Madeleine hastened to open the door to him.

"The British signaled the attack with one of their new rockets," he said. "The redcoats came up in a thick, broad column to the left of the American line. The Tennessee

riflemen opened fire, and I could see hundreds of those red specks upon the field become still! Hundreds!

"It looked like a pantomime," he went on. "There was a thin brown-and-green line on one side. It curved with the canal. That was the American line. There were many thick red squares on the other. They were the British platoons. They came, one after another, to the thin American line. Then, one after another, they shattered into red specks, some still, some moving."

Again I could not quiet my fear about my father. "And the Lafittes' men? Are they fighting, too?" I asked.

"Ho, are they fighting!" he cried. "The British have already learned to stay away from Batteries Three and Four! Those pirates can fight!"

The man hurried off then, to tell others the news he had brought; and I sat at the window, not daring to leave, for fear I should miss the next messenger as he came through the street. It was almost fifteen minutes later when a slave came running through the street. Sister Marie Madeleine sent me to stop him. He came in, glad of a moment of rest after his long run. Between excitement and breathlessness the man could hardly talk. His face glistened as he babbled out his story.

"The British general is seriously wounded. Jackson has almost a thousand Americans guarding the outskirts of the woods and another line beyond the first defense at the canal. We have another eight hun-

96

dred on the right bank of the Mississippi, but they are not in fighting condition, and some of the British are attacking them."

Sister Marie Madeleine asked him where he was going.

"I'm going back," he said, "to see what I can see. Jackson's doing fine, and the Lafittes' men are going strong. They are shouting and singing as they fire, turning back the British as fast as they come. If we can just hold out on the right bank—"

We thanked the man and let him go on his way. When I reached the door of the chapel again, Sister Saint Angela was waiting for me.

"What is it, Elise?" she entreated. I told her the story the two messengers had told me, adding, "Let me stay here, Sister! I must see each messenger as he arrives, then bring you the news. I am praying, though!"

Almost three quarters of an hour had passed since the first signal rocket of the British. By this time I was feverish with excitement and worry, and my hands were nervously fingering my rosary, as I stood at the window. My thoughts flew from Jackson's bravery and skill to the Lafittes' daring men. If only my father is safe, I thought.

It seemed hours before the next messenger came, although actually it was only about ten minutes. He was running, too, and stopped only a moment when I called to him from the door.

"The British general is dead, I think," he said, "and the British have suffered great losses. So far we have very few dead and a few wounded. We have had no news of the men on the right bank of the river. They are weak with fatigue, and if the British got through, the right bank may have fallen."

He hastened on to spread the news. Just at that moment Father Dubourg came to the convent door, to offer Mass. I could hardly realize that it was only eight o'clock in the morning. I felt that I had lived half a lifetime in a few hours—but I knew that the battle was not yet over.

Sister told me to come in for Mass. As I entered the chapel, I saw the girls and the women, wan with their night's watch and worry, waiting for the news of the battle and for the beginning of Mass.

With the end of the battle so close, I tried not to think of the results. I could not bear to think of defeat, and I dared not dream of victory. God's will would decide,

97

I told myself, and all would be for the best, even though defeat should come. All through the Mass my thoughts were distracted by my desire to know the outcome of the battle, but my petitions were all the more fervent when I prayed.

At the Gospel, Mother Marie Olivier stood and made a solemn vow to have a Mass of Thanksgiving sung each year should we be victorious. This moved many of the women to tears, and I felt even more strongly that we had to win.

The Communion of the Mass came. I had just risen from my seat to walk up the aisle when a man rushed in at the door. Seeing that Mass was being offered, he hesitated. I whispered, "What is it? It it over? Where are Jackson's men?"

In his excitement the man did not lower his voice. "Victory!" he gasped. "The British have withdrawn from the left bank! New Orleans is safe!"

New Orleans was safe! My father was safe!

Almost everyone in the chapel heard him. Anxious faces became bright as the news of our victory spread. Girls and women were radiant as they moved toward the altar rail.

I was relieved of tension, and so full of thanksgiving that I faltered on the way up the aisle to Holy Communion. Never before had I been so grateful to God, and, from the devout expressions on the faces around me, I concluded that I was not alone in my gratitude and relief.

After Mass, Sister Saint Angela stopped me outside the chapel and whispered, "A work well done, Elise! And Our Lady has heard our prayers again!"

III. GENERAL JACKSON COMES

My only concern now was the fate of my father; but oh! what a deep concern it was! Was he still safe, or had he fallen during the bitter events of the night? We had had up to that time no news of losses, but Sister Saint Angela was hurrying about, taking care of last-minute details in preparation for the coming of the wounded.

Then, swiftly, word ran among us that General Jackson himself was stopping at our academy. He was coming, someone said, to speak to Father Dubourg, who had given him so much help in making ready for the battle, and to thank the Sisters for their promise of aid for the wounded. Sister Saint Angela lined us up in a double row in the halls as the general came in.

A tall, thin man, he looked gaunt and worn; but his courtesy, even in these hours after his most terrible battle, was as perfect as if he had learned it in the bygone court of the king of France. He bowed low to Father Dubourg. He spoke quietly, seriously to the Superior, to Sister Marie Madeleine, to Sister Saint Angela. He talked to Sister Saint Angela longer than to any of the others and stood back to let her go before him as he moved between our curtsying lines.

I had no thought of speaking to him, but as he came close to me I could think of nothing but my father. What had happened to him? Surely a man who had been at Chalmette would know! "General Jackson," I gasped, then could say no more, as I saw hundreds of eyes watching me with amazement.

"Yes?" he said and bent toward me.

"I—I—"

"Her father was with you," Sister Saint Angela said. "You ask news of him, do you not, Elise?"

"Oh, yes, Sister," I told her gratefully.

"Who is your father?" the general asked.

I could see all those eyes upon me, the kindly eyes of the Sisters, the curious eyes of the strangers, the watchful eyes of the girls who had scorned me for being the daughter of a Baratarian. There was a time when I would have hung my head before them. Now I lifted it proudly. "My father is Louis Rigaud. He came with Jean Lafitte from Barataria. He was on Battery Four."

"I know him," the general smiled. "Little fellow with a big

99

voice and an aim good as Daniel Boone's. He's all right. Don't worry about him. Will you tell him I thank him for all he did on Battery Four?"

I thought the general was passing me, but he paused again. "What did you do to help us win victory?" he asked me. The question was so sharp, so sudden, that I had no answer for it. "Why—why —," I said, "I only picked the jasmine."

"The jasmine?" he repeated, not understanding—as who would?—my answer.

"Elise means," said Sister Saint Angela, "that she brought her own special gift of God's beauty to the feet of Our Lady of Prompt Succor while we prayed."

"Then you did your part," General Jackson said. "And you did it bravely, my dear."

He went on, and I leaned back against the wall. I was too tired to speak even when Adèle spoke to me. "You must be very proud of your father," she said.

We went to breakfast together. I think that every girl in the school, even Delphine, spoke to me as we went by. Sister Saint Angela spoke to me as I passed her at the refectory door. "Another battle is over,"
she said, "your own battle. I always knew that, in time, you would win it, Elise. People are good at heart. They need only remember that we must all love one another because we love God. Sometimes, though, it takes a great danger to make them remember."

"We are all one now," I said. "Not Louisianians or Baratarians. Americans."

"Let us be worthy of our victory. We have earned this one." Then her voice went low, and I saw tears in her eyes. "My only brother was killed at Chalmette," she said. "He was General Jackson's aide. The general came to bring me the news."

We are still busy here at the academy, for the wounded are being brought to us. I have carried messages, and rolled bandages, and answered calls all through the day; but Sister Saint Angela has said that I should write down my memories of last night. It will, she says, be an exercise in the class where we learn to write English. I will ask her if I may not show it to my father. He will be glad, I think, to know that I did something for our country while he was facing the enemy out on the plain of Chalmette.

100

Dividing Words into Syllables

Using the words in the list below, find the word which fits the description given and write it on your paper. Then use your dictionary to find the meaning of each word, and write it on your paper. You will not use all the words in the Word List.

Word List

inviolate	infirmary	horizon	conqueror
plain	breathlessness	dismounted	academy
fervent	alcove	victorious	pantomime
niche	guarantee	platoon	dormitory

1. A four-syllable word with a prefix and the accent on the second syllable.
2. A three-syllable word with the accent on the last syllable.
3. A word that is a homonym.
4. A word having two suffixes.
5. A three-syllable word with the accent on the middle syllable.
6. A one-syllable word with a silent *e*.
7. A three-syllable word having a prefix and a suffix.
8. A two-syllable word with the accent on the last syllable.
9. A three-syllable word with a suffix.
10. A four-syllable word whose suffix changes it from a noun to an adjective.

Writing a Character Sketch

You can tell much about a person's character from listening to what he says and observing what he does. From what you read in this story, write a character sketch of either *Sister Saint Angela* or *Elise*.

101

The Magnolia Tree

I AM the tall magnolia tree
At the western side of the Treasury,
Where President Jackson planted me
In eighteen hundred and thirty-three,
And I bloom in every springtime.

Set deep in earth by Old Hickory,
I clamp my feet on this soil of the free,
And stand in the quiet dignity
Of what God has made in majesty,
And I bloom in every springtime.

Across the street, on the White House grass,
The long processions of Presidents pass.
Ashes to ashes, dust to dust,
They go their way, as all men must,
But I bloom in every springtime.

Around me in April the city roars,
And the planes fly low on Potomac shores,
Times change, and customs, and even flowers,
But God is the same through the changing hours,
And I bloom in every springtime.

I am the old magnolia tree
That stands in the yard of the Treasury,
I am the dream of Old Hickory,
I am the faith and the hope of the free,
And I bloom in every springtime.

Anchors Aweigh!

KEVIN COLEMAN had never seen the United States Naval Academy but, for most of his seventeen years, he had wanted to be a midshipman.

When Kevin was an infant, his father, a young naval lieutenant, had died aboard a destroyer on the December day the Japanese attacked the American naval base at Pearl Harbor. Although Kevin could not remember his father, he had a clear picture in his mind of the smiling young lieutenant. He had treasured all his life a little album of snapshots that had belonged to John Coleman who had perished at Pearl Harbor.

In the album were happy mementos of another time—a snapshot of his father in the uniform of a smiling seaman standing in front of Bancroft Hall on the Academy grounds; a later picture, showing a midshipman standing beside a small craft in the Severn River. There were a dozen or more photographs—a class marching in formation, a group of "middies" on a North Atlantic cruise, a close-up of John Coleman, standing before the statue of the Indian Tecumseh, making the traditional plea for help in passing Academy exams.

There was another picture, not a snapshot. It was a faded clipping from a weekly magazine of the year 1940 and it showed the midshipmen and their guests at the annual "Ring Dance" at the Academy. Around the likeness of the prettiest girl in the group was drawn a penciled circle, and below the picture John Coleman had written with pride, *My Mary*.

John Coleman's "Mary" became Kevin Coleman's mother. One year later, holding her infant son in trembling arms as the enemy attack demolished American naval base and ships, she prayed for help as radio bulletins flashed news to the world of America's greatest naval defeat. Then, as armored trucks from the nearest United States Army base rolled past the shambles of Pearl Harbor, she was led with wives of other navy personnel to the planes that would evacuate survivors to the American mainland.

World War II had begun!

Mary Coleman died in a San Francisco hospital when Kevin was five years old. "Take care of him for me, Father Tom," she had begged the hospital chaplain. "Let me make you his legal guardian."

"There must be some close relative," protested the young priest.

"There's no one left," she said.

On a day of bright California sunlight, the child walked through the door of his new home. A smiling, gray-haired woman held out her arms to him. "I'm Father Tom's mother," she said, "and I love little boys."

Father Tom led the child around the little house, from room to room. "I grew up here, Kevin," he told him. "From now on this is your home."

"Will you come and see me?" pleaded the boy.

"Every day," Father Tom promised him, and the pledge was kept throughout the years.

Often, as the priest and the boy stood together on the top of a hill that overlooks the wide bay, they would watch the ships of the fleet come and go. "Someday I'll be a sailor," Kevin would say.

"Your father would like that," the priest would answer.

"How did my father get into Annapolis?" the boy once asked.

"I don't know," Father Tom told him. "All that I remember is that your mother once said that John Coleman did it the hard way."

"Which way was that?"

"By competitive examination, I suppose," the priest explained. "He was an enlisted man before he entered the Academy. I believe that one hundred and sixty enlisted Navy and Marine personnel are selected annually that way."

"I'll get there, too," said the boy.

Through grade school, through high school, through years of affectionate ties with Father Tom and the priest's mother, Kevin Coleman held to his dream of service. The salt breath of the sea, the tang of ocean spray was tonic to his spirit. In the month of June that marked his graduation and his seventeenth birthday, he knew that the time had come to follow in his father's footsteps.

On a "Visiting Day," as bright as the gleaming battleships that swung at anchor in the blue waters of the harbor, Kevin went aboard a United States aircraft carrier. At first no one noticed the boy who walked with eyes shining, pulse throbbing, along the deck of the great leviathan of the sea. He listened to the orders of the officers. He watched sailors going about their duties. He touched shining brass, fingering it with loving pride. He looked up at the bridge and imagined how he would act if he were the ranking officer. He pictured himself in command of the carrier during a great storm or a great battle.

At first he did not hear the voice beside him. "Would you like to see the rest of the ship?"

Startled, Kevin turned to look at a boy his own age, dressed in the regulation summer uniform of the Navy. "Could I see everything?" he asked.

"Let's go," said the sailor.

"What is your job?" Kevin queried.

"I'm an apprentice seaman," explained the sailor. "My name's Jimmie Taylor."

Jimmie showed Kevin the details of operation as they walked the length and breadth of the carrier—the galleys, the living quarters, the elevators that bring planes up to the flight deck, the catapult that shoots planes off the carrier. Kevin asked a hundred questions, and Jimmie Taylor laughed. "Thinking of joining us?" he asked.

"I've been waiting for the chance for seventeen years," Kevin told him.

"The recruiting office is on Sutter Street," said Jimmie.

Kevin said nothing that night until Father Tom was about to leave for the hospital. Then he asked, "May I serve Mass for you tomorrow morning?"

"Seven o'clock," Father Tom reminded him, and looked sharply at the boy.

"I'll be there," said Kevin.

From *Gloria* to the Last Gospel the boy's fervent responses rang out through the quiet hospital chapel. Only when they were taking off their vestments in the sacristy did the priest and the boy openly acknowledge that the time had arrived for frank and final confidences.

"What's on your mind, Kevin?" Father Tom asked, as he folded his chasuble.

"I'm enlisting in the Navy today," Kevin said.

Father Tom took off his long white alb. "Do you believe in slogans? Such as 'Join the Navy and see the world'?"

Kevin's jaw stiffened. "I could see the world other ways," he said. "I'm joining the Navy because it's where I belong. My folks were Navy people and proud of it."

"Do you intend to make a career of it, or just put in a tour of duty?"

"I want the Navy for as long as the Navy wants me," the boy protested.

"It isn't all glamour," Father Tom warned him. "It isn't all dress parades, or the big football game with Army, or a desk in the Pentagon, or gay cruises in the Mediterranean."

"I know. I'm not asking for those things."

"It's hard work," said the priest.

"I can take it," said the boy, and added sharply, "my father did."

Father Tom placed his hands on Kevin's shoulders. "Your father was a graduate of Annapolis, Kevin," he said. "By enlisting today you won't be stepping into a wardroom or the officers' quarters as he did after graduation from the Academy. You'll be on the forecastle side of the dividing line between officers and enlisted men."

"It's a line that can be crossed," said the boy, "if you've got what the Navy needs. Experience as a seaman will help me."

The priest's grip on Kevin's shoulders did not relax. "Has it ever occurred to you that there's an easier way than enlistment as a seaman to reach Annapolis?" he asked.

"Do you mean by Presidential appointment?"

"Yes," said Father Tom. "You're the son of a naval officer who gave his life for his country. Each year the President of the United States can select forty sons of men or women who were killed in action. You could be one of those forty candidates."

"I know that, Father," Kevin told him, "but I'm choosing the hard way."

"Why?" Father Tom's voice lifted sharply. "This Presidential appointment isn't charity. It's a tribute—and a debt of honor—to the valor of American heroes. Your father was one of them."

"I like to think of my father as a boy who started at the foot of the ladder and rose through his own ability. I want to prove to him that I can do it the same way."

Father Tom's eyes filled with tears. "Don't think for a minute that I'm trying to stop you, Kevin," he said. "I've known for years that this day would come, and I've hoped it would come in this way. I've only been testing your vanity and your courage."

"Do you think I'll make the grade?" asked Kevin.

Father Tom laughed. "You'll be an admiral someday," he said.

"Maybe the ghost of Old Tecumseh is waiting for me on the Academy grounds," said the boy.

"You'll find much more than the statue of an Indian warrior. You'll be conscious of the spirit of a fine young man who once sailed out the Chesapeake Bay the summer before Pearl Harbor. He'll say, 'Welcome home, my son!'"

Kevin reached for his jacket. "Will you go to the recruiting office with me?" he asked.

"I'll be proud to go with you," said Father Tom.

They left the sacristy, genuflected before the chapel altar, and walked down the wide halls of the busy California hospital. "What'll I take with me?" asked the boy.

Father linked his arm with that of the future admiral. "Your faith and your courage," he said.

They came to the door that looks down upon the city and the sea and the great gray ships in harbor. "I'll take Dad's snapshot album of Annapolis, too," said Kevin Coleman. "I'll need it for a road map."

Below them from the harbor rose the faint chime of a ship's bell and the low, soft wail of a ship's horn.

Can You Find the Main Idea?

Read carefully from your text the paragraphs indicated. Then choose for each section the *best* main idea from those listed.

Page 103, paragraphs 1–5. (1) John Coleman dies at Pearl Harbor (2) The Navy in Kevin Coleman's background (3) Pictures of the United States Naval Academy

Page 104, paragraphs 9–10. (1) Kevin's mother's death (2) Father Tom's mother provides a home for Kevin (3) Kevin's dreams of following in his father's footsteps

Page 104, paragraphs 16–17. (1) Kevin's joy in viewing the ship and the seamen at work (2) Kevin's graduation and his seventeenth birthday (3) Kevin meets Jimmie Taylor

Page 106, paragraphs 1–6. (1) Father Tom points out the difficulties of Navy life (2) Kevin serves Father Tom's Mass (3) Kevin's desire to enlist in the Navy

Page 106, paragraphs 7–12. (1) Father Tom tests Kevin's desires (2) Father Tom goes to the recruiting office with Kevin (3) Kevin proves that he has high ideals

What Was Your Reaction?

Adults and those approaching adulthood react emotionally to their surroundings, to the things they observe and read. Your answers to these questions will show your emotional reactions to situations in the story.

1. At any time in the story did you pity Kevin? Why?
2. Did you admire Kevin? Why?
3. What did you think of his wanting to work his way up in the Navy?
4. How did you feel about Father Tom? Give two reasons.

JOHN HAY

Mother of God

MOTHER of God! as evening falls
    Upon the silent sea,
And shadows veil the mountain walls,
    We lift our souls to thee!
From lurking perils of the night,
    The desert's hidden harms,
From plagues that waste, from blows that smite,
    Defend thy men-at-arms.
Mother of God! thy starry smile
    Still bless us from above!
Still save each soul from guilt apart
    As stainless as each sword;
And guard undimmed in every heart
    The image of our Lord!

In desert march or battle's flame,
    In fortress and in field,
Our war-cry is thy holy name,
    Thy love our joy and shield!
Mother of God! the evening fades
    On wave and hill and lea,
And in the twilight's deepening shades
    We lift our souls to thee!
In passion's stress—the battle's strife,
    The desert's lurking harms,
Maid-Mother of the Lord of Life,
    Protect thy men-at-arms!

The First Captain of the Navy

In THE January days of 1781, nearly six years after the outbreak of the War for Independence, the Continental Congress faced a major crisis.

In the camps the Continental soldiers were demanding payment in coin, since the Continental paper money was without value. Only through the aid of France could these coins be obtained. American envoys must be sent to France. Already General George Washington, commander in chief of the armies, had chosen three men in whom he could place his trust to carry out this mission. They were hopeful that, if they could reach France in safety, they could gain the help. But how could speed and safety be assured them?

Remembering the treason of Benedict Arnold, who had once done so much for the cause of the colonies but who had been unable to endure defeats and hardships, General Washington insisted that the captain of the ship which should bear the envoys to France should be absolutely trustworthy.

"Whom can we trust now?" he asked sadly.

Instantly the Continental Congress made answer, "Captain John Barry," and gave to that patriot command of the best and fastest ship of the Continental Navy, the *Alliance*.

Captain John Barry, by notable deeds, had already won fame as a man to be trusted. A Catholic, born in Ireland, he had gone to sea as a cabin boy when he was fifteen. When he was eighteen, he had come to Philadelphia. By the time he was twenty-one years old, he was captain of a schooner. Ten years later he was the captain of the *Black Prince*, one of the finest trading vessels that sailed from the Atlantic ports.

Barry was on a cruise to London when the battle of Lexington was

fought. He returned to find the colonies aflame with determination to win their independence. On the day of his arrival Congress resolved to fit out two armed cruisers for the capture of British vessels that were bringing supplies to the British army. Congress bought two ships, the *Lexington* and the *Reprisal*. To Barry they gave command of the *Lexington*. His was the first naval commission issued by the Continental Congress. The *Lexington* was the first ship to bear the Continental flag to victory on the seas. Barry brought back to Philadelphia the first prize won in the war, the British ship *Edward*.

Then came the terrible winter after the Declaration of Independence, when General Washington had to retreat from Cornwallis, crossing New Jersey from New York. Barry, seeing that the need on land was greater than the need at sea, organized a company of volunteers and went to Washington's aid. He helped to transport the Continental Army across the ice-locked Delaware on that fateful Christmas of 1776. He served in the battles of Princeton and Trenton, which drove the British back to New York. When Cornwallis asked for permission to send relief to his wounded men, General Washington, in Christian charity, sent John Barry to assure safe conduct to surgeons to care for the British wounded.

With that task done, John Barry went back to his old job. It was Barry who, when the British came up the Delaware, worked out the plan of filling kegs with gunpowder, and sending them downstream to explode against wharves and warships. This was the famous "Battle of the Kegs."

Then, with only twenty-seven men in open rowboats, Barry captured in the Delaware River a British ship of ten guns. With it he took four convoys and one hundred and fifty prisoners.

In the sixth year of the war Barry was given command of the *Alliance,* the ship on which he took the American envoys to France. On his way to France, he captured the British privateer *Alert.* He waited at a French port while the three envoys presented their case to King Louis XVI with such success that they came back with enough money to make it possible for General Washington to win the Yorktown campaign.

Then, on the way home, Captain Barry almost met disaster. Just off France, he captured two British privateers. Weeks later, two other vessels attacked the American ship. Barry was badly wounded. Surrender seemed almost certain.

Below decks, knowing the vital importance of his mission, the captain prayed—as he did all things—openly. Afterward he was to say that his answer came from God as direct as his pleading to his Maker. For, when all hope seemed lost, a wind arose, filling the sails of his ship. "Swing her around," Barry ordered. The ship ran between her two enemies firing broadsides upon them from her guns until the two ships lowered their flags. The wounded captain brought not two, but four prizes into port.

Barry was rewarded by an order to take Lafayette, who had already won the grateful devotion of the colonies, back to France upon a mission for the Congress. The success of that mission brought about the treaty of peace between England and the colonies. Barry, not knowing it had been signed, was bringing back a large amount of coin from Havana when he met the British sloop of war *Sybil.* He fought her until she was ready to surrender, but two other English ships came up, and the *Alliance* had to find safety in flight. This was the last battle of the War for Independence.

At the end of the War for Independence, Barry retired. Afterward he was brought back from private life to become the first captain of the *United States,* the first ship built by an act of Congress for the United States Navy. General Washington, then President, gave further honor to Barry by making him the first commander-in-chief of the Navy.

After a long life of service to his country John Barry died during the administration of Thomas Jefferson. In Old St. Mary's Churchyard in Philadelphia, near the graves of other great Catholics of the Revolution, Thomas FitzSimons, who signed the Constitution of the United States, and George Meade, and Captain John Rosseter, the first captain of the Navy of the United States lies at rest.

Skimming for Information

Skim to find the answers to the following questions. On your paper copy the questions and after each write the number of the page and the paragraph in which you found the answer. Then write the answer in your own words, using complete sentences.

1. What country was the only one from which coins could be obtained so that the soldiers in the Continental Army might be paid?

2. What battle was fought while John Barry was on a cruise to London?

3. What was Captain Barry's religion and where was he born?

4. What was the name of the first ship built by an Act of Congress?

5. How many prisoners did Barry and his men take when they captured a British ship and four convoys in the Delaware?

6. Where was John Barry's body buried?

7. What was the name of the ship Barry captured on his way to France?

8. What was the date (day and year) on which the Continental Army crossed the Delaware?

9. Who betrayed his country because he was unable to face hardships and defeat?

10. How did Barry and his men fight against the British when they attempted to come up the Delaware?

3. American Laughter

You can't pin a label on American humor. It must speak for itself. There is one thing certain about it—it is on a grand scale, immense as our rivers, violent as our tornadoes, fantastic as Disneyland.

Earlier than the covered wagon is the tall tale of America. In country stores, around prairie campfires, in lonely woods, at roaring camp meetings, men told these stories that are based on a little bit of fact and a fearful amount of fiction. From the beginning, Americans have liked their heroes big.

Today our tales of laughter are more sophisticated, but modern heroes of fiction remain counterparts of other days. There is still horse sense in the horseplay. You can still find the sly humor, the tall talk, the breakdown of the pretentious and the pompous. Modern American laughter is up to its old tricks. Time has not changed the grand American scale.

KENNETH ALLEN ROBINSON

American Laughter

OH, THE men who laughed the American laughter
Whittled their jokes from the rough bull-pines;
They were tall men, sharpened before and after;
They studied the sky for the weather-signs;
They tilted their hats and they smoked long-nines!

Their laughter was ladled in Western flagons
And poured down throats that were parched for more;
This was the laughter of democrat wagons
And homely men at the crossroads store
—It tickled the shawl that a lawyer wore!

It hurt the ears of the dainty and pretty
But they laughed the louder and laughed their fill,
A laughter made for Virginia City,
Springfield, and Natchez-under-the-Hill,
And the river that flows past Hannibal still!

American laughter was lucky laughter,
A coonskin tune by a homespun bard;
It tasted of hams from the smokehouse rafter
And locust trees in the courthouse yard,
And Petroleum Nasby and Artemus Ward!

And the corn grew tall and the fields grew wider,
And the land grew sleek with the mirth they sowed;
They laughed the fat meat into the spider,
They laughed the blues from the Wilderness Road,
—They crossed hard times to the Comstock Lode!

How Pecos Bill Became a Cowboy

Ask any oldtimer in Texas about Pecos Bill and he'll tell you that Bill was the rootin'est, tootin'est cowboy of all time. He was a mighty man. You'll hear that he taught the broncho how to bust, that he dug the Rio Grande one dry year when he grew tired of packin' water from the Gulf of Mexico, and that once he rode an Oklahoma cyclone.

The brave deeds of Pecos Bill have been told for generations by men of the Southwest ranges. No one believes these stories, but cowboys have a lot of fun telling them. If you ask what happened to the hero of the Pecos River, they'll tell you that one day he met a man from Boston, wearing a mail-order cowboy outfit and asking fool questions about the West, and poor old Pecos Bill lay down and laughed himself to death.

No WONDER Pecos Bill was so brave. His mother was a very brave woman. One morning before breakfast she swept forty-five Indian chiefs out of her yard with her broom.

When Davy Crockett heard how brave she was, he sent her a Bowie knife as a present. All her eighteen children cut their teeth on that Bowie knife.

Her nearest neighbor lived one hundred miles away. When one day she heard that a new neighbor had moved in only fifty miles away, she decided, "This part of Texas is getting too crowded. We must move out where we will have more room."

So Pecos Bill's father hitched the old spotted cow and the old red mule to the old covered wagon. The father and mother put their eighteen children into the wagon, and they started out across the prairie. Their son Bill was four years old then. He sat in the very end of the wagon, with his feet hanging out.

When they were driving through the low waters of the Pecos River, one wheel of the wagon hit a rock, and the jolt threw Bill right out of the wagon and into the sand of the river. No one saw him fall or heard him call, "Wait for me!"

After Bill saw that the wagon was going on without him, he got up and ran after it. But his short little legs could not go so fast as the wagon. Soon it was gone, and Bill was left all alone.

There were still seventeen children in the wagon, and no one noticed that little Bill was gone, until his mother counted the children at dinner time.

"Where is Bill?" she asked.

No one had seen him since they crossed the river. So the family all hurried back to the river and hunted for little Bill. They looked and looked, but they could not find him. Because they had lost him at the Pecos River, they always spoke of him after that as their little lost Pecos Bill.

Little Pecos Bill was not lost long. His father and mother never did find him, but he was found by an old grandfather Coyote, named Grampy.

Grampy showed little Pecos Bill berries to eat, dug up roots for him, and found mesquite beans for him, too. At night Grampy led Pecos Bill to his cave in the mountain where he could curl up and sleep safe and warm.

Grampy showed his man-child to each of the other hunting animals, and asked all of them not to hurt little Pecos Bill. The Bear grunted, "W-f-f-f! I will not hurt your man-child. I will show him where to find wild honey in the bee trees."

The Wolf yelped, "I will not hurt your man-child. Let him come play with my cubs."

But the Rattlesnake just shook his rattles, "Th-r-r-r!" and hissed, "S-s-s-s! Keep him out of my way! I bite anybody that crosses my path, but I give fair warning first. Th-r-r-r! S-s-s-s!"

The Mountain Lion yowled, "Get your child out of my way before I eat him up! A nice fat man-child is what I like to eat best of all!"

So all the hunting animals except the Rattlesnake and the Mountain Lion promised to be good to little Pecos Bill. He learned to talk to all the animals and birds in their own languages.

But the Coyotes liked Pecos Bill best of all. They taught him how to hunt. When he grew older, he was able to run so fast that he could catch the long-eared Jack Rabbit and the long-tailed Road-Runner. Finally he grew big enough to catch the Deer, and even the Antelope, which runs fastest of any animal.

He grew strong enough to pull down a Buffalo for his friends, the Coyotes. He climbed to the mountaintops and jumped about from crag to crag to catch the Mountain Sheep.

In all the years while Pecos Bill was living with the Coyotes, he had never seen a human being. Then one day, Bill's brother Chuck came riding along on his cowpony and found Bill. Bill was a tall young man by now, his skin was a dark brown color, and his black hair hung long and tangled. But Chuck knew him at once, and cried, "Why, you are my long-lost brother, Pecos Bill!"

Bill looked at Chuck and agreed, "We do look alike. Perhaps I am your brother!"

Chuck said, "Brother, you must put on some clothes and come with me to the ranch where I work and be a cowboy too. But I don't have any extra clothes with me. I don't know what we can do!"

Pecos Bill laughed. "If anything has to be done, I can do it! Just wait a minute, and I'll have some clothes!"

He looked around until he found a big old steer with horns measuring six feet from tip to tip. He grabbed it by the tail, yelled loudly, and scared it so badly that it jumped clear out of its skin! (That didn't hurt the old steer; it wanted to grow a new hide anyhow.) From the hide Pecos Bill made himself a leather jacket, using a yucca thorn for a needle. He made some boots, too. Then he made himself a pair of leather pants, the kind that are now called chaps. Other cowboys wear them now, to keep from getting scratched when they ride through thorny bushes. They learned that from Pecos Bill.

When Bill had put on his clothes, Chuck told him, "Get up behind me on my cowpony, and he will carry both of us to the ranch."

But Pecos Bill laughed. "Ride your pony, and I'll go afoot, and I'll beat you to the ranch."

Sure enough, Bill galloped along easily, faster than Chuck's cowpony could run.

Chuck disagreed, though, "You really must not go up to the ranch on foot. Nobody walks in the ranch country. We must find you some old pony to ride and a quirt to whip him along with."

Just then Bill nearly stepped on the Rattlesnake that lay in the trail. It was fifteen feet long, and had thirty rattles on its tail.

"Get out of my way," hissed Pecos Bill in snake language.

"I won't," the Snake hissed back. "I told Grampy long ago to teach you to stay out of my way."

The Snake spit poison at Pecos Bill, hitting him right between the eyes. Bill said, "I'll give you three chances at me, before I even begin to fight."

The three shots of poison didn't even blister Pecos Bill's skin. Next, Bill spit back at the Snake, right on top of the Snake's head, and the Snake fell over, unable to move for a moment.

Bill jumped on the Snake and stamped it before it had time to bite him. He caught the Snake up by the throat and asked, "Had enough yet?"

The Snake cried, "I give up!" Pecos Bill wrapped it around his arm for a quirt and galloped on ahead of Chuck's pony.

Soon they met the Mountain Lion. He was the largest Mountain Lion in all the world, twice as large as Chuck's cowpony. The Mountain Lion growled, "I said I would eat you up if ever you got in my way, and now I will!"

He jumped at Pecos Bill, but Bill dodged and pulled out a handful of the Mountain Lion's fur as he went by. The fight lasted for two hours, since they were evenly matched. Every time the Mountain Lion tried to jump on Pecos Bill, Bill pulled out some more of his hair. The sky was so full of the Mountain Lion's hair that it was almost as dark as night. Finally the Lion lost all of his hair except just a little on the tips of his ears and under his chin.

Then he begged, "Please, Pecos Bill, will you not hurt me any more?"

"Very well," agreed Pecos Bill, "but you must let me ride you for a cowpony."

So Pecos Bill jumped on the Mountain Lion's back, and using the Rattlesnake for a quirt to whip him along with, rode on to the ranch with Chuck.

Just at sundown, Pecos Bill rode up to the cowboy's camp on the Mountain Lion, twice as big as a cowpony, and he was still using the Rattlesnake fifteen feet long for a quirt. The cowboys around the campfire were too surprised to say a word. Chuck announced proudly, "Boys, this is my brother, Pecos Bill."

The cowboys' supper was cooking over the campfire—a big kettle of beans and a big pot of coffee, both boiling hot. Pecos Bill stuck his hands into the boiling bean kettle, pulled out a double handful of beans, and stuck them into his mouth. Then he washed them down with boiling coffee, lifting the big coffee pot from the fire, and swallowing down a gallon. He wiped his mouth on a prickly pear leaf.

Then he asked, "Who is the boss here?"

A big man seven feet tall and wearing three guns stepped forward. "I was," he said, "but you are now, Pecos Bill. Anybody that can ride a Mountain Lion and use a Rattlesnake for a quirt is boss here as long as he wants to be."

Giving Your Impressions

1. On your paper write three sentences telling why you liked or disliked the story.

2. The author of this story, Leigh Peck, wanted to amuse his readers with this "tall tale" of the West. Humor can be achieved in many ways. One author may choose dialect; another might have the characters in his story tell jokes; another might use exaggeration; and still another might paint funny word pictures. Which method do you think this author used?

On your paper write five examples which prove the answer you gave to the question above.

Cattle Brands

THERE was a law upon the range when Western lands were new,
The law of Double-Diamond, and Bar X, and Lazy U,
The law which set the brands upon the roving, milling herds,
And marked them for their owners better than a thousand words.

There were U V, and D B L, and X I T, and Y,
And U-Bar-U, and E-Cross-M, and One-Star-in-the-Sky;
And F-Bar-C, and One-O-One, and dozens more to spare,
And Diamond C, and L O S, and the old Rocking Chair;

O X, L S, and L I T, and V set upside down,
The Pitchfork and the Shovel that were known in every town,
These were the brands the irons marked. No cattleman could fail
To know the owners of the herds upon the Chisholm Trail.

The fences hold the cattle now, the wires rise high and strange,
The old law of the branding-iron no longer rules the range;
But all the way from Texas to Dakota runs the tale
Of cattle brands which marked the herds upon the Chisholm Trail.

Treasure

THERE comes a time in every rightly constructed boy's life when he has a raging desire to go somewhere and dig for hidden treasure. This desire suddenly came upon Tom Sawyer one day. He sallied out to find his friend Joe Harper, but had no luck. Next he sought Ben Rogers; Ben had gone fishing. Presently he stumbled upon Huckleberry Finn. Tom took him to a private place and opened the matter to him confidentially. Huck was willing.

"Where'll we dig?" said Huck.

"Oh, 'most anywhere."

"Why, is it hid all around?"

"No, indeed it ain't. It's hid in mighty particular places, Huck."

"Who hides it?"

"Why robbers, of course. Who'd you reckon?"

"I don't know. If 'twas mine I wouldn't hide it; I'd spend it and have a good time."

"So would I. But robbers don't do that way. They always hide it and leave it there."

"Where you going to dig first?"

"Well, I don't know. S'pose we tackle that old dead-limb tree on the hill t'other side of Still House branch?"

"I'm agreed."

So they got a crippled pick and a shovel, and set out on their three-mile tramp. They arrived hot and panting. They worked and sweated for half an hour. No result. They toiled another half-hour. Still no result. Then Tom remembered, "Oh, Huck, I know what the matter is. You got to find out exactly where the shadow of the limb falls at midnight, and that's where you dig!"

Nothing daunted, the boys were back on the hillside that night. When they judged that twelve had come, they marked where the shadow fell, and began to dig. Their hopes commenced to rise. Their interest grew stronger, and their industry kept pace with it. The hole deepened and still deepened, but every time their hearts jumped to hear the pick strike something, they only suffered a new disappointment. It was only a stone or a chunk.

At last Tom said: "It ain't any use, Huck. We're wrong again."

"Let's try somewhere else, Tom."

"All right, I reckon we better."

"What'll it be?"

Tom considered a while, and then said: "The ha'nted house. That's it!"

But Huck was unwilling to disturb the haunted house at night when ghosts might be about; so the boys decided to tackle it in the daytime on Saturday.

When they reached the haunted house shortly after noon, there was something so weird and grisly about the dead silence that reigned there under the baking sun, and something so depressing about the loneliness and desolation of the place, that they were afraid, for a moment, to venture in. Then they crept to the door and took a trembling peep. They saw a weed-grown, floorless room, unplastered, with an ancient fireplace, vacant windows, a ruinous staircase; and here, there, and everywhere hung ragged, abandoned cobwebs. They presently entered very softly, with quickened pulses, talking in whispers, ears alert to catch the slightest sound, and muscles tense and ready for instant retreat.

They gave the place a critical and interested examination. Next

they wanted to look upstairs. This was something like cutting off retreat, but they got to daring each other, and of course there could be but one result—they threw their tools into a corner and made the ascent. Up there were the same signs of decay. In one corner they found a closet that promised mystery, but the promise was a fraud —there was nothing in it. Their courage was up now and well in hand. They were about to go downstairs again and begin work when—

"Sh!" said Tom.

"What is it?" whispered Huck, turning pale with fright.

"Sh! . . . There! . . . Hear it?"

"Yes! . . . Oh, my! Let's run!"

"Keep still! Don't you budge! They're coming toward the door."

The boys stretched themselves upon the floor with their eyes to knotholes in the planking, and lay waiting in a misery of fear.

"They've stopped. . . . No— coming. . . . Here they are. Don't whisper another word, Huck. My goodness, I wish I was out of this!"

Two men entered. Each boy said to himself: "There's the old deaf and dumb Spaniard that's been about town once or twice lately— never saw t'other man before."

"T'other" was a ragged and unkempt creature, with nothing very pleasant in his face. The Spaniard was wrapped in a serape; he had bushy white whiskers; long white hair flowed from under his sombrero, and he wore green goggles. When they came in, "t'other" was talking in a low voice; they sat down on the ground, facing the door, with their backs to the wall, and the speaker continued his remarks. His manner became less guarded and his words more distinct as he proceeded.

"No," said he, "I've thought it all over, and I don't like it. It's dangerous."

"Dangerous!" grunted the "deaf and dumb" Spaniard—to the vast surprise of the boys. "Milksop!"

This voice made the boys gasp and quake. It was Injun Joe's!

There was silence for some time. Then Joe said: "Well, what's more dangerous than coming here in the daytime! Anybody would suspicion us that saw us."

"I know that. But there warn't any other place as handy. I want to quit this shanty. I wanted to yesterday, only it warn't any use trying to stir out of here with those infernal boys playing over there on the hill right in full view."

"Those infernal boys" quaked again under the inspiration of this remark.

The two men got out some food and made a luncheon.

Presently Joe said, "I'm dead for sleep! It's your turn to watch."

He curled down in the weeds and soon began to snore. His comrade stirred him once or twice and he became quiet. Presently the watcher began to nod a bit; his head drooped lower and lower; both men began to snore now.

The boys drew a long, grateful breath. Tom whispered: "Now's our chance—come!"

Huck said: "I can't—I'd die if they was to wake."

Tom urged—Huck held back. At last Tom rose slowly and softly, and started alone. But the first step he made wrung such a hideous creak from the crazy floor that he sank down almost dead with fright. He never made a second attempt. The boys lay there counting the dragging moments till it seemed to them that time must be done and eternity growing gray; and then they were grateful to note that at last the sun was setting.

Now one snore ceased. Injun Joe sat up and stared around—smiled grimly upon his comrade, whose head was drooping upon his knees —stirred him up with his foot and said: "Here! *You're* a watchman, ain't you! It's all right, though— nothing's happened."

"My! Have I been asleep?"

"Oh, partly, partly. Nearly time for us to be moving, pard. What'll we do with what little swag we've got left?"

"I don't know—leave it here as we've always done, I reckon. No use to take it away till we start south. Six hundred and fifty in silver's something to carry."

"Well—all right—it won't matter to come here once more."

"No—but I'd say come in the night as we used to do—it's better."

"Yes, but look here—it may be a good while before I get the right chance at that job; accidents might happen. 'Tain't in such a very good place; we'll just regularly bury it— and bury it deep."

"Good idea," said the comrade, who walked across the room, knelt down, raised one of the hearthstones and took out a bag that jingled pleasantly. He subtracted from it twenty or thirty dollars for himself and as much for Injun Joe and passed the bag to the latter, who was on his knees in the corner, now, digging with his bowie knife.

The boys forgot all their fears, all their miseries in an instant. With gloating eyes they watched every movement. Luck!—the splendor of it was beyond all imagination! Six hundred dollars was enough to make half a dozen boys rich! Here was treasure-hunting in the easiest way possible—there would not be any bothersome uncertainty as to where to dig. They nudged each other at every moment—eloquent nudges and easily understood—for they simply meant, "Oh, but ain't you glad *now* we're here!"

Joe's knife struck upon something.

"Hello!" said he.

"What is it?" said his comrade.

"Half-rotten plank—no, it's a box, I believe. Here—bear a hand and we'll see what it's here for. Never mind, I've broken a hole."

He reached his hand in and drew it out. "Man, it's money!"

The two men examined the handful of coins. They were gold. The boys above were as excited as themselves, and as delighted.

Joe's comrade said: "We'll make quick work of this. There's an old rusty pick over amongst the weeds in the corner the other side of the fireplace. I saw it a minute ago."

He ran and brought the boys' pick and shovel. Injun Joe took the pick, looked it over critically, shook his head, muttered something to himself, and then began to use it.

The box was soon unearthed. It was not very large; it was iron-bound and had been very strong before the slow years had injured it. The two men contemplated the treasure a while in blissful silence.

"Pard, there's thousands of dollars here," said Injun Joe.

" 'Twas always said that Murrel's gang used to be around here one summer," the stranger observed.

"I know it," said Injun Joe, "and this looks like it, I should say."

"What'll we do with this—bury it again?"

"Yes. (Extreme delight overhead.) No! by the great sachem, no! (Profound distress overhead.) I'd nearly forgot. That pick had fresh earth on it! (The boys were sick with terror in a moment.) What business has a pick and a shovel here? What business with fresh earth on them? Who brought them here—and where are they gone? Have you heard anybody? —seen anybody? What! bury it again and leave them to come and see the ground disturbed? Not exactly—not exactly. We'll take it to my den."

"Why, of course! Might have thought of that before. You mean Number One?"

"No—Number Two—under the cross. The other place is bad—too common."

"All right. It's nearly dark enough to start."

Injun Joe got up and went about from window to window cautiously peeping out. Presently he said: "Who could have brought those tools here? Do you reckon they can be upstairs?"

The boys' breath forsook them. Injun Joe put his hand on his knife, halted a moment, undecided, and then turned toward the stairway. The boys thought of the closet, but their strength was gone. The steps came creaking up the stairs. The boys in desperation were about to spring for the closet, when there was a crash of rotten timbers, and Injun Joe landed on the ground amid the debris of the ruined stairway. He gathered himself up cursing, and his comrade said: "Now what's the use of all that? If it's anybody, and they're up there, let them stay there. Who cares? It will be dark in fifteen minutes."

Joe grumbled awhile; then he agreed with his friend that what daylight was left ought to be economized in getting things ready for leaving. Shortly afterward they slipped out of the house in the deepening twilight, and moved toward the river with their precious box.

Tom and Huck rose up, weak but vastly relieved, and stared after them through the chinks between the logs of the house. Follow? Not they. They were content to reach the ground again without broken necks, and head for the townward track over the hill. They did not talk much. They were too much absorbed in hating themselves— hating the ill luck that made them take the spade and the pick there. But for that, Injun Joe never would have suspected. He would have hidden the silver with the gold and then he would have had the misfortune to find that money turn up missing. Bitter, bitter luck that the tools were ever brought there!

They resolved to keep a lookout for that Spaniard when he should come to town and then follow him to "Number Two," wherever that might be.

[It was some days, however, before the boys were able to continue their search for the Spaniard and the treasure. Exciting events intervened. Tom and his friend Becky Thatcher became separated from the rest of a picnic party and were lost for several days in the vast underground chambers of McDougal's cave. While searching a corridor as a means of escape, Tom caught a fleeting glimpse of Injun Joe. He backed away in terror and did not tell Becky of his discovery. Shortly afterward, Tom found a hole that brought them out upon the side of a bluff, five miles below the valley where they had entered the cave. Here they were rescued by some men in a skiff.

Becky's father, not knowing Injun Joe was in there, put a locked door at the mouth of the cave, and there one day Injun Joe was found, dead.]

As soon after his funeral as possible, Tom took Huck to a private place to have an important talk.

"Huck, the money's in the cave!"

Huck's eyes blazed. "Say it again, Tom."

"The money's in the cave!"

"Tom—honest injun, now—is it fun, or earnest?"

"Earnest, Huck—just as earnest as ever I was in my life. Will you go in there with me and help get it out?"

"I bet I will! I will if it's where we can blaze our way to it and not get lost."

"All right. We want some bread and meat, and a little bag or two, and two or three kite strings, and some of these newfangled things they call lucifer matches. I tell you, many's the time I wished I had some when I was in there before."

A trifle after noon the boys borrowed a small skiff, and got under way at once. When they were several miles below Cave Hollow, Tom said: "Now you see this bluff here looks all alike all the way down from Cave Hollow—no houses, no wood-yards, bushes all alike. But do you see that white place up yonder where there's been a big landslide? Well, that's one of my marks. We'll get ashore now."

They landed.

"Now, Huck, where we're a-standing you could touch that hole I got out of with a fishing-pole. See if you can find it."

Huck poked and searched all over the place and found nothing. Tom proudly marched right into a thick clump of sumac bushes and said: "Here you are! Look at it, Huck; it's the snuggest hole in this country. We've got it now, and we'll keep it quiet, only we'll let Joe Harper and Ben Rogers in—because of course there's got to be a gang, or else there wouldn't be any style about it. Tom Sawyer's Gang —it sounds splendid, don't it, Huck?"

By this time everything was ready and the boys entered the hole, Tom in the lead. They toiled

their way to the farther end of the tunnel, then made their spliced kite strings fast and moved on. A few steps brought them to the spring, and Tom felt a shudder quiver all through him. He showed Huck the fragment of candlewick perched on a lump of clay against the wall, and described how he and Becky had watched the flame struggle and expire.

The boys began to quiet down to whispers, now, for the stillness and gloom of the place oppressed their spirits. They went on, and presently entered and followed Tom's other corridor until they reached the "jumping-off place." The candles revealed the fact that it was not really a precipice, but only a steep clay hill twenty or thirty feet high.

Tom whispered: "Now I'll show you something, Huck." He held his candle aloft and said: "Look as far around the corner as you can. Do you see that? There—on the big rock over yonder—done with candle smoke."

"Tom, it's a cross!"

"Now where's your Number Two? 'Under the cross,' hey? Right yonder's where I saw Injun Joe poke up his candle, Huck!"

Huck stared at the mystic sign a while, and then said with a shaky voice: "Tom, let's get out of here!"

"What! and leave the treasure?"

"Yes—leave it. Injun Joe's ghost is round about there, certain."

"No, it ain't, Huck. No, it ain't. It would ha'nt the place where he died—away out at the mouth of the cave—five mile from here."

"No, Tom, it wouldn't. It would hang around the money. I know the ways of ghosts, and so do you."

Tom began to fear that Huck was right. Misgivings gathered in his mind. But presently a new idea occurred to him.

"Lookyhere, Huck, what fools we're making of ourselves! Injun Joe's ghost ain't a-going to come around where there's a cross!"

The point was well taken. It had its effect.

"Tom, I didn't think of that. But that's so. It's luck for us, that cross is. I reckon we'll climb down there and have a hunt for that box."

Tom went first, cutting rude steps in the clay hill as he descended and Huck followed. Four avenues opened out of the small cavern which the great rock stood in. The boys examined three of them with no result. They found a small recess in the one nearest the base of the rock, with a pallet of

131

blankets spread down in it; also an old suspender, some bacon rind, and the well-gnawed bones of two or three fowls. But there was no money box. The lads searched and researched this place, but in vain.

Tom said: "He said under the cross. Well, this comes nearest to being under the cross. It can't be under the rock itself, because that sets solid on the ground."

They searched everywhere once more, and then sat down discouraged. Huck could suggest nothing.

By and by Tom said: "Lookyhere, Huck, there's footprints and some candle grease on the clay about one side of this rock, but not on the other sides. Now what's that for?

I bet you the money is under the rock. I'm going to dig in the clay."

Tom's barlow knife was out at once, and he had not dug four inches before he struck wood.

"Hey, Huck—you hear that?"

Huck began to dig and scratch now. Some boards were soon uncovered and removed. They had concealed a natural chasm which led under the rock. Tom got into this and held his candle as far under the rock as he could, but said he could not see to the end of the rift. He proposed to explore. He stooped and passed under; the narrow way descended gradually. He followed its winding course, first to the right, then to the left, Huck at his heels. Tom turned a short curve, by and by, and exclaimed: "Oh, my goodness, Huck, lookyhere!"

132

It was the treasure box, sure enough, along with an empty powder keg, a couple of guns in leather cases, two or three pairs of old moccasins, a leather belt, and some other rubbish, well soaked with the water drip.

"Got it at last," said Huck, plowing among the tarnished coins with his hands. "My, but we're rich, Tom!"

"Huck, I always reckoned we'd get it. It's just too good to believe, but we have got it, sure! Say—let's not fool around here. Let's snake it out. Lemme see if I can lift the box."

It weighed about fifty pounds. Tom could lift it, after an awkward fashion, but could not carry it conveniently.

"I thought so," he said; "they carried it like it. was heavy, that day at the ha'nted house. I noticed that. I reckon I was right to think of fetching the little bags along."

The money was soon in the bags and the boys took it up to the cross rock.

They presently emerged into the clump of sumac bushes, looked warily out, found the coast clear, and were soon lunching in the skiff. As the sun dipped toward the horizon, they pushed out and got under way. Tom skimmed up the shore through the long twilight, chatting cheerily with Huck, and landed shortly after dark.

"Now, Huck," said Tom, "we'll hide the money in the loft of the widow's woodshed, and I'll come up in the morning, and we'll count it and divide. Just you lay quiet here and watch the stuff till I run and borrow Benny Taylor's little wagon; I won't be gone a minute."

He disappeared, and presently returned with the wagon, put the two small sacks into it, threw some old rags on top of them, and started off, dragging his cargo behind him.

[Tom's and Huck's windfall made a mighty stir in the poor little village of St. Petersburg. When the money was counted, it came to a little over twelve thousand dollars. Every empty or "haunted" house in St. Petersburg and the neighboring villages was examined, plank by plank, and its foundations dug up and ransacked for hidden treasure. Wherever Tom and Huck appeared they were courted, admired, and stared at.

The Widow Douglas put Huck's money out at six per cent, and Judge Thatcher did the same with Tom's at Aunt Polly's request.]

Drawing Inferences from Your Reading

To get the most out of a story we often have "to read between the lines." This exercise will give you practice in doing so. Write the answers to the following questions on your paper.

1. Which of the boys gave evidence of possessing the stronger character? Give reasons for your answer.

2. What was his outstanding trait? Find three sentences to prove it.

3. Find an example to prove that the other boy was the weaker character.

4. Do you think Tom and Huck are typical boys? Give three examples to prove your answer.

5. Injun Joe told his companion, "I want to quit this shanty." Why was he so anxious to leave?

6. Both Tom and Huck disliked going into the cave, but each dreaded it for a different reason. What were Tom's and Huck's reasons for disliking the cave?

7. Why didn't the boys ask friends or townspeople to help them search for the treasure which Injun Joe had hidden at "Number Two"?

8. Was the money used in the way the boys said they would use the treasure if they found it?

9. You notice that the author uses dialogue (conversation) to unfold the story. What would you say about the English Tom and Huck use? Write three grammatical errors they use and beside them give the correct usage.

Using Your Glossary

Find the exact meaning of the following words in the glossary of your reader: *serape, bowie knife, pallet, barlow knife, intervened.*

134

The Big Rock Candy Mountain

ONE summer's day in the month of May
 A weary man came hiking;
Down a shady lane near the sugar cane
 He was looking for his liking.
As he strolled along, he sang a song
 Of a land of milk and honey,
Where a man can stay for many a day
 And never think of money.

O, the buzzing of the bees and the cigarette trees,
 And the soda-water fountain,
Where the blue bird sings near the lemonade springs
 In the Big Rock Candy Mountain.

Apple pies grow on bushes below,
 And the crust is flaky and light;
Roast pigeons fly into your mouth
 And the skies are always bright.
There's a lake with stew and dumplings, too;
 Cakes to be had for the asking;
Time seems to fly 'neath a sugar sky
 As you spend your whole life basking.

O, the buzzing of the bees and the cigarette trees,
 And the soda-water fountain,
Where the blue bird sings near the lemonade springs
 In the Big Rock Candy Mountain.

WILD WEST SHOW

Buffalo Bill's "Wild West" Prairie Exhibition and Rocky Mountain Show

A Dramatic-Equestrian Exposition of Life on the Plains, with Accompanying Monologue and Incidental Music, the Whole Invented and Arranged by William F. Cody.

WILLIAM F. CODY AND N. SALSBURY,
PROPRIETORS AND MANAGERS,
WHO HEREBY CLAIM AS THEIR SPECIAL PROPERTY
THE VARIOUS EFFECTS INTRODUCED IN THE PUBLIC
PERFORMANCES OF

BUFFALO BILL'S "WILD WEST SHOW"

Enter the RINGMASTER. *Bugle Call.* RINGMASTER *speaks.*

RINGMASTER: Ladies and Gentlemen: I respectfully request your attention and your silence. Our agents will pass among you the history of the life of the Honorable William F. Cody, whom you know and love as Buffalo Bill. There is nothing but accuracy in this history which you are privileged to read and buy—twenty-five cents a copy —for the management of the "Wild

136

West" Exhibition speaks the truth, the whole truth, and nothing but the truth. Before the entertainment begins I wish to impress upon your minds that the performance you are about to witness is not a performance in the common use of that term; it is an exhibition of incomparable skill. Skill, ladies and gentlemen! Skill, skill, skill! Nowhere else, either in the East or in the West, is there a show to equal this exhibition. Nowhere is there such courage, such stamina, such daring. (*Bugle call.*) At the conclusion of the overture our performance will begin with a grand processional parade of the "Wild West." I hope you have all purchased the history of the life of Buffalo Bill.

(*Overture: "Stars and Stripes Forever"*)

Grand processional parade of COWBOYS, MEXICANS, *and* INDIANS, *with incidental music.*

RINGMASTER: I will now introduce the different groups and the individual celebrities as they pass before you in review.

Enter a group of PAWNEE INDIANS, *war-bonneted.* (*Tom-toms.*)

Enter PAWNEE CHIEF, *in full war regalia.* (*War-whoops.*)

Enter a large group of MEXICAN VAQUEROS. (*Music: "Santa Anna March"*)

RINGMASTER: These are *vaqueros,* ladies and gentlemen. Pronounced *vah-kay' ros,* and the boldest, bravest Mexican cowboys who ever spurred on their horses under the Mexican stars.

Enter a group of WICHITA INDIANS, *eagle feathers dipping.* (*Tom-toms.*)

Enter WICHITA CHIEF, *armed with bow and arrow.* (*Tom-toms.*)

Enter a group of AMERICAN COWBOYS. (*Music: "Red River Valley"*)

Enter KING OF THE COWBOYS. (*Music: "The Broncho Buster"*)

Enter COWBOY SHERIFF *of the Platte.* (*Music: "Git Along, Little Dogies"*)

Enter a group of SIOUX INDIANS. (*Tom-toms.*)

RINGMASTER: Listen to the names of these Indians from the Rosebud Reservation: Lone Wolf, Stands First, Slow Bear, Young Mule, Wamba-Gee-Sapa, Black Bear, Moccasin, Cha-Sha-Sha, and Opaga. With them are three Indian policemen—Fast Horse, Iron Crow, and Bear Run. Following them is their chief, Old Chief Red Cloud.

Enter CHIEF RED CLOUD. (*War-whoops. Tom-toms.*)

RINGMASTER: I now have the honor of introducing a man whose record as servant of the government, whose skill and daring as a frontiersman, whose place in history as the chief of scouts of the United States Army, under such generals as Sherman, Sheridan, Hancock and Miles, and whose name as one of the avengers of the murderous attack upon General Custer, and whose steadfast belief throughout an eventful life in the principle of loyalty to friend and foe have made him so famous throughout the world. You all know to whom I allude. Ladies and Gentlemen, I give you Buffalo Bill.

(*Roll of drums. Blare of bugles.*) *Enter* CODY, *tall, handsome, with white goatee and silver hair, dressed in fringed white buckskin, riding a white Arabian stallion.* CODY *bows to right and left.* (*Bugle call.*)

CODY (*turning toward the performers*): Wild West, are you ready?

Performers shout their readiness.

138

CODY: Wild West, get set! (*Gunfire.*) Wild West, go!

(*Music: "The Old Chisholm Trail."*) COWBOYS, MEXICANS, INDIANS, *with* BUFFALO BILL *bringing up the rear, ride off in triumph.*

RINGMASTER: They are gone, but they will return. *Exeunt omnes,* as in Latin; it means, "Everyone departs." Now, first on our programme after this magnificent introduction, there will be a mile race between a cowboy, a Mexican, and an Indian. You will please notice that these horses carry the heaviest trappings and that no rider weighs less than 145 pounds.

(*Drums. Thunder of hoofs.*) COWBOY *wins the race.*

RINGMASTER: Next on our programme, the Pony Express. The Pony Express, ladies and gentlemen, was established long before the Union Pacific railroad was built across this mighty continent. The Pony Express came before telegraph poles were set. It came in a time of national crisis, when Abraham Lincoln was elected President of the United States and it was vital to the nation that the election returns from California be brought across the mountains as quickly as possible. And who was better equipped to accomplish this fearless work than the young men who volunteered to ride seventy-five to one hundred miles a day to carry the United States mail? Now Mr. Billy Johnson will illustrate for you the mode of riding the Pony Express, mounting, dismounting, and changing the mail to fast horses.

(*Music: "The Yellow Rose of Texas."*) *Enter* MR. BILLY JOHNSON. *He changes horses in front of the grandstand, then exits.*

RINGMASTER: Next on our programme, a one hundred yard race between an Indian on foot and an Indian on an Indian pony. They start at a given point, run fifty yards, then return to the starting point—actually a race of one hundred yards.

Race as described above. (*Tomtoms.*)

RINGMASTER: Again I ask your silence and your attention, ladies and gentlemen. You will now see a performance that has even been witnessed by the kings and queens of Europe. It is an historical representation of a duel fought during the battle at War Bonnet Creek, Dakota, shortly after the massacre

139

of General Custer and his five companies of United States cavalry. And who will engage in this duel you are about to see? (*Roll of drums.*) Watch and see! Here they come now! Give them a great big round of applause, for they are none other than Buffalo Bill and Chief Yellow Hand!

CODY *enters, riding Arabian stallion. Bows to right and left.*

CHIEF YELLOW HAND *enters, riding Indian pony. Looks neither to right nor to left.*

COWBOYS *and* INDIANS *follow.*

(*Music: "Bury Me Not on the Lone Prairie" followed by crescendo of drums.*)

CODY *dismounts.* CHIEF YELLOW HAND *dismounts.*

They meet. They engage in duel. CODY *wins.*

Exit CODY, YELLOW HAND, INDIANS, COWBOYS.

RINGMASTER: Next on our programme, I present Miss Annie Oakley, the celebrated wing and rifle shot. Miss Oakley will give an exhibition of her skill, shooting at clay pigeons.

ANNIE OAKLEY *shoots at pigeons sprung from trap.*

Shoots double, from two traps sprung at the same time.

Picks up the gun from the ground after the trap is sprung.

Shoots as above.

Shoots double in the same manner.

Shoots three composition balls, thrown in the air in rapid succession, the first with the rifle held upside down upon the head, the second and the third with the shotgun.

Shoots as above. Exit.

RINGMASTER: Next on our programme, the cowboy's fun, or the riding of bucking ponies and mules. I suppose you think, for this is a common error, that these horses are trained to buck. You may even suspect that foreign substances are placed under their saddles. This, however, is not a fact. Bucking, the same as balking, or running away, is a natural trait of the animal.

RIDERS *are announced and mount the horses.*

(*Music: "Hack-Drivers' Quadrille."*)

RINGMASTER: Watch Mr. Taylor pick up his hat.

MR. TAYLOR *rides by at full speed, leans out of his saddle and picks hat from the ground.*

Watch Mr. Taylor pick up his handkerchief.

MR. TAYLOR *rides by at full speed, leans from saddle and picks up handkerchief.*

Horses buck. Other riders shout Yip-EE-I-O-I-Ay.

All exit.

RINGMASTER: Next on our programme you will see the Deadwood stagecoach, the famous coach that traveled between Deadwood in the Dakotas and Cheyenne in Wyoming. This coach, ladies and gentlemen, has an immortal place in the history of the United States. It has gone through fire and blood. Days when the coach did not arrive at its station were days of harrowing anxiety for the people in that isolated land of Indian reservations. Who could tell what had been its fate and the fate of its passengers? Indians could have waylaid it; desperados of the badlands could have attacked it. The story of the Deadwood coach is the saga of American courage. And now you will see, holding the reins, an old stagecoach driver, Mr. John Higby. Seated beside him is Mr. Con Croner, the Cowboy Sheriff of the Platte, the sheriff who brought peace and quiet to Lincoln County, Nebraska. It was Con Croner who drove out the cattle thieves and the hoodlums who had terrorized the people of Lincoln County. Now our coach will start upon its journey. It will be attacked from ambush by a band of fierce and warlike Indians, who in their turn will be repulsed by a party of scouts and cowboys, under the command of

Buffalo Bill. Will two or three ladies in the audience volunteer to ride as passengers?

LADIES *volunteer. All passengers are seated in coach.*
One lady waves to friend in audience.

RINGMASTER: It is customary to deliver parting instructions to the driver before he starts on his perilous journey, something in the following words: Mr. Higby, I have intrusted you with valuable lives and property. Should you meet with Indians or other dangers, *en route,* put on the whip, and, if possible, save the lives of your passengers. Now, if you are all ready, go!

Coach is driven down track. Meets INDIANS. *Turns back.*
Coach is followed by INDIANS.
INDIANS *attack. Battle rages.*
INDIANS *give war-whoop.*
Lady passengers scream.
MR. JOHN HIGBY, MR. JOHN HANCOCK, MR. CON CRONER *engage in struggle.*
COWBOYS *and* SCOUTS, *led by* BUFFALO BILL, *appear on scene.*
INDIANS *retreat in haste.*
BUFFALO BILL *and* COWBOYS *pursue them.*
Exit coach.

RINGMASTER: Next on our programme, a one-quarter mile race between Sioux boys on barebacked ponies and Mexican boys on Mexican thoroughbreds. All up now, boys! No jockeying! Get ready! Go!

Race as described. (Music: "We Won't Go Home Until Morning.")

RINGMASTER: Now a portion of the Pawnee and Wichita tribes will introduce their native sports and pastimes, giving their tribal war dance.

War dance by INDIANS.
Grass dance by INDIANS.

RINGMASTER: Next on our programme, the roping, tying, and riding of wild Texan steers by cowboys and Mexicans.

Performance as above. (Music: "Old Dan Tucker.")

RINGMASTER: Now comes the climax of our exhibition. This is the attack upon a settler's cabin by a band of marauding Indians and their repulse by a party of scouts and cowboys, under the command of our brave Buffalo Bill. After this entertainment, and before you leave the grounds, you are invited to visit our Wild West camp. The admission fee is but a pittance. We thank you for your polite attention and bid you all good afternoon.

SETTLER'S *camp attacked.* SETTLERS *scream for help.*
BUFFALO BILL *and* COWBOYS *arrive.*
INDIANS *repulsed.*
SETTLERS *take bows, as do* COWBOYS *and* INDIANS.

This is followed by a grand review of all entertainers around the ring.
Farewell speech delivered by MR. CODY.

(*Music:* "*The Washington Post March.*")

FINIS

What Is Your Opinion?

The selection "Wild West Show" is a script for a stage production. Do you think it would be difficult for amateurs to present for an audience? Why? In order to enjoy "Wild West Show," which of your mental powers did you have to use especially?

Recall circuses or fairs you have attended. From what you remember, would you say that a real picture of a Wild West Show is presented in this selection? Is the ringmaster a real character? Explain.

How would you describe "Buffalo Bill"? Do you think you would enjoy knowing him? Give a reason for your answer.

Finding Facts

Using your history book or the encyclopedia, write five sentences about each of the following topics, choosing the most important facts about them.

Winfield Scott Hancock
George Armstrong Custer
The Pony Express
William F. Cody
General William Tecumseh Sherman

143

PHYLLIS McGINLEY

Love Letter to an Institution

OF ALL museums,
I've a pet museum,
And it's not the Morgan
Or the Met Museum,
Or the Frick Museum,
Which steals the heart,
Or a trick museum
Like the Modern Art.
I must confess
It's a queer museum,
A more or less
Done-by-ear museum,
But it suits my nature
As knife suits fork:
The Museum of the City
   of New York.

A bit like an auction,
A bit like a fair,
Everything is cozy
   that's collected there.
Everything is cheerful
   as a Currier & Ives:
Capes made for gentlemen,
Caps for their wives;
Lamps lit at dark
By Great-Grandmama;
Central Park
In a diorama
(Where boys are sledding
And their runners curl);
A brownstone wedding
With a flower girl;
Doll-house parlors with carpet
   on the floor;
Patriotic posters from
   the First World War;
A solitary spur
That belonged to Aaron Burr;
And a small-scale model
Of a ten-cent store.

144

There for the dawdler,
Yesterday is spread—
Toys that a toddler
Carried once to bed;
Hoopskirts, horsecars,
Flags aplenty;
Somebody's dance dress,
    circa '20;
Somebody's platter,
    somebody's urn;
Mr. and Mrs.
Isaac Stern—
All gaily jumbled
So it's automatic
To believe you've stumbled
On your great-aunt's attic.
Helter-skelter
But large as life,
A room by Belter
And a room by Phyfe;
A period spinet,
A period speller;
The rooms that soured
    Mr. Rockefeller;
Rooms you can stare at,
    rooms you can poke in,
And a tenderhearted lobby
You can even smoke in.

It's a fine museum,
Not a new museum,
But a neighborly
Sort of old-shoe museum,
Not a class museum
Where the pundits go
Or a mass museum
With a Sunday show,
Not vast and grand
Like the Natural History.
How it ever got planned
Is a minor mystery.
But it fits my fancy
Like applesauce and pork,
The Museum of the City
    of New York.

The Doughnuts

ONE Friday night in November Homer overheard his mother talking on the telephone to Aunt Agnes over in Centerburg. "I'll stop by with the car in about half an hour and we can go to the meeting together," she said, because tonight was the night the Ladies' Club was meeting to discuss plans for a box social and to knit and sew for the Red Cross.

"I think I'll come along and keep Uncle Ulysses company while you and Aunt Agnes are at the meeting," said Homer.

So after Homer had combed his hair and his mother had looked to see if she had her knitting instructions and the right size needles, they started for town.

Homer's Uncle Ulysses and Aunt Agnes have a very up and coming lunch room over in Centerburg, just across from the court house on the town square. Uncle Ulysses is a man with advanced ideas and a weakness for labor-saving devices. He equipped the lunch room with automatic toasters, automatic coffee maker, automatic dish washer, and an automatic doughnut maker. All just the latest thing in labor-saving devices. Aunt Agnes would throw up her hands and sigh every time Uncle Ulysses bought a new labor-saving device. Sometimes she became unkindly disposed toward him for days and days. She was of the opinion that Uncle Ulysses just frittered away his spare time over at the barber shop with the sheriff and the boys, so, what was the good of a labor-saving device that gave you more time to fritter?

When Homer and his mother got to Centerburg they stopped at the lunch room, and after Aunt Agnes had come out and said, "My, how that boy does grow!" which was what she always said, she went off with Homer's mother in the car. Homer went into the lunch room and said, "Howdy, Uncle Ulysses!"

"Oh, hello, Homer. You're just in time," said Uncle Ulysses. "I've been going over this automatic doughnut machine, re-oiling and cleaning the works . . . wonderful things, these labor-saving devices."

"Yep," agreed Homer, and he picked up a cloth and started polishing the metal trimmings while Uncle Ulysses tinkered with the inside workings.

"Opfwo-oof!!" sighed Uncle Ulysses and, "Look here, Homer, you've got a mechanical mind. See if you can fit these two pieces in. I'm going across to the barber shop for a spell, 'cause there's somethin' I've got to see the sheriff about. There won't be much business until the double feature is over and I'll be back before then."

As Uncle Ulysses went out he said, "Uh, Homer, after you get the pieces in place, would you mix up some doughnut batter and put it in the machine? You could turn it on and make a few doughnuts to have on hand for the crowd after the movie . . . if you don't mind."

"O.K." said Homer, "I'll take care of everything."

A few minutes later a customer came in and said, "Good evening, Bud."

Homer looked up from putting the last piece in the doughnut machine and said, "Good evening, sir, what can I do for you?"

"Well, young feller, I'd like a cup o' coffee and some doughnuts," said the customer.

"I'm sorry, Mister, but we won't have any doughnuts for about half an hour, until I can mix some dough and start this machine. I could give you some very fine sugar rolls instead."

"Well, Bud, I'm in no real hurry so I'll just have a cup o' coffee and wait around a bit for the doughnuts. Fresh doughnuts are always worth waiting for is what I always say."

"O.K.," said Homer, and he drew a cup of coffee from Uncle Ulysses' super automatic coffee maker.

"Nice place you've got here," said the customer.

"Oh, yes," replied Homer, "this is a very up and coming lunch room with all the latest improvements."

"Yes," said the stranger, "must be a good business. I'm in business too. A traveling man in outdoor advertising. I'm a sandwich man; Mr. Gabby's my name."

"My name is Homer. I'm glad to meet you, Mr. Gabby. It must be a fine profession, traveling and advertising sandwiches."

"Oh no," said Mr. Gabby, "I don't advertise sandwiches, I just wear any kind of an ad, one sign on front and one sign on behind, this way. . . . Like a sandwich. Ya know what I mean?"

"Oh, I see. That must be fun, and you travel too?" asked Homer as he got out the flour and the baking powder.

"Yeah, I ride the rods between jobs, on freight trains, ya know what I mean?"

"Yes, but isn't that dangerous?" asked Homer.

"Of course there's a certain amount of risk, but you take any method a travel these days, it's all dangerous. Ya know what I mean? Now take airplanes for instance . . ."

Just then a large shiny black car stopped in front of the lunch room and a chauffeur helped a lady out of the rear door. They both came inside and the lady smiled at Homer and said, "We've stopped for a snack. Some doughnuts and coffee would be simply marvelous."

Then Homer said, "I'm sorry, Ma'm, but the doughnuts won't be ready until I make this batter and start Uncle Ulysses' doughnut machine."

"Well now, aren't *you* a clever young man to know how to make *doughnuts!*"

"Well," blushed Homer, "I've really never done it before but I've got a recipe to follow."

"Now, young man, you simply must allow me to help. You know, I haven't made doughnuts for years, but I know the best recipe for doughnuts. It's marvelous and we really must use it."

"But Ma'm . . ." said Homer.

"Now just *wait* till you taste these doughnuts," said the lady. "Do you have an apron?" she asked, as she took off her fur coat and her rings and her jewelry and rolled up her sleeves. "Charles," she said to the chauffeur, "hand me that baking powder. And, young man, we'll need some nutmeg."

So Homer and the chauffeur stood by and handed things and cracked the eggs while the lady mixed and stirred. Mr. Gabby sat on his stool, sipped his coffee, and looked on with great interest.

"There!" said the lady when all of the ingredients were mixed. "Just *wait* until you taste these doughnuts!"

"It looks like an awful lot of batter," said Homer as he stood on a chair and poured it into the doughnut machine with the help of the chauffeur. "It's about ten times as much as Uncle Ulysses ever makes."

"But wait until you taste them!" said the lady with an eager look and a smile.

Homer got down from the chair and pushed a button on the machine marked *Start*. Rings of batter started dropping into the hot fat. After a ring of batter was cooked on one side an automatic gadget turned it over and the other side would cook. Then another automatic gadget gave the doughnut a little push and it rolled neatly down a little chute, all ready to eat.

"That's a simply *fascinating* machine," said the lady as she waited for the first doughnut to roll out.

"Here, young man, *you* must have the first one. Now isn't that just *too* delicious? Isn't it simply marvelous?"

"Yes, Ma'm, it's very good," replied Homer as the lady handed doughnuts to Charles and to Mr. Gabby and asked if they didn't think that they were simply divine doughnuts.

"It's an old family recipe!" said the lady with pride.

Homer poured some coffee for the lady and her chauffeur and Mr. Gabby, and a big glass of milk for himself. Then they all sat down at the lunch counter to enjoy another few doughnuts apiece.

"I am so glad you enjoy my doughnuts," said the lady. "But now, Charles, we really must be going. If you will just take this apron, Homer, and put two dozen doughnuts in a bag to take along, we'll be on our way. And, Charles, don't forget to pay the young man." She rolled down her sleeves and put on her jewelry, then Charles managed to get her into her big fur coat.

"Good night now, young man, I haven't had so much fun in years. I *really* haven't!" said the lady, as she went out the door and into the big shiny car.

149

"Those are sure good dough-nuts," said Mr. Gabby as the car moved off.

"You bet!" said Homer. Then he and Mr. Gabby just stood and watched the automatic doughnut machine make doughnuts.

After a few dozen more dough-nuts had rolled down the little chute, Homer said, "I guess that's about enough doughnuts to sell to the after-theater customers. I'd better turn the machine off for a while."

Homer pushed down the button marked *Stop* and there was a little click, but nothing happened. The rings of batter kept right on drop-ping into the hot fat, and an auto-matic gadget kept right on giving them a little push and the dough-nuts kept right on rolling down the little chute, all ready to eat.

"That's funny," said Homer, "I'm sure that's the right button!" He pushed it again, but the auto-matic doughnut maker kept right on making doughnuts.

"Well I guess I must have put one of those pieces in backwards," said Homer.

"Then it might stop if you pushed the button marked *Start*," said Mr. Gabby.

Homer did, and the doughnuts still kept rolling down the little chute, just as regular as a clock can tick.

"I guess we could sell a few more doughnuts," said Homer, "but I'd better telephone Uncle Ulysses over at the barber shop." Homer gave the number and while he waited for someone to answer he counted thirty-seven doughnuts roll down the little chute.

Finally someone answered "Hel-lo! This is the sarber bhop, I mean the barber shop."

"Oh, hello, sheriff. This is Ho-mer. Could I speak to my Uncle Ulysses?"

"Well, he is playing pinochle right now," said the sheriff. "Any-thin' I can tell 'im?"

"Yes," said Homer. "I pushed the button marked *Stop* on the doughnut machine, but the rings of batter keep right on dropping into the hot fat, and an automatic gad-get keeps right on turning them over, and another automatic gadget keeps giving them a little push, and the doughnuts keep right on rolling down the little chute! It won't stop!"

"O.K. Wold the hire, I mean, hold the wire and I'll tell 'im." Then Homer looked over his shoul-der and counted another twenty-

150

one doughnuts roll down the little chute, all ready to eat. Then the sheriff said, "He'll be right over.... Just gotta finish this hand."

"That's good, Homer answered. "G'by, sheriff."

The window was full of doughnuts by now so Homer and Mr. Gabby had to hustle around and start stacking them on plates and trays and lining them up on the counter.

"Sure are a lot of doughnuts!" said Homer.

"You bet!" said Mr. Gabby. "I lost count at twelve hundred and two and that was quite a while back."

People had begun to gather outside the lunch room window, and someone was saying, "There are almost as many doughnuts as there are people in Centerburg, and I wonder how in tarnation Ulysses thinks he can sell all of 'em!"

Every once in a while somebody would come inside and buy some, but while somebody bought two to eat and a dozen to take home, the machine made three dozen more.

By the time Uncle Ulysses and the sheriff arrived and pushed through the crowd, the lunch room was a calamity of doughnuts! Doughnuts in the window, doughnuts piled high on the shelves, doughnuts in stacks on plates, doughnuts lined up twelve deep all along the counter, and doughnuts

still rolling down the little chute, just as regular as a clock can tick.

"Hello, sheriff, hello, Uncle Ulysses, we're having a little trouble here," said Homer.

"Well, I'll be dunked!!" said Uncle Ulysses.

"Dernd ef you won't be when Aggy gits home," said the sheriff. "Mighty fine doughnuts though. What'll you do with 'em all, Ulysses?"

Uncle Ulysses groaned and said, "What will Aggy say? We'll never sell 'em all."

Then Mr. Gabby, who hadn't said anything for a long time, stopped piling doughnuts and said, "What you need is an advertising man. Ya know what I mean? You got the doughnuts, ya gotta create a market... Understand?... It's balancing the demand with the supply . . . That sort of thing."

"Yes!" said Homer, "Mr. Gabby's right. We have to enlarge our market. He's an advertising sandwich man, so if we hire him, he can walk up and down in front of the theater and get the customers."

"You're hired, Mr. Gabby!" said Uncle Ulysses.

Then everybody pitched in to paint the signs and to get Mr. Gabby sandwiched between. In big letters they painted a sign, "SALE ON DOUGHNUTS," on the window as well.

Meanwhile the rings of batter kept right on dropping into the hot fat, and an automatic gadget kept right on turning them over, and another automatic gadget kept right on giving them a little push, and the doughnuts kept right on rolling down the little chute, just as regular as a clock can tick.

"I certainly hope this advertising works," said Uncle Ulysses, wagging his head. "Aggy'll certainly throw a fit if it don't."

The sheriff went outside to keep order, because there was quite a crowd by now—all looking at the doughnuts and guessing how many thousand there were, and watching new ones roll down the little chute, just as regular as a clock can tick. Homer and Uncle Ulysses kept stacking doughnuts. Once in a while somebody bought a few, but not very often.

Then Mr. Gabby came back and said, "Say, you know there's not much use o' me advertisin' at the theater. The show's all over, and besides almost everybody in town is out front watching that machine make doughnuts!"

"Zeus!" exclaimed Uncle Ulysses.

"We must get rid of these dough-nuts before Aggy gets here!"

"Looks like you will have ta hire a truck ta waul 'em ahay, I mean haul 'em away!!" said the sheriff who had just come in. Just then there was a noise and a shoving out front and the lady from the shiny black car and her chauffeur came pushing through the crowd and into the lunch room.

"Oh, gracious!" she gasped, ignoring the doughnuts, "I've lost my diamond bracelet, and I know I left it here on the counter," she said, pointing to a place where the doughnuts were piled in stacks of two dozen.

"Yes, Ma'm, I guess you forgot it when you helped make the batter," said Homer.

Then they moved all the dough-nuts around and looked for the diamond bracelet, but they couldn't find it anywhere. Meanwhile the doughnuts kept rolling down the little chute, just as regular as a clock can tick.

After they had looked all around the sheriff cast a suspicious eye on Mr. Gabby, but Homer said, "He's all right, sheriff, he didn't take it. He's a friend of mine."

Then the lady said, "I'll offer a reward of one hundred dollars for that bracelet! It really *must* be found! . . . it *really* must!"

"Now don't you worry, lady," said the sheriff. "I'll get your bracelet back!"

"Zeus! This is terrible!" said Uncle Ulysses. "First all of these doughnuts and then on top of all that, a lost diamond bracelet . . ."

Mr. Gabby tried to comfort him, and he said, "There's always a bright side. That machine'll prob-ably run outta batter in an hour or two."

If Mr. Gabby hadn't been quick on his feet Uncle Ulysses would have knocked him down, sure as fate.

Then while the lady wrung her hands and said, "We must find it, we *must!*" and Uncle Ulysses was moaning about what Aunt Agnes would say, and the sheriff was eye-ing Mr. Gabby, Homer sat down and thought hard.

Before twenty more doughnuts could roll down the little chute he shouted, "SAY! I know where the bracelet is! It was lying here on the counter and got mixed up in the batter by mistake! The bracelet is cooked inside one of these dough-nuts!"

"Why . . . I really believe you're right," said the lady through her tears. "Isn't that *amazing?* Simply *amazing!*"

"I'll be durn'd!" said the sheriff.

"Ohh-h!" moaned Uncle Ulysses. "Now we have to break up all of these doughnuts to find it. Think of the *pieces!* Think of the *crumbs!* Think of what *Aggy* will say!"

"Nope," said Homer. "We won't have to break them up. I've got a good plan."

So Homer and the advertising man took some cardboard and some paint and printed another sign.

And that's not all. Everybody bought coffee to dunk the doughnuts in too. Those that didn't buy coffee bought milk or soda. It kept Homer and the lady and the chauffeur and Uncle Ulysses and the sheriff busy waiting on the people who wanted to buy doughnuts.

When all but the last couple of hundred doughnuts had been sold, Rupert Black shouted, "I GAWT IT!!" and sure enough . . . there was the diamond bracelet inside of his doughnut!

FRESH DOUGHNUTS
2 *for* 5¢
WHILE THEY LAST
$100 *PRIZE*
FOR FINDING A *BRACELET*
INSIDE A *DOUGHNUT*
YOU HAVE TO GIVE THE *BRACELET* BACK

They put this sign in the window, and the sandwich man wore two more signs that said the same thing and walked around in the crowd out front.

THEN . . . the doughnuts began to sell! *Everybody* wanted to buy doughnuts, *dozens* of doughnuts!

Then Rupert went home with a hundred dollars, the citizens of Centerburg went home full of doughnuts, the lady and her chauffeur drove off with the diamond bracelet, and Homer went home with his mother when she stopped by with Aunt Aggy.

As Homer went out of the door he heard Mr. Gabby say, "Neatest trick of merchandising I ever seen," and Aunt Aggy was looking sceptical while Uncle Ulysses was saying, "The rings of batter kept right on dropping into the hot fat, and the automatic gadget kept right on turning them over, and the other automatic gadget kept right on giving them a little push, and the doughnuts kept right on rolling down the little chute just as regular as a clock can tick—they just kept right on a comin', an' a comin', an' a comin', an' a comin'."

Arranging Events in Order

Arrange these statements in the proper order and copy them on your paper.

1. Mr. Gabby comes into the lunch room and orders coffee and doughnuts.

2. The lady comes and reports the loss of her diamond bracelet.

3. Uncle Ulysses says he is going to the barber shop to discuss business with the sheriff.

4. Mother and Aunt Agnes go to a Ladies' Club meeting.

5. A big black car stops in front of the lunch room.

6. The double feature is over and people begin to gather outside the lunch room.

7. Homer hears his mother talking on the telephone with Aunt Agnes.

8. After making and eating some doughnuts, the lady puts on her jewelry and leaves with her chauffeur.

9. Homer finishes cleaning and putting the doughnut machine together.

10. Homer calls the barber shop and the sheriff takes the message for Uncle Ulysses.

11. Uncle Ulysses hires Mr. Gabby to advertise the doughnuts at the theater.

12. Rupert Black finds the bracelet in one of the doughnuts.

13. Aunt Agnes looks skeptically at Uncle Ulysses.

155

Every Day Is Monday

MONDAY is the day that everything starts all over again,
Monday is the day when just as you are beginning
    to feel peaceful you have to get up and get dressed and put on
    your old gray bonnet and drive down to Dover again,
It is the day when life becomes grotesque again,
Because it is the day when you have to face your desk again;
It is a day with no fun about it,
Because it is the first of a series of days filled with one task
    or another that something has to be done about it.
When the telephone rings on Saturday or Sunday you are pleased
    because it probably means something pleasing
    and you take the call with agility,
But when it rings on any other day it just usually means
    some additional responsibility,
And if in doubt,
Why the best thing to do is to answer it in a foreign accent
    or if you are a foreigner answer it in a native accent
    and say you are out.
Oh, there is not a week-day moment that can't wring a sigh from you,
Because you are always being confronted with people who want
    to sell you something, or if they don't want to sell you something,
    there is something they want to buy from you,
And every shining hour swaggers arrogantly up to you
    demanding to be improved,
And apparently not only to improve it, but also to shine it,
    is what you are behooved.
Oh for a remedy, oh for a panacea, oh for a something,
    oh yes, oh for a coma or swoon,
Yes, indeed, oh for a coma that would last from
    nine A.M. on Monday until Saturday noon.

The Country Boy from Claremore

WILL ROGERS, a cowboy from the Oklahoma Territory, swung his lariat and spoke his lines and became the symbol of American laughter.

Today only the older generation can remember Will Rogers. They still speak of his rumpled clothes, his sheepish grin, and the drawling way he'd stand on a Broadway stage and voice his opinions of public men and public affairs. He spoke without malice and with homespun philosophy. There were no bitter stings that men could neither forget nor forgive. Rogers smiled as he did his rope tricks and chewed a wad of gum, while he appraised human nature with a kindly wit that released public fear and public anger by the safety valve of laughter.

"I'm just a country boy trying to get along," he used to say. "I've been eating pretty regular, and the reason I have is because I've stayed a country boy."

A country boy he surely was, for Rogers was born in Indian Territory that later became a part of Oklahoma. Choctaw, Chickasaw, Creek, Seminole, and Cherokee lived within its borders, and Will Rogers was proud of the strain of Cherokee in his blood. When a man would boast that he came of Colonial ancestry, Will Rogers would laugh and say, "My ancestors didn't come over on the *Mayflower;* they *met* the boat."

There is a distance greater than miles between the lights of Broadway and the wide sunlit stretches of Oklahoma. Will Rogers was born in 1879 in a little settlement, not far from Claremore. Great herds of cattle and a fine string of cow ponies, owned by his father, grazed on the vast range and, almost before he could walk, young Rogers learned to ride. When he was ten, he owned a buckskin pony that he called Comanche, and he was already practicing the simple lariat throws that were to make him famous.

The boy started to school in a one-room log cabin across the river from his father's ranch. From there he went to a school in Muskogee, but Will and the principal's son were the only boys in an academy filled with girls, so he soon returned to a school in the capital of the Indian nation. By this time his mother was dead—the mother whom he always credited for whatever humor he possessed and whose kindness he long remembered. With her death passed the boy's incentive for further formal education.

His life as a cowboy began in earnest. At a ranch on the Canadian River near Higgins, Texas, the boss hired young Rogers as a wrangler. This was the life Will Rogers knew and loved. Up with the sun, roping cattle, riding in the roundups, branding and shipping with the other cowboys was the answer, he believed, to his restlessness. It is possible that he would never have left a Texas ranch if it hadn't been for a trip to the West Coast. "Old Man Ewing," the man who'd hired him, shipped Rogers and another cowboy to California with a load of cattle. San Francisco was a stopover on their way home; unfortunately, they did not know that gaslight in a hotel room was to be turned off, not blown out, and they barely survived.

Sick and sad, and very much wiser, the young cowboy went back to his father's ranch in Indian Territory. The wide lands of the Five Civilized Tribes no longer seemed familiar. Homesteaders had begun to cast envious eyes at the broad, fertile ranges, and the greatest "land run" of all time began when the Cherokee Outlet was opened for settlement in 1893. "Aren't there any wide open spaces left in the world?" young Rogers complained. Then someone told him about the Argentine, and he headed south. The Argentine opportunity wasn't what he expected. Penniless, young Rogers got a job on a cattle boat bound for South Africa, but Zululand was not for him and he struck out for a city called Ladysmith.

Ladysmith is a long way from Texas, but it was there that Will Rogers found Texas Jack and his Wild West Circus. In the tents the homesick lad found horse-riding, broncho-busting Americans. He stayed with them for supper and found himself in show business for life.

After two years during which audiences all over the world cheered his rough-riding, lasso-throwing tricks, Rogers came back to the United States. He soon joined Colonel Zach Mulhall's show in St. Louis. Dressed in chaps, a colored shirt, and a wide Stetson hat, the former cowboy went on into a career that included a three-rope catch, a nose catch, a figure eight, and the sensational "Big Crinoline," a loop that Rogers would circle over his head, very small at first, then gradually growing wider and wider until a full hundred feet of rope was swinging out over the heads of the audience.

It didn't take long for news of the sensational act to reach New York and soon Rogers was acting his part on a New York stage. The first time he ever spoke his lines, he thought the audience was laughing at him, not with him, and he wanted to walk off into the wings. "Take a bow," shouted the stage manager, and that was the beginning of the cowboy's fame. His slow drawling voice, his shy smile,

the untamed lock of hair that dangled on his forehead, and the simple wisdom of his speech endeared him to the American public. The boy from Oklahoma moved on to the most glittering, extravagant, spectacular production in the history of the American theatre, the Ziegfeld *Follies*.

Perhaps it was the contrast of Broadway glamour with the homespun qualities of the cowboy from Oklahoma that helped put his name in headlines, but today few Americans can remember by name the glittering girls who helped make the *Follies* the showpiece of the New York stage; they have never forgotten the man who tossed a rope and laughed at life.

New York loved him. So did the wide, wide world. Rogers traveled a half million miles by plane in the last seven years of his life, and countless more miles on trains and ocean liners and in automobiles. He came to be known, not wholly in jest, as "the unofficial ambassador from the United States to the world."

Twenty years after his first appearance on a Broadway stage, Will Rogers felt he had earned a vacation. It was then that Wiley Post, a famous flyer and an old friend, urged him to join a survey flight by air to map a route to Russia. Rogers met Wiley Post in Seattle. On Tuesday, June 7, 1935, they took off in flight along the coast of Canada. From Anchorage they flew over Mt. McKinley, the highest peak on the American continent. To his wife and family Will Rogers wired, "Going to Point Barrow tomorrow. Furthest point of land on American continent. Lots of love. Don't worry. (Signed) Dad." It was Rogers' last message.

Fifty miles from Fairbanks the fog closed in. Wiley Post set down the plane on a little inlet to get directions from some Eskimo seal hunters. Rogers waved at them. Then Post gunned the ship and the plane began to lift. Suddenly its motor cut out. Post fought for control, but he didn't have enough altitude. The plane crashed on its back in chill northern waters.

The news made headlines, but no one smiled that day. They remembered with tears the unforgettable prelude to all of Will Rogers' monologues: "All that I know is what I read in the papers." The country boy from Oklahoma Territory was gone, but the legend of the man and his gift of laughter remain as part of the American tradition.

Matching Headlines and Paragraphs

The newspaper is read by all types of people, many of whom do not have much time to read. In order to save time for them, the newspaper writer composes headlines which give a summary of the story. If it is a long story, he gives additional assistance by writing subheads which give the main ideas contained in a group of paragraphs. Subheads are written at the beginning of the paragraphs. They do not break into them.

Below is a headline and several subheads. Copy them on your paper and then skim the story to determine where you would place the subheads. Beside the subhead write the number of the page and the paragraph where you think it should be placed. Also write the first and last words of the paragraph. Underline on your paper the headline which summarizes the whole story.

1. Disillusioned Wanderer
2. Proud of Background
3. Cowboy-Humorist Dies in Crash
4. Takes to Show Business
5. Vacation Ends in Tragedy
6. Laughs with Them; Not at Them
7. Little Formal Schooling

Drawing Conclusions

Choose the two *best* answers to complete this statement:

From this brief biography of Will Rogers, we can conclude that
   a. wholesome entertainment is to be encouraged;
   b. a cowboy's life is full of adventure;
   c. Will Rogers traveled to many parts of the world;
   d. everyone loves the person who tries "to be himself."

4. Pioneers! O Pioneers!

THE FRONTIERS of America were high and wide. Thousands of settlers left the Eastern shores. Their wagons moved westward, piled with bedding and clothing, with pots and pans, with Bibles and fiddles, with clocks and jugs and children and chickens. Long on hardships and short on food as they often were, many of the pioneers died on the long, long trail.

The spirit of America was in the saddle. Across the Platte River, through the hunting grounds of the savage Pawnees, down the Santa Fe Trail or on to Fort Laramie rode men and women and children as America grew. They didn't know much about the West or the North, where they were going, but they cleared the land and they built their cabins and they tilled the soil. "Only the doubters stayed home," they said. With hope and courage and great faith, these hardy pioneers proved that they were right.

Pioneers!   O Pioneers!

Come, my tan-faced children,
Follow well in order, get your weapons ready,
Have you your pistols? have you your sharp-edged axes?
    Pioneers!   O pioneers!

For we cannot tarry here,
We must march, my darlings, we must bear the brunt of
    danger,
We, the youthful sinewy races, all the rest on us depend,
    Pioneers!   O pioneers!

O you youths, Western youths,
So impatient, full of action, full of manly pride and
    friendship,
Plain I see you, Western youths, see you tramping with the
    foremost,
    Pioneers!   O pioneers!

Have the elder races halted?
Do they droop and end their lesson, wearied, over there
    beyond the seas?
We take up the task eternal, and the burden and the lesson,
    Pioneers!   O pioneers!

Till with sound of trumpet,
Far, far off the daybreak call—hark! how loud and clear
    I hear it wind,
Swift! to the head of the army!—swift! spring to your places,
    Pioneers!   O pioneers!

Our Lady's Lantern

THE OREGON country was the promised land of the western pioneer. Across plains and mountains it called men and women to its fast-flowing rivers, its green forests, its sheltered valleys. If it was far, it was also friendly. For within it waited Doctor John McLoughlin, already earning, by his welcoming justice and charity, his title of "the Father of Oregon."

Six feet and four inches tall, with flowing white hair and white beard, which led the Indians to call him White Eagle, Doctor John Mc-Loughlin commanded the Northwest as a "factor," or manager, of the territory of the Hudson's Bay Company. So good was his management that in the twenty-two years while he was the factor, no Indian trouble broke out in Oregon. British in his own citizenship and Anglican in his religion, he was nevertheless the friend and helper of American settlers, and, in particular, of the American missionaries, Catholic, Methodist, and Presbyterian.

The coming of settlers to the Oregon valleys brought the need for schools. Father Pierre-Jean De Smet of the Society of Jesus, apostle of the Rockies and missionary to all the American Northwest, believed with Doctor McLoughlin that a Catholic school must be started in one of the new settlements. There were no Sisters then available in the United States; and so Father De Smet went back to his native Belgium to find a community willing to send teaching Sisters to the Oregon country.

He found them in Namur. The Sisters of Notre Dame de Namur offered to send six of their number out to the Western wilderness. With the blessing of the Papal Nuncio, Archbishop Joachim Vincent Pecci, whom the world was later to know as Pope Leo XIII, they set out from Antwerp. As the ship drew away from the wharf, the Sisters saw a crescent moon gleaming in the western sky. "Our Lady's Lantern," said Sister Mary Catherine. "It will light us on our way."

They were to see the crescent

moon seven times before they came to the end of their voyage in far-away Oregon.

The Sisters took with them their habits, the tools of their teaching, and a few cherished holy pictures and statues. They took the piano of Sister Aloysia, and it served as an altar during the long voyage across and down the Atlantic, around Cape Horn, and up the Pacific. Most amazing of all their baggage, they took a goat which Father De Smet had bought for them in one of the Netherlands towns where the boat put in before facing the storms of the North Sea.

The goat, Father De Smet told them, would give them milk, so that they would not have to drink the strong black coffee which was part of the ship's meals. The trouble was that no one of the Sisters had ever milked a goat. Sister Loyola, leader of the band, assigned the actual milking task to Sister Mary Catherine. With the help of Sister Norbertine, who held the goat's horns, and Sister Albertine, who held the bucket for the milk, the task was done; but there were many times when the combination of bucking goat and bucking ship caused the Sisters to be entirely willing to drink black coffee.

The voyage from Amsterdam to Oregon took seven months. Off the coast of France storms raged over the sailing ship. The Sisters saw a spouting whale, a beautiful dolphin cast on deck, a shark, a school of fish following the vessel. Shipwrecked sailors from a French boat promised that they would take back messages to Namur. On Valentine's Day they crossed the equator. They saw the play with which the sailors gaily greeted the pretended appearance of Neptune, the old Greek god of the sea; and they were soaked by the deluge of water which the sailors threw on everyone on board the ship.

166

For a day they were followed by a pirate ship. The captain armed the crew. Father De Smet led the Sisters in prayer until the pirate craft disappeared.

Floating icebergs of the South Atlantic rose around them. Masses of ice rose like mountains out of the sea. As they rounded Cape Horn, terrible winds struck the little ship. The hurricane tore the furled sails into ribbons. For an entire week no one but the sailors could go on deck. Death stared them in the face.

Off the rocky shores of Patagonia the most terrible of all the storms struck the ship. Father De Smet went to the Sisters, offering to hear their confessions. He found them calm and unterrified. "Nothing troubles us, Father," Sister Aloysia said. "The Lord may dispose of us as He pleases."

The wind changed, and the sea fell quiet. As the clouds lifted, the sailors saw that the ship had almost run on treacherous rocks. Another quarter-hour would have rushed them to destruction. One of the ship's officers asked Sister Mary Catherine if she had felt no fear.

"No," she said. "Our Superiors did not send us to be the food of fishes. They sent us to teach the children of Oregon."

On the west coast of South America, Valparaiso, rising terrace on terrace, with flowering gardens and beautiful houses like the homes of Spain, offered them a pleasant rest from the long voyage. It offered them more than that when the citizens of the city asked them to remain. Messengers from Rio de Janeiro invited them to go to Brazil. When they arrived at Lima, the Peruvian authorities begged them to remain there in the lovely city of Saint Rose. These invitations must have been tempting, for the South American cities had already flowered into fine civilization, with splendid buildings, libraries, universities; but the Sisters of Notre Dame de Namur had been sent to teach the children of Oregon, and on to Oregon they went.

They crossed the equator for the second time. Then their provisions gave out. The sailors grumbled. The captain fell ill. Even when they started to disembark, their landing was delayed by ill winds. At last, on the feast day of Saint Ignatius Loyola, they came to the Oregon shore.

Through Astoria, the old American fur-trading post, they made their way to Fort Vancouver. There they were welcomed by Dr. John McLoughlin. Doctor McLoughlin had already become a Catholic, led to the Faith by the noble example of Father De Smet's work among the Indians. He himself had given aid to all immigrants to Oregon, both Canadians and Americans. He had fed and clothed them, lent to them farm implements and farm animals, given them credit for food and supplies. In every possible way he helped the settlers of Oregon to build their community. He helped the Sisters as he had helped others, even having a large boat built for them so that they would not have to travel the river in frail Indian canoes.

In this boat they went to the place on the Willamette River which was to be the site of their school. They spent a night on a sandbank, where they were drenched by mists and tormented by mosquitoes. At the Mass of Thanksgiving for safety the insects were so thick that the Sisters could not see the priest. The last five miles of their journey had to be made by wagon over roads rougher than the oceans.

They came at last to their destination, a large and dirty shack which had been the home of thirty half-breed boys. Like Saint Teresa of Avila, they spent their first hours of residence in their new convent by giving it a thorough cleaning. Sister Mary Catherine undertook the community washing. Luckily some good-natured squaws came to her aid. Other squaws helped Sister Mary Cornelia to find, under a coating of years of dirt, the floor of a building which could be used for a church. Three of the Sisters fell ill with malaria, and Mother Loyola cared for them.

For weeks the house of the Sisters had no doors or windows. It was not plastered. The Sisters brought moss from the woods to stop up the holes in the roof. They hung matting on the walls of the chapel to shut out the cold.

With their own hands they built a new house and a new school. They took in hundreds of pupils, Indians and whites. They cared for them, protected them. Mountain lions and wolves prowled near the little school. Once a panther leaped into the garden, but leaped out again. The Sisters taught— and did all the work. Their pupils, one of the Sisters wrote home to Namur, acted like spectators rather than helpers.

Little by little, the Sisters planted an orchard in the wilderness into which they had come. The school prospered. So did the farm which the teachers worked, spading and irrigating the hard soil. In time, Sister Norbertine planted thirteen hundred fruit trees in the orchard. The fruit of these trees was a forerunner of the great crop which Oregon now sends all over the world.

"These trees began to bear," one of the Sisters wrote, "the year we left for California."

For, driven by circumstances over which they had no control, they had to give up their Oregon mission. First of all, their friend and benefactor, Doctor John McLoughlin, was forced out of his factor's post with the Hudson's Bay Company on the charge that he had favored Americans too much. Through all the years of McLoughlin's rule there had been no Indian trouble. Then came the massacre, when the Protestant missionary Whitman and his wife were killed by several Indians who had been living at the Whitman mission. A Catholic missionary saved the life of Whitman's associate, Spalding, but Spalding's misrepresentations about Catholic missionaries caused trouble which lasted a long time in Oregon.

In spite of all this trouble, the school kept on. Then, suddenly, came the good news of the finding of gold in California. Immediately all the Oregon settlements boiled with excitement. Men from every part of the world were coming to the gold fields. Why should not the men of Oregon, with the least distance to go, set out for them? On foot or in ships they started for the gold fields of California, leaving their wives to manage their farms in Oregon and trusting their children to the care of the Sisters of Notre Dame. Few of the men ever came back.

The women managed the farms poorly, so the harvest was small. Fuel was scarce that winter. Sister Mary harnessed an old blind horse and, with two children, broke her way through the forests, gathering firewood while they heard the cries of wolves.

Sister Mary Cornelia and the other Sisters went out into the fields in the next year. They tilled the ground, sowed seeds, and cultivated the fields. Then, when the harvest was ready, they reaped it with scythes. By their work they saved not only themselves, but the whole community from famine.

In the next year that dreaded disease, cholera, attacked the mission. First the children fell ill. To nurse them the Sisters went without any sleep for days and nights. Then they too fell ill. When they recovered, they found the mothers and children gone from the settlement. Sadly the Sisters realized that there was no further need for their missionary service.

After eight years of struggle they closed the school. They said good-by sadly to the few Indians left there. Even more sadly they said good-by to the old doctor, already suffering those injustices which for a long time clouded his great fame. Wet and cold,—as they had been on the first night of their coming to Oregon,—they went out from the place that they had made holy, the place where other missionaries would one day come.

Sadly they went aboard the boat which was to take them away from the Oregon country. They were going to California because California was then the place of greatest need for their services. As they went, a crescent moon shone over the Oregon pines.

"Our Lady's Lantern," said Sister Mary Catherine. "It lighted us here. It will light us the rest of the way."

Arranging Main Ideas in Order

These are the major ideas contained in this story. Arrange them on your paper in the order of their occurrence. If it is necessary, reread the selection.

Men of Oregon sought gold
Difficulties with the goat
Oregon reached
Sisters had variety of baggage
Journey to the mission
Oregon was land of promise
Dangers of voyage
Sister's work in agriculture
Farewell to Oregon
Sights seen on voyage
School closed
The new home in Oregon

Sisters built school in which they taught
Welcomed by Doctor McLoughlin
Schools needed in Oregon
Cholera patients nursed by Sisters
Sisters of Notre Dame secured for teachers
Doctor McLoughlin deprived of position
Sisters prevented famine by farming
Invitations to remain in South America

171

ALFRED BARRETT, S.J.

Pioneer Sister

All the way across the United States, in old settlements and in young territories, pioneer Catholic Sisters have helped to build the nation. Like the Sisters in Oregon, Sisters in other places cut down trees, cleared fields, put up houses and schools. All the while they labored at their greater task, the teaching of children. Their double work has been well described in this poem about Mother Seton at Emmitsburg.

> HERS was a country where the axes rang
> To hew a vista letting in the sun;
> The logs had hardly fallen when they sprang
> Foursquare and fragrant—and the house was done.
> Something is lost that she knew when our land
> Had to be cleared and set with barriers,
> For wheat-fields wave only when fences stand,
> And water only flows from springs like hers.
> Thickets of tangled thought are on us now,
> The springs are choked and all the fences down.
> She must have known, and planned with placid brow
> Outposts in many a countryside and town,
> Where nuns in softer days might still pioneer—
> Facing in each young mind a new frontier.

Comanche

THE FIRST rays of the morning sun touched the tops of the cottonwood trees along the river bank, and from the parade ground at the army post came the clear call of a bugle. Down in the cavalry shed Comanche pawed the wooden floor of his stall impatiently. It was time for his oats and he was happy.

The days always began like this at Fort Lincoln. First the notes of the bugle, then the voices of the men at the troopers' quarters and a stamping and nickering of the horses in the cavalry shed. Comanche had been with the regiment for eight years now, and he knew all these sounds well.

He knew that soon the man would come to feed him, the man who walked with a limp and who always had a pat and a friendly word for him. Putting his ears forward, Comanche listened. Some soldiers were coming toward the cavalry shed, and in a moment he heard the low half-door at the back of his stall swing open. Turning his head he whinnied softly. The man had come at last.

"I'm giving you double rations today, Comanche," the man said, "double rations to remember me by when you're out in the plains country fighting Indians."

Limping over to the feed box, the old soldier poured a pail of oats into it and then stood looking at the horse approvingly. "Not so handsome as some," he said presently. "Body too stocky, neck too thick, legs too short and heavy for speed. But you've got plenty of strength and endurance," he added, giving Comanche a friendly slap on the rump.

This man was Trooper Briggs. He had served under General Custer back in Civil War days, and it was in one of the last battles of this war that he had received the wound which made him lame.

These were stirring days out in the Indian country. The long struggle between the red men and the white men had been going on for more than two centuries, and it was not yet finished. In the land of the warlike Sioux and Cheyenne Indians there were still powerful

173

tribes who dared to take the war-path and fight the white man. And so the United States Government built forts and army posts and sent soldiers to subdue these last un-conquered tribes. For the white man needed even these far lands.

To one of these army posts, Fort Lincoln, Comanche had been sent when he was a fine young horse. At the Fort he had been assigned to the famous Seventh Cavalry, commanded by General Custer, the greatest Indian fighter of them all. Many times since then Comanche had gone into battle, ridden by Captain Miles Keough, whose fa-vorite mount he was, and always he and his rider had come through each battle safely.

For several weeks scouts had been bringing to Fort Lincoln alarming reports from the western plains. Sitting Bull was on the warpath again. And so, on this fine spring morning, the regiment moved out of Fort Lincoln, on its way to the Sioux country. The Seventh Cavalry went first, led by General Custer. He was a striking figure, sitting very straight in his saddle, his long yellow hair falling to his shoulders under his wide-brimmed hat. Behind him rode Captain Miles Keough mounted on Comanche, and following the cav-alry came the marching soldiers. Bands were playing, bright banners were flying. It was a splendid mili-tary procession.

It was late in June when the regiment reached the land of the Sioux Indians in the rugged Black Hills country. Here it divided into detachments of several companies each, and each detachment then followed the line of march assigned to it. General Custer, with four companies, proceeded cautiously toward the Little Big Horn River, on whose banks it was thought the Indians would make their stand. At the head of one of these companies rode Captain Miles Keough on Comanche.

General Custer was not familiar with this country, but the red men knew the region very well, for it was their home and the home of their fathers. On every hillside the Sioux chiefs had stationed keen-eyed watchers, and scouts slipped among the trees. Slowly a net of red warriors was drawn round the white men. And then one day, outnumbered ten to one, General Custer and his men rode into the deadly trap prepared for them.

Just exactly what happened that day no one will ever know. A rifle cracked, then another and another, and the air was suddenly filled with the dreadful war whoops of the Indians. It was quickly over. The shouting ceased, the firing died away, and all was quiet again. A great battle had been fought—the battle of the Little Big Horn.

It was not until two days later that General Terry arrived with his command. He had reached the river on the day agreed upon beforehand, but he had come too late. As he and his men came over the brow of the hill and looked down into the valley, a worried frown appeared on General Terry's face.

"I don't like the look of this," he said.

On every hand there were signs that many Indians had passed that way, but now there were none to be seen. A moment later a scout came hurrying toward him. "I bring bad news, General," he said, "Custer

175

and his men have been defeated; the loss is heavy, sir."

"How many are dead?" asked General Terry.

"Many," said the scout. "It was a terrible disaster, sir."

"And what of Custer?" General Terry asked anxiously.

The scout shook his head. "Dead, sir," he answered.

For a moment General Terry could not trust himself to speak. "The wounded must be cared for without delay," he said. "You may report back to your captain now."

But the scout did not move. "There are no wounded, sir," he said slowly.

General Terry looked at him in horror. "You mean—"

The scout nodded sadly. "All are dead, sir," he said. "It was a gallant stand. There was no retreat. Custer's men fought until the very last trooper had given his life."

The scout turned to go, but faced about again and addressed the General. "There is one horse that still lives, sir," he said, "the only life left on the field. You may know him—he's been with the regiment a long time. It's Comanche, the horse that Captain Keough always rode. The horse is wounded, but the men are doing what they can to make him comfortable."

And so it happened that the small river steamboat, *Far West,* which had arrived with additional supplies and ammunition and had started back again to Fort Lincoln, had aboard her one wounded horse, the only survivor of the battle of Little Big Horn.

On a night in July Old Briggs sat by the river smoking thoughtfully. It had been more than a month since General Custer and his men had left Fort Lincoln to fight the Indians. Before long he heard a sound up the river that brought him to his feet with a start. It was the whistle of a steamboat. He emptied his pipe and, going to the very edge of the water, stood looking upstream.

"It's the *Far West,*" he thought, "I know her whistle. She will be bringing us news of the regiment."

To Old Briggs that night seemed, ever after, like a dream: the dim gray shape of the steamboat coming out of the dark; the sparks from her funnels floating high in the air; the steady throb of her engine; and the swish of water thrown up by the paddle wheel.

A number of troopers, wakened by the steamboat's whistle, came hurrying across the parade ground toward the river. For many days they had been eagerly awaiting the arrival of the *Far West.* Old Briggs joined them, and they all climbed into two small boats, and started across the river. No one spoke. Each man was wondering what news they would hear.

They put their little boat ashore just below the wharf and went aboard the *Far West* at once. Captain Marsh, her commander, stood on deck talking to a group of people gathered around him. "Three hundred men killed," he was saying. "Four companies of the famous Seventh Cavalry, the flower of the regiment, and not a man left alive. They died as troopers should die, with their rifles at their shoulders."

For a moment Old Briggs could not believe he had heard these words. Not a man left alive of the three hundred who rode away with General Custer on that memorable day! Slowly he turned away. He did not want to hear more just then.

The unhappy trooper's shoulders drooped as he went down to the lower deck and he felt, all at once, very tired and alone. General Custer gone, Captain Keough gone, and Captain Keough's mount, Comanche. But suddenly he straightened up with a jerk. He had heard the low nicker of a horse; a nicker he had learned to know from all others.

Hurrying along the deck Old Briggs came upon a deck hand dozing in a chair. "Have you got a horse here?" he asked excitedly.

"Yes, sir," answered the deck hand, rubbing his eyes. "There's a horse on board, but he's pretty badly done for. The Indians got him with half a dozen bullets, in the big battle when Custer and his men were killed. Comanche, they call him, and they found him wandering around the battlefield alone. He's back yonder in a stall we fixed up for him."

But Old Briggs was already on his way. "I'm coming, Comanche!" he shouted. "It's your old friend Briggs, Comanche! It's your old friend Briggs!"

Back home once more came Comanche, the Indian-fighting horse. When the little steamboat carried him across the river to Fort Lincoln next morning, the men and officers of the fort welcomed him as a hero. Old Briggs scarcely left him, day or night, until Comanche's wounds were healed.

One day a special order went out from Army Headquarters.

Headquarters Seventh U.S. Cavalry
  Fort A. Lincoln, D.T.
    April 10, 1878

GENERAL ORDERS No. 7

1. The horse known as "Comanche" being the only living representative of the bloody tragedy of the Little Big Horn, his kind treatment and comfort shall be a matter of special pride and solicitude on the part of every member of the Seventh Cavalry to the end that his life shall be preserved to the utmost limit. Wounded and scarred as he is, his very existence speaks in terms more eloquent than words, of the desperate struggle against overwhelming numbers, of the hopeless conflict, and the heroic manner in which all went down on that fatal day.

2. The commanding officer of Company I will see that a special and comfortable stall is fitted up for him, and he will not again be ridden by any person whatsoever, under any circumstances, nor will he ever be put to any kind of work.

3. Hereafter, upon all occasions of ceremony of mounted regimental formation, Comanche, saddled and bridled and draped in mourning, and led by a mounted trooper of Company I, will be paraded with the regiment.

By command of Colonel Sturgis.

E. A. Garlington
First Lieutenant and Adjt.
Seventh Cavalry

Comanche's fighting days were over. He had earned a rest and now he was to have it. There was a meadow not far from the army post where the grass was soft and green. This was now Comanche's own field, and here he spent his days nibbling the tender grass and listening to the familiar sounds that came to him from the fort. He had his own shed, too, and his own comfortable stall to stay in when the weather was cold and stormy. And, as before, he had his good friend Briggs, the trooper, to look after him. Here Comanche lived on for many years. Each day Old Briggs limped over to carry him some dainty or other.

"You haven't changed much, old fellow," Briggs said to him one morning as he opened the gate to Comanche's field. "You haven't changed much, old soldier, in spite of all the hard fighting you have seen."

Comanche whinnied softly and began to eat the corn husks Briggs had brought. When he had finished he rested his muzzle on the top of the gate and blinked contentedly while the trooper stroked his neck and talked to him.

Suddenly, over on the parade ground, the army band began to

They stood there together, the old trooper and the old horse, and watched another splendid procession march away from the army post, with banners flying, rifles glistening in the sunshine, and the big ammunition wagons rumbling along the river trail. After a time Old Briggs picked up his empty basket. "Well, I must be getting back to quarters now," he said and limped slowly away.

Comanche looked after him for a

lay, and Comanche raised his head uickly. Mounted troopers were iding out and pack horses and mmunition wagons were being rought up. "They are off to the ndian country again," Old Briggs aid half to himself. "But you and are not going, Comanche. Our ighting days are done."

moment and then glanced once more at the marching regiment. It had been a fine exciting life, fighting Indians out on the wide plains, and he had enjoyed it. But here in this meadow the grass was fresh and tender. Comanche lowered his head and began to browse.

Can You Recall Details?

How well do you recall the details of what you have read? This exercise is designed to help you recall details. On your paper write the number of the statement and beside it the letter of the phrase which completes it correctly.

1. Comanche had been with the regiment for (a) seven years; (b) five years; (c) eight years; (d) three years.

2. Old Trooper Briggs limped because of a wound he received (a) in the battle of Little Big Horn; (b) in one of the last battles of the Civil War; (c) in the battle led by Captain Keough; (d) while tending the horses in the cavalry shed.

3. The famous Seventh Cavalry was led by (a) General Custer; (b) General Terry; (c) Captain Marsh; (d) Captain Keough.

4. Comanche was injured in battle against the (a) Cheyenne Indians; (b) Iroquois Indians; (c) Sioux Indians; (d) Potawatomi Indians.

5. The cavalry reached the Black Hills country in (a) late June; (b) early July; (c) early spring; (d) late autumn.

6. The Seventh Cavalry was defeated because (a) General Custer was not a good leader; (b) they were outnumbered ten to one by the Indians; (c) General Terry did not arrive on time; (d) their scouts were not alert.

7. Comanche was carried home, the only survivor of the encounter with the Indians, aboard the steamboat (a) Mississippi; (b) Fort Lincoln; (c) Far West; (d) S. A. Arlington.

8. In the battle of Little Big Horn, the American troops lost (a) two hundred men; (b) four companies of the Seventh Cavalry; (c) General Terry and his command; (d) all their leaders, cavalrymen, and horses.

ROSEMARY AND STEPHEN VINCENT BENÉT

Western Wagons

THEY went with ax and rifle, when the trail was still to blaze,
They went with wife and children, in the prairie-schooner days,
With banjo and with frying pan—Susannah, don't you cry!
For I'm off to California to get rich out there or die!

We've broken land and cleared it, but we're tired of where we are.
They say that wild Nebraska is a better place by far.
There's gold in far Wyoming, there's black earth in Ioway.
So pack the kids and blankets, for we're moving out today!

The cowards never started and the weak died on the road,
And all across the continent the endless campfires glowed.
We'd taken land and settled—but a traveler passed by—
And we're going West tomorrow—Don't ever ask us why!

We're going West tomorrow, where the promises can't fail,
O'er the hills in legions, boys, and crowd the dusty trail!
We shall starve and freeze and suffer. We shall die, and tame
    the lands.
But we're going West tomorrow, with our fortunes in our hands.

Trail to the West

THE OLD WEST was a land of mighty men: Lewis and Clark, pushing their way northwestward over plains and mountains; Father De Smet, walking or riding nearly two hundred thousand miles to win the Indian to God; Mike Fink, the fabulous killer of bears; Jim Bridger, strongest of the Mountain Men; Kit Carson, greatest of all guides and scouts, the man who held open the road to California for the wagon trains that helped to build America; and a hundred others, some of less fame but of no less courage, whose deeds made a pattern as bright as sunlight on the Rockies.

No one, venturing into the land where these men had blazed the trails, could long forget their dangers and their daring. What they had done, others could do. What they had endured, others must endure, if need came. That was the code of the men who followed them; and Edward Creighton, mounting to the box of the westbound stage-coach at the South Platte Crossing on a winter day of 1860, remembered that code, although he did not yet know that he was on his own way to join the heroic crew of America's destiny.

With creaking of wheels and cracking of whip, the coach rattled through the freezing waters of the muddy, yellow river. Creighton, carefully watching for quicksands that might swallow up coach and horses and passengers, never once looked back at the piles of mail sacks which topped the swaying vehicle. It was his job to take the mail through rivers, over plains, over mountains, past hostile Indians, all the way to Salt Lake City. Colorado, Wyoming, Utah lay before him, wilderness, with a few forts and stage-stations the only dots of safety upon it. He would carry out his orders.

The conductor, seated beside him, was the official authority of the caravan. He made the reports to the division superintendent on the safe transport of mails, express, and passengers, but the driver assumed the responsibility for a safe journey. He spoke little to the passengers. His hours were long,

his route always dangerous. No matter what happened, the coach had to go on—and it was his job to keep it going.

Wind was rising, and snow was beginning to blow down from the high eaves of the world, as Creighton steadily drove his four horses. There were few stage-stations and still fewer settlements between the South Platte Crossing and Fort Laramie. He was due for relief at the fort; but when he arrived there, the driver who was to take his place was ill. Creighton would have to take the passengers and mail on to the next stage-station.

There were Indians around Laramie, Sioux who had come down from the Black Hills, whose pine-clad slopes showed over the wintry plains of Wyoming. Only a little while before the Sioux had massacred men at Fort Laramie. Little Thunder and his braves had been defeated, but there were rumors that the Sioux were again ready to go on to the warpath. Creighton, driving westward, peered toward every ridge to see signs of Indian scouts.

The coach was on the Oregon Trail. For years hundreds of thousands of men and women had been going over that trail. Sixty thousand gold-seekers had moved upon it in one wild year. In another year seventy-five thousand oxen and more than six thousand Conestoga wagons had plodded over it. Sixteen thousand Mormons had once marched through its ruts. Now a daily coach service, bridging Atchison, Kansas, with Salt Lake City, ran upon it; and the Pony Express was soon to come. Nearly a mile wide at some points, with broken wagons and bleached bones marking its course, the trail was the one great highway to green Oregon and golden California.

Keeping westward, Creighton came to Independence Rock. A relief driver should have been waiting there, but again there was no one. Creighton still held the reins, although the horses had been replaced time and again.

On the way the coach rolled past prairie-dog towns, past herds of buffaloes, past deer and antelope grazing on the cold, short grass of the wintry hills. Several times it went through hostile Indian country. Then the conductor pulled down the shades and stood guard over the passengers; but Creighton drove on.

Coyotes howled throughout the night while passengers tried to sleep upon piled mail sacks. Winds whistled endlessly. Sometimes a wolf loped across the trail. Night, the vast, star-studded night of the West, brought dangers from nature, as soon as the daylight dangers from Indians had ended. Through every danger the coach continued westward.

As Creighton drove into the mountains the snow fell deeper and the going grew slower. Wrapped in a great buffalo coat, Creighton held the reins in freezing hands. He took the coach through South Pass, climbing to the sky. There came a day when he paused upon the summit of the Rockies and saw the glory of that world of high peaks, white with snow and ice. The Continental Divide! The top of the Western world! Behind him lay one land of dangers passed. Before him lay another land of dangers to come.

Near the Wind River Mountains he passed the grave of Sakajawea, the Indian woman who had guided Lewis and Clark. At Fort Bridger a driver offered to take the stage on to Salt Lake City; but Creighton, almost as if he knew what chance of fortune awaited him in that town, refused. He let his horses take their own course through the twenty miles of Echo Canyon, the one good road of the long journey. Then, one day at sunset, he came to the summit of Big Mountain, and saw Salt Lake City, fifteen miles away, in the heart of a vast picture of glowing mountain peaks.

Salt Lake City was then only a little more than ten years old, but it was already a busy and thriving town. The Mormons, driven out of some of the Eastern states, had journied far across the plains and mountains, and, after fearful hardships, had built this city. It had continued its growth under the leadership of Brigham Young, head of the Mormon Church. It was then a town of good buildings and the promise of better ones. Open streams of clear water flowed at the sides of its wide streets. Homes, schools, church buildings, and business blocks were already filling its broad acres.

"Here's the end of our road," Edward Creighton said to his conductor; but it was not to be the end of the road for him.

Three years later Edward Creighton came again into Salt Lake City. He came at the crucial time when a group of men was trying to find a way to link the Far West with the East by means of the telegraph. The telegraph line already crossed the plains. Creighton knew more about the building of telegraph lines than most men. He had left his native Ohio for a job of setting telegraph poles through Missouri and Kansas. He had done more of that work in Nebraska. In Salt Lake City, he happened to meet men who were interested in building a telegraph line. He spoke to them with authority.

He told these men that, first of all, they needed a survey of the country between Salt Lake City and the Pacific Coast. How could they estimate the cost of poles, the cost of labor, the cost of equipment, unless they knew the conditions under which the builders would work? Did they have someone to make that survey, someone whose judgment and experience they could trust?

They had no one. They needed such a man, and needed him immediately, for already there was a rumor that a group of Californians would try to come eastward with a telegraph line. Creighton was not interested in that situation, but he had another more important reason for wishing to see the telegraph reach the Pacific Coast. It was almost certain that the nation would soon be torn apart by a civil war.

If it came, it was vital that the Union should be certain that California was part of that Union. The lack of communication was keeping that new state apart from the East. If the telegraph line could be built soon, it might hold the Golden State in the Union.

"You'll have to move fast," Creighton told the telegraph promoters, "as fast as you can get your man."

Through Salt Lake City they sought the man for the surveying job. Everywhere they went they got one answer: Edward Creighton. What if he did not know the country to the westward? Had he not brought in the stagecoach all the way from the South Platte Crossing? Had he not finished any job he had undertaken? Get Creighton, said the Mormons. Get Creighton, said the others.

Creighton himself said he could not do the job. He knew the great plains, the Black Hills, and the towering Rockies. He did not know the flat Nevada deserts, the Humbolt River country, or the rugged Sierras. Since he was not their man, he was returning to Nebraska.

He did not go back to Nebraska for a long, long time. Instead he set out from Salt Lake City to the westward. This time he was not driving the four horses of a coach, horses which would be changed at each stage-station. He was riding a horse, and that horse would have to carry him all the way to California.

After skirting the edge of the Great Salt Lake he crossed an alkali desert, waterless for miles upon miles. He rode all day and every day, stopping at night at a stage-station or camping out beside the trail. Sometimes the California coach, going or coming, passed him; but he kept his way alone.

That way led him through the Utah desert, a vast, treeless place which looked like an ocean with ashes for its waves. Even the sagebrush and the Joshua trees were forever gray with its eternal dust. Sometimes the great sunset clouds looked like lakes; but the water he glimpsed in this way was never real. Creighton carried water for himself and his horse in his saddlebags and got what food he could at the stage-stations; but there came a time when he had to go off the stagecoach trail to find a shorter route for the telegraph. Then he faced dangers of hunger, thirst, and the loss of his horse. Twice the horse fell, but the rider got him up. Once, walking, he led the tired animal for many miles across the desert.

He met hostile Indians more savage than the Sioux. and went through canyons where desperadoes lay in wait for passing travelers. He followed the twists and turns of the Humboldt River. He crossed the Great American Desert, vaster and more terrifying than the desert in Utah, a limitless plain of sagebrush and greasewood. Winter winds drove sand and alkali dust against him, and three times pulled the skin from his face. By the time he came to Carson City he was so bruised and battered that miners there begged him to wait until he was healed; but as soon as his horse was rested, he went on.

He climbed the high Sierras and saw the camps of the Forty-niners. Then, below him, he saw the valley of the Sacramento and knew that the worst of his journey was done. He dismounted from his horse and knelt upon the mountainside. "Thank God," he said. "Thanks

be to God!" That was all he ever told of his own story.

The rest of Edward Creighton's story is a tale, not of one man, but of many men. In San Francisco he met the Californians who were planning to bring the telegraph from west to east, and brought back to Salt Lake City the terms that they offered the eastern promoters. These men asked Creighton to undertake the building of the line westward from his own surveys. He started the project on July 4, 1861.

That work was a gigantic task. Everything was hard to get—poles, equipment, laborers. Some Mormons, who undertook some of the job, worked as they pleased, not as the task demanded. They were, they said reasonably, farmers, not road laborers. In despair Creighton went to Brigham Young, explaining to him the national need of the telegraph. Young gave out orders that every Mormon should stay on his job. The telegraph was finished; and California linked with the East.

Edward Creighton's work in the surveying and building of the telegraph across deserts and mountains of the West did more than open a quick means of communica-tion. The telegraph was one of the most important elements in the unification of East and West in that time of national peril, the Civil War. Had it not been for the telegraph, there could not have existed the speed of communication which caused quick, unified action; and had it not been for this unified action, the Civil War might have had a different ending, an ending which could have split the nation in two. Edward Creighton's work was therefore far more than adventure. It was a great national service in citizenship.

Today shining streamliners flash past long miles of telegraph poles on deserts and mountains between the Missouri River and the Golden Gate. Most of the tens of thousands who travel every year over the road Edward Creighton pioneered have never heard of him. There is, however, hardly one of them who does not owe something of his ease in travel to the man who once used his freedom to finish his job of self-chosen service for the nation he loved. Mule-skinner and stagecoach-driver, ranger and scout, builder of highways and telegraph trails, Edward Creighton, son of an Irish farmer, linked the Old West of the plains and mountains, of Indians and buffalo-hunters, of Carson and Bridger, of the Mountain Men, and Father De Smet, with the New West of vast ranches, of great power plants, of airplanes gleaming in the sun, the New West which is still the clean slate of the wide-flung world.

Making a Summary

As you already know, the topic sentence in a paragraph is the sentence which tells what the paragraph is about. You will be able to prepare a very good summary of a story, your history lesson, or geography lesson, by selecting the topic sentence from each paragraph. Skim this story quickly and pick out the topic sentences. You will see how well they summarize the story for you.

Explaining Colorful Expressions

Locate the following colorful phrases in the story and figure out their meanings from the way in which they are used.

fabulous killer of bears

deeds made a pattern as
   bright as sunlight

pine-clad slopes

vast, star-studded night

dots of safety

clean slate of the wide-flung
   world

speak with authority

over the trail that he blazed

skirted the edge

the high eaves of the world

Extra Credit Work

You might like to divide into groups and rewrite this story as a radio drama and present it to the class. Edward Creighton was a real "Lone Ranger" and you should stress the contribution of lasting worth which he made to the American way of life in addition to his deeds of adventure.

ARTHUR GUITERMAN

Kit Carson

I WAS nine when my father died,
    Killed by a falling limb;
Daniel Boone was my father's friend—
    Maybe you've heard of him.

He and his kind were my teachers, then—
    Trapper, hunter, and guide;
They taught me to shoot and to speak the truth;
    I taught myself to ride.

Woodsman I was till I saw the plains,
    And I saddled and rode away
To the little old Injun town of Taos
    And the city of Santa Fe.

Plainsman I was till I saw the hills
    And the trails that westward ran
To the farther hills and the farthest hills—
    And I am a mountain man.

Mine were the days of the mountain men,
    The days that are now a dream;
As once we followed the buffalo track
    We followed the beaver stream.

None knew the roads through the desert dust,
    The trails of cliff and glen,
None knew the paths to the western sea
    But we that were mountain men!

Rooms for Tourists

From a letter of Nora Norton in Alaska to her friend Rita Rowan in the State of Washington.

DEAR RITA:

Here we are, the Norton family in a new home, in the new state of Alaska. We live not far from Fairbanks, almost at the end of the Alaska Highway. We are three hundred miles northwest of the Canadian border, and that means that we are very far northwest.

I sound, I know, like a lesson in geography, but you come to think a lot about geography when you have traveled as far as we have. It is not very long since I said good-by to you in Bellingham, but it seems a long time because we have come so far.

Maybe you remember how we started. Mother and I went ahead in the car and Father and the boys followed with the truck. We kept that order all the way up through British Columbia to Prince George, and all the way over the Hart Highway to the Alaska Highway. The traffic there was so heavy that we were separated occasionally.

From the hour we struck the highway, everyone was friendly. Somehow there seemed to be a feeling of going on together. Mother said it reminded her of the stories her grandmother told of going West in a covered wagon when she was a little girl. There weren't any Indians along our way except a few peaceful Siwash, but the meadows and the mountains and the rivers and the lakes must have looked about the same to the pioneers of a hundred years ago as they did to us.

As we rode along, Mother told me that many of the places on the Alaska Highway were historic. We saw the blood-red banner of the Honorable Company of the Hudson's Bay flying bright above Fort St. John and Fort Nelson. They had been, before the highway was built, frontiers of civilization. We went through Whitehorse from which roads led out to Skagway and Juneau. Then, to our right, a road led off through the Klondike to Dawson, which had once been the greatest gold rush town in the world. Thousands of men had come over these trails, hoping to find gold in the streams of the Klondike. Few of them found it; but the stories about the Klondike piled up faster than did the gold.

Nowadays there are not so many people seeking gold. Most of them have come for oil or for uranium. In Canada the government owns the mineral rights to the lands and rents their use to prospectors. There must be plenty of prospectors, for we kept seeing the big trucks which carried supplies coming to or going from the oil fields. When we saw men carrying picks and rather odd-looking instru-

ments, Mother said they were looking for uranium. If they came near a field of uranium, the instruments began to click like crazy. I think Ted knows more about this than Mother does.

Ted says the Alaska Highway is over fifteen hundred miles long. He says that the United States and Canada built it together during World War II. Canada now owns over twelve hundred miles of it and we own the rest. I don't mean our family. I mean our country. All we Nortons own is a couple of hundred feet of land on the highway, with some buildings back of the sign, *Motel: Rooms for Tourists*.

We did not come to Alaska merely to run a motel. Father is a

mining engineer, and plans to work in this new state. Mother wants him to do that, but she thinks it will take a while for him to get into that work, and so she talked about having a motel. Her grandfather used to have a hotel near Glacier Park. All the family used to help in the work there, and Mother says the Nortons can do the same here.

We have started already.

We didn't have to build a house. There is one here. In fact, there are five. Four of them are cabins. But the fifth, a big, rambling, two-story place, has rooms enough for our family and for sixteen other persons. Father and Mother bought it just from seeing its picture. I think they were dumfounded when they saw it.

"How will we heat it in the Alaskan winter?" Mother cried.

"We're not too far from the oil fields," Father said.

Then we found that there was no oil heater. Round black stoves and big fireplaces furnish the heat. We furnish the logs. There were electric fixtures, but there was no electricity. "We'll fix that," Father said. "We'll get a battery and start an electrical system of our own."

He was lucky in finding an oil camp that was closing down. There he bought the battery and a lot of furniture. The houses still looked pretty bare, so Mother and I went to work making curtains and bedspreads. I don't know what we'd have done without our electric sewing machine. I wonder how much Mother's grandmother sewed by hand when she settled in Oregon. Nothing like what we did; but then she wasn't getting ready to run a motel on the Oregon Trail.

We weren't prepared for guests when the first ones came. We had finished our after-dinner work—for it stays light up here until nearly midnight at this time of the year—and we were saying our evening prayers when a car drew up at the gate. Someone knocked on the door, and Father opened it. There stood a man and woman and seven children.

193

"I'm sorry," Father began, but the woman said quickly, "Oh, please, you must find room for us. We've been driving hours and hours, and the children are so tired we can't go any farther."

"It isn't room we lack," Father said. "We aren't ready for customers. We haven't sheets or blankets."

"We'll manage somehow," the woman said, "if you'll just take us in for the night."

Father looked as if he were going to refuse, but Mother said, "I think we can arrange something," and so we arranged it. We divided the blankets from our beds and took our best sheets and pillow cases out of the cedar chest we had brought on the truck. Then Mother found cookies for the children and you should have seen them eat!

They had come, the man and woman told us, from Ohio. They were going far beyond Fairbanks, all the way north to the coast

194

where the woman's brother had a salmon-canning factory. They had been traveling for days and days, and they were kind of dizzy from it. The children didn't even know that they had come through Alberta, although they had stopped in Calgary and in Edmonton. "Didn't you see the Mounties?" Ted asked them. But they couldn't remember, and we hurried them off to bed.

They left early next morning, and we rushed to get the place ready for other travelers. They came so fast that we were out of breath keeping ahead of them. At first the boys and I thought it was fun to see the cars pulling up at the gate, but after a while we stopped watching.

Once I went into Fairbanks with Mother. It is a bigger town than I had expected. There are shops and houses and many cars. There are churches, one of them Catholic, and there is a Catholic school.

"Can't we go to school there?" I asked Mother.

"I wish you could," she said, "but it's too far from home. Some day, when you're older, perhaps we'll live here in Fairbanks, and you can go to the school here."

There is a Catholic chapel not very far from our motel. The priest comes there every Sunday, and people come from miles and miles around. It reminds me of stories of pioneer times, but I guess we are the pioneers now. Mother says that pioneering sometimes brings you nearer to God. I feel that way when I go into the chapel. It is always shining clean, and there are always flowers on the altar. This means that someone is always taking care of it.

The boys and I go to a school about a mile from our house. There are eight grades, but only two teachers for them. They make us work hard, but I think we all like it. I don't know what we are going to do when winter comes. We hear the school often has to close for weeks. It is dark then most of the hours of the day. I don't know if I'm going to like going to school in the dark, but perhaps I will.

After we come home from school we do the chores, and there are plenty of chores to do. Ted does the heavy work. Father is away a good part of the time now, and so Ted's work is heavier. There's hardly a night when all the rooms of the motel, both in the little cabins and in the big house, are not taken by tourists. We see all sorts of people. Some of them are very fine. Others of them aren't; but, as Ted says, "It's a living."

I've forgotten to tell you about how beautiful the country is. The trees are so green, and there are flowers everywhere in the forest near us. We're near the Arctic Circle, but you'd never know it now. Sometimes we catch sight of wild animals, mostly deer, although I saw a bear the other day. Ted says he isn't afraid of bears, but I am. I hope none comes too close to the house. Sometimes they do.

Father says that perhaps in another year we can sell what we own here, and move into Fairbanks.

Mother shakes her head. I should be glad to go to the Catholic school there, but I'd miss the place here. I like it, for I like the people who keep coming. They all seem so free, so happy in their traveling. Our teacher says that Americans are always "on the move." Perhaps we are—but what are we going to do when we get as far west and as far north as we can go?

Write to me soon. Give my love to Sister Frances. And tell Martha Laydon that she can keep my book about Mexico. I won't be going that way for a long, long time.

Your friend,
Nora Norton.

Proving Statements

From what you remember of the story, write a sentence that proves each statement given below.

1. Many people have sought their fortune in Alaska.
2. The trip which Nora and her mother made along the Alaska Highway was quite pleasant.
3. The Alaska Highway is not very old.
4. The Nortons had an important reason for going to Alaska.
5. Mrs. Norton was kind-hearted and generous.
6. Nora was sometimes reminded of the story her mother told her of the pioneer days.
7. Nora enjoyed meeting and dealing with people.

The Plainsmen

MEN of the older, gentler soil,
    Loving the things that their fathers wrought—
Worn old fields of their fathers' toil,
    Scarred old hills where their fathers fought—
Loving their land for each ancient trace,
Like a mother dear for her wrinkled face,
      Such as they never can understand
      The way we have loved you, young, young land!

Born of a free, world-wandering race,
    Little we yearned o'er a half-turned sod.
What did we care for the fathers' place,
    Having ours fresh from the hand of God?
Who feared the strangeness or wiles of you
When from the unreckoned miles of you,
      Thrilling the wind with a sweet command,
      Youth unto youth called, young, young land?

When the last free trail is a prim, fenced lane
    And our graves grow weeds through forgetful Mays,
Richer and statelier then you'll reign,
    Mother of men whom the world will praise.
And your sons will love you and sigh for you,
Labor and battle and die for you,
      But never the fondest will understand
      The way we have loved you, young, young land.

Lion of the North

JOHN IRELAND was the archbishop of St. Paul in the days when Minnesota was still an outpost of the nation. He was one of the great pioneering priests of our country, and one of the greatest patriots of his time. He built churches and schools and communities of homes. He led causes of right with splendid courage and fought so bravely for justice that men called him "the Lion of the North."

He had come to Minnesota as an immigrant boy. He and his parents reached the Mississippi Valley while the smoke of Indian fires still lingered on the horizon and the memory of the Indian chief, Black Hawk, still rode in the river mists. The westward migration was pushings settlers into the wide prairies of the great valley. The Ireland boy caught the pioneering spirit of the time, and added to it something of his own.

While he plowed with his father, and hunted and fished for food, rather than for pleasure, he saw the little homes of the settlers, log houses and sod houses, far apart from one another, far from schools and churches. Men and women and children needed more, he thought, than the lonely life of the frontier farm. They needed neighbors, education, and religion.

Even when he went to college in France the boy did not forget his dream of settlements on the American frontier. Soon after his return and ordination he became chaplain of the Fifth Minnesota Regiment of the Union Army in the Civil War. There he came to know hundreds of men from the northern cabins, and he realized that they

198

longed, not only for home, but for better conditions in their homes.

In time John Ireland became a bishop and later an archbishop. He was able now to make his dream come true. He started settlements in Minnesota for Catholic immigrants, families from Ireland, from Germany, from Belgium. In all of these settlements he built churches and schools. He also established community centers where families might come for simple pleasures.

His archdiocese was large and some of his settlements were difficult to reach. The archbishop often rode rickety railway trains, drove creaking buggies, or walked for miles to get to his destination. Often his visit was a surprise, not always welcomed by those who had fallen below his standards. He knew every pastor and curate; it was said that he knew every telegrapher and brakeman along the line of the Great Northern Railway.

He also knew the Sisters in the schools. When he visited a parish he made a tour of the schoolrooms. He flung out questions about geography and arithmetic and American history; but, most often, he questioned about catechism. And woe betide the teacher whose pupils made mistakes! There were never any mistakes, however, in answer to his thundering query, "Who made you?" "God," the children would thunder just as loudly. No one finished any of the schools of the St. Paul Archdiocese without realizing his duty and responsibility. He was to love and serve God.

One way of service was in patriotism. John Ireland knew the code of the soldier, and he set that code for all citizens. A citizen must give allegiance to his nation. He must be ready to die for her, if necessary. He must live to promote her welfare at all times.

The archbishop came to realize that the need for Catholic settlements went beyond the boundaries of his own archdiocese. The time was one of large immigrations into the United States. For greater freedom, for better work opportunities, hundreds of thousands of people were every year leaving the old lands of Europe. Many of them, particularly the Irish, were staying in the cities of the Eastern seaboard. They should, Archbishop Ireland believed, be placed upon the farms of the land.

He knew that the main reason for their clinging to the cities was the presence there of the Church. He decided that the Church must precede these people, not follow. With this in mind, he started the Catholic Colonization Society.

This Society spread its work far beyond the boundaries of Minnesota. It established settlements as far west as Nebraska and as far south as Mississippi. To these new settlements the Society brought immigrants under the archbishop's plan. It was a remarkable plan of transportation that has never been bettered. He sent ships to Europe for the immigrants and had trains waiting to take them to the settlements. Many of these settlements have become important centers of American patriotism and of Catholic faith. The Society was eventually disbanded, but its broad influence lived long after its founders.

As the frontier moved northward and westward, conservation—care of the natural resources which God has given for the use of mankind—became a national problem. Men were cutting down the great forests for their own profit, ignoring the rights of both individuals and nation. Minnesota was one of the first states to suffer from this vandalism, and the archbishop of St. Paul was one of the first citizens to oppose it. His campaign for conservation was locally successful, but it went farther. It was not by accident that the nationwide conservation movement started in Archbishop Ireland's diocese.

Archbishop Ireland traveled over the country, preaching love of God and love of country. He came to know the most important leaders of his time. Statesmen, financiers, and educators sought his counsel. A national organization of public-school teachers invited him to speak at their convention. He helped to organize a World Congress of Religious where thinkers from all over the world spoke on man's need to worship God. He was one of the founders of The Catholic University.

As one of the great orators of his day, he was the leading speaker at hundreds of meetings. He always spoke with fiery zeal. He always lifted the two flags, the banner of our nation and the flag of our Faith. No one ever doubted that the Archbishop of St. Paul was a staunch American as well as a staunch Catholic.

He lived to see the upper Mississippi Valley become a land of many homes, of prosperous settlements, of fine churches and schools. He lived to see his nation grow in numbers and in strength. He lived to see thousands of Catholic churches and schools where there had been only hundreds. He himself never claimed credit for his share in that building; but everyone who knew him knew that, without the Lion of the North, the work would not have been done.

Can You Complete an Outline?

Copy this outline on your paper. Then complete it by supplying the minor ideas for the major ideas given below.

    I. John Ireland's Background
        A.
        B.
        C.

    II. His Vocation to the Priesthood
        A.
        B.
        C.

    III. Early Accomplishments as Archbishop
        A.
        B.
        C.

    IV. Interest in Education
        A.
        B.
        C.

    V. Teaching Concerning One's Duty to Country
        A.
        B.
        C.

    VI. Promotion of the Work of Church and Nation
        A.
        B.
        C.
        D.

    VII. Achievements Seen by "Lion of the North"
        A.
        B.
        C.
        D.

5. Roll of the Drums

JOHN BROWN, a tall strange man with flaming red hair and a burning desire to free the slaves, came out of Kansas and lit fires of rebellion that led to the War Between the States.

The flames spread. Abraham Lincoln in the White House, through feverish days and anxious nights, tried to unite a bitter people while bells in the South were melted into cannon and Massachusetts regiments marched toward Virginia. The battles of Bull Run ended in Confederate victory. The *Monitor* and the *Merrimac,* ironclad ships, fought their bitter duel. Calls came for volunteers, and men left their plows and workshops, their wives and children, to fight for a common freedom.

The War Between the States was a war of many battles, of many years. Then, at the courthouse at Appomattox, the greatest American tragedy came to an end. The war was ended. Five days later, as he sat in the Presidential box at Ford's Theatre in Washington, the President of the United States was shot. Across the street, in the little red-brick house of a stranger, the man who guided the destiny of the nation breathed a deep sigh, and was still.

Abraham Lincoln was dead, but his cause had triumphed and freedom was marching on.

ROSEMARY AND STEPHEN VINCENT BENÉT

Nancy Hanks

IF Nancy Hanks
Came back as a ghost,
Seeking news
Of what she loved most,
She'd ask first
"Where's my son?
What's happened to Abe?
What's he done?
Poor little Abe,
Left all alone
Except for Tom,
Who's a rolling stone;
He was only nine
The year I died.
I remember still
How hard he cried.

Scraping along
In a little shack,
With hardly a shirt
To cover his back,
And a prairie wind
To blow him down,
Or pinching times
If he went to town.
You wouldn't know
About my son?
Did he grow tall?
Did he have fun?
Did he learn to read?
Did he get to town?
Do you know his name?
Did he get on?"

A Child Looks Back

THE boy, Abe, had his thoughts, some running ahead wondering how Indiana would look, some going back to his seven little years in Kentucky. Here he had curled around his mother's apron and watched her face and listened to her reading the Bible at the cabin log-fire, her fingers rambling through his hair, the hands patting him on the cheek under the chin. God was real to his mother; he tried to make pictures in his head of the face of God far off and away in the sky, watching Kentucky, Hodgenville, Knob Creek, and all the rest of the world He had made. His thoughts could go back to the first time on a winter night around the fire when he lay flat on his stomach listening to his father as he told about his brothers, Mordecai and Josiah, and their father, Abraham Lincoln, who had staked out claims for more than 2000 acres of land on the Green River. One day Abraham Lincoln and his three boys were working in a field; all of a sudden the father doubled up with a groan of pain and crumpled to the ground, just after the boys had heard a rifle-shot and the whining of a bullet. "Indians," the boys yelled to each other.

As Mordecai ran to a cabin, Josiah started across the fields and woods to a fort to bring help, while Tom Lincoln—little knee-high Tom—stooped over his father's body and wondered what he could do. He looked up to see an Indian standing over him, and a shining bangle hanging down over the Indian's shoulder close to the heart.

The Indian clutched upward with his hands, doubled with a groan, and crumpled to the ground; Mordecai with a rifle at a peephole in the cabin had aimed his rifle at the shining bangle hanging down close to the Indian's heart, and Tom was so near he heard the bullet plug its hole into the red man.

And for years after that Mordecai Lincoln hated Indians with a deadly hate; if he heard that Indians were loose anywhere in a half-day's riding, he took his best rifles, pistols, and knives, and went Indian-killing.

Then there was Dr. Christopher Columbus Graham from Louisville, telling how the Indians were chasing Daniel Boone, and Boone saw a grapevine climbing high up a big oak; and he cut the grapevine near the root, took a run and a swing and made a jump of forty feet, so the Indians had to lose time finding sight and smell of his foot-tracks again.

And there were caves, worth remembering about in that part of Kentucky, and especially the biggest one of all, Mammoth Cave, fifty miles south; they said a thousand wagons could drive in and there would be room for another thousand.

And there was the foxy Austin Gollaher, his playmate. Up a tree he climbed one time, Abe dropped a pawpaw down into a coonskin cap; he guessed it was Austin's cap he was putting a smear of pawpaw mash in, but Austin had seen the trick coming and changed caps. So he had to wipe the smear out of his own cap.

Once he was walking on a log across Knob Creek when the rains had raised the creek. Just under the log, and under his feet, was the rush of the yellow muddy water.

206

The log was slippery, his feet went up in the air, he tumbled to the bottom of the creek; he came up, slipped again, came up with his nose and eyes full of water, and then saw Austin Gollaher on the bank holding a long pole. He took hold of the pole, and Austin pulled him to the bank.

Maybe he would grow up; his feet would be farther away from his head and his chin if he grew up; he could pick apples without climbing a tree or throwing clubs —if he grew up. Maybe then, after growing up, he would know more about those words he heard men saying, "in-de-pend-ent" and "ab-o-li-tion." Daniel Boone—yes, he could understand about Daniel Boone—wearing moccasins and a buckskin shirt. But George Washington and Thomas Jefferson, and President Madison in Washington, —they were far off; it was hard to make pictures of their faces.

And there was his mother, his "mammy," the woman other people called Nancy or Nancy Hanks. . . . It was so dark and strange about her. There was such sweetness. Yet there used to be more sweetness and yet fresher sweetness. There had been one baby they buried. Then there was Sally— and him, little Abe. Did the children cost her something? Did they pull her down? . . . The baby that came and was laid away so soon, only three days after it came, in so little a grave: that hurt his mother; she was sick and tired more often after that. . . . There were such lights and shadows back in her eyes. She wanted—what did she want? There were more and more days he had to take care of her, when he loved to bring cool drinking water to her—or anything she asked for.

Well—a boy of seven years old isn't supposed to know much; he goes along and tries to do what the big people tell him to do. . . . They had been young and seen trouble: maybe they know. . . . He would get up in the morning when they called him; he would run to the spring water. . . . He was only seven years old—and there were lots of frisky tricks he wanted to know more about.

He was a "shirt-tail boy." . . . Three boys teased him one day when he took corn to Hodgen's Mill; they wouldn't be satisfied till he had punched their noses. . . . A clerk in the store at Elizabeth-town gave him maple sugar while his mother bought salt and flour.

And the clerk was the only man he knew who was wearing store clothes, Sunday clothes, every day in the week. ... The two pear trees his father planted on the Rock Spring Farm ... the faces of two goats a man kept down in Hodgenville ... Dennis Hanks saying, "Abe, your face is solemn as a papoose."

It wouldn't be easy to forget that Saturday afternoon in corn-planting time when other boys dropped the seed-corn into all the rows in the big seven-acre field—and Abe dropped the pumpkin seed. He dropped two seeds at every other hill and every other row. The next Sunday morning there came a big rain in the hills; it didn't rain a drop in the valley, but the water came down the gorges and slides, and washed ground, corn, pumpkin seeds, and all clear off the field.

A dark blur of thoughts, pictures, memories, and hopes moved through the head of little seven-year-old Abe. The family was going to move again. There was hope of better luck up north in Indiana. Tom's older brother, Josiah, was farming along the Big Blue River. Rich black corn-land was over there in "Indianny," more bushels to the acre than anywhere in Kentucky.

Taking Notes

Reread the selection and make a few notes on each of the main paragraphs which will help you to remember what you have learned. Below is an example of what to do.

Paragraph 1. Abe—seven years old—Hodgenville, Ky.—father tells how his own father was killed by an Indian.

Paragraph 2.

Using New Words

Look up the exact meaning of the words given below and use them in interesting sentences.

| whining | bangle | gorges |
| crumpled | independent | abolition |

208

To Mrs. Bixby

The *Army and Navy Journal,* in its issue of December 3, 1864, published a message from the President of the United States to a Mrs. Bixby with this explanation: "Mrs. Bixby is a poor widow living in the Eleventh Ward of Boston. Her sixth son, who was severely wounded in battle, is now lying in the Readville Hospital." This wartime message has become one of the most famous letters in American history.

Executive Mansion, Washington
November 21, 1864

Mrs. Bixby,
Boston, Massachusetts

Dear Madam:

I have been shown in the files of the War Department a statement of the Adjutant-General of Massachusetts that you are the mother of five sons who have died gloriously on the field of battle. I feel how weak and fruitless must be any words of mine which should attempt to beguile you from the grief of a loss so overwhelming. But I cannot refrain from tendering to you the consolation that may be found in the thanks of the Republic they died to save. I pray that our Heavenly Father may assuage the anguish of your bereavement and leave you only the cherished memory of the loved and lost and the solemn pride that must be yours to have laid so costly a sacrifice upon the altar of freedom.

Yours very sincerely and respectfully,

Abraham Lincoln

The Gettysburg Address

FOUR score and seven years ago our fathers brought forth on this continent, a new nation, conceived in Liberty, and dedicated to the proposition that all men are created equal.

Now we are engaged in a great civil war, testing whether that nation, or any nation so conceived and so dedicated, can long endure. We are met on a great battlefield of that war. We have come to dedicate a portion of that field, as a final resting place for those who here gave their lives that that nation might live. It is altogether fitting and proper that we should do this.

But, in a larger sense, we cannot dedicate—we cannot consecrate—we cannot hallow—this ground. The brave men, living and dead, who struggled here, have consecrated it, far above our poor power to add or detract. The world will little note, nor long remember what we say here, but it can never forget what they did here. It is for us the living, rather, to be dedicated here to the unfinished work which they who fought here have thus far so nobly advanced. It is rather for us to be here dedicated to the great task remaining before us—that from these honored dead we take increased devotion to that cause for which they gave the last full measure of devotion—that we here highly resolve that these dead shall not have died in vain—that this nation, under God, shall have a new birth of freedom—and that government of the people, by the people, for the people, shall not perish from the earth.

HAROLD J. HEAGNEY

The Capture of the Robert E. Lee

Long before he was converted to the Roman Catholic Faith and became Father John Banister Tabb, the poet of the South was known as "young Johnny Tabb." Because of weak eyesight he was unable to join the Confederate Army with his brothers and friends. His disappointment was turned to joy when his cousin, Captain John Wilkinson, took him as clerk on the most famous of the Confederate blockade runners, the *Robert E. Lee.* Twenty-one times the *Lee* eluded the Yankee blockade and sailed to England, the Bermudas, and the West Indies to secure ammunition and medical supplies for the men in gray.

When Captain Wilkinson was transferred to a Confederate man-of-war, Johnny Tabb reluctantly but bravely remained at his post on the *Lee.*

THE return voyage began with fair weather, bright sunshine, and balmy breezes. But even in the smooth waters the *Robert E. Lee* rode heavily. Unlike the other captain and crew, Captain Knox was constantly at odds with his. But they were lucky in that they had sailed for three days without sighting a vessel. When they did, it proved to be a United States Navy cruiser, but luckily, the sun was setting and the blockade runner slipped away before the enemy warship detected her.

Johnny's heart grew lighter. They were nearing home and the sense of foreboding was leaving him. But he knew they had still to run the blockade.

"Look, Johnny," said Ben Magruder. "The breakers! We're just a little north of Wilmington."

The foam-covered waves were clearly before them and they could hear the boom of the surf. Just to the southward was the entrance to New Inlet and safety.

Lieutenant Rooks joined them. "Is that the North Carolina coast?"

"Yes, sir," replied Johnny, "and we should direct our course that way. I can't understand why we are delaying."

211

"There's Yankee ships to the westward, three of them," shouted Clay Bragg from the crow's-nest.

"We'd better dive into the shoals," cried Magruder, "or we may be captured."

Johnny ran to the stern. Three armored cruisers were looming up, but it was hard for him to see them distinctly, since night was falling. He was surprised to feel the ship lurch and swing northward.

Captain Knox was pacing up and down, a worried frown creasing his brow.

Johnny turned to him in desperation. "Let Clay Bragg take the helm, sir," he begged. "He can make it through."

"I'm in command, Tabb," retorted Knox gruffly. He strode away without another word.

Their only chance for escape now lay in the darkness which was rapidly deepening. Under cover of night they would be able to elude the Federals, but Johnny's heart was like lead despite this hope. For the *Lee* was moving northward, away from Wilmington, moving steadily towards enemy waters. He knew it was useless to appeal to Captain Knox, who would only turn a deaf ear to his plea.

Hours passed. Still the pilot held the vessel in a northerly direction. Johnny could not sleep; he jumped up and hurried on deck. At sunrise he saw the lighthouse on Cape Lookout over towards the east and knew they were at least eighty miles north of Wilmington. Directly south was a Yankee warship. Black smoke poured from her funnels as she steamed towards them. The *Lee* was in a deep bay of the coast, bottled up! Never before had they been in such a serious predicament. Oh, if only Captain Wilkinson were aboard!

The warship was gaining rapidly.

Only a mile separated them. The *Lee* was doing her best to speed away, when bang! the terrific report of a big gun brought home to the crew their great danger. A huge splash of white foam showed them that the cannon ball had fallen short by no more than three hundred yards.

Bang! Another gun was loosed on them. This time the shot was only fifty yards distant. The Yankee gunners were getting their range. The next shot went through the *Lee's* rigging. There was a rush of men on deck. It was the engine crew, who were deserting their duty in this hour of extreme need. Captain Knox confronted them and Johnny saw him draw his pistol. "Get back, you cowards," he cried.

Bang! Bang! Shells from the big guns on the battleship were breaking all around them.

"We're not going to die like rats in a trap," screamed the leader of the engine crew.

"Boom! Boom! Boom!" The Yankee cruiser let loose a rain of shells as she swooped nearer and nearer. There had been no direct hit as yet, but the roar of the giant guns was deafening. Knox turned sharply aside, the hand holding the revolver faltered.

"The next one will send us to the bottom," cried the engine crew's spokesman.

"Raise the white flag," shrieked another of the crew. "It's our only chance."

Ben Magruder leaped forward, his face red with rage. "We're not going to surrender."

John Tabb, Moncrief, and old Clay ranged themselves beside Magruder.

"We're ready, Captain," announced Johnny, stepping forward. "We can fight and go down fighting. The *Lee* has a nine-pound gun. With luck a direct hit on the Yankee might blow up her magazine powder."

"Haul up the Stars and Bars, sir," pleaded Clay. "Let's go down with our colors flying. We'll die like men, not like yellow curs."

The Union cruiser was driving very close. Her rail was thick with men, swords drawn, ready to board the Confederate ship. Knox hesitated, lowering his pistol. Johnny made a leap for the gun, closely followed by the three Confederate sailors. They stopped midway at a sudden command from Captain Knox. "Heave to! Run up the white flag."

Johnny could scarcely believe his ears when Knox barked the order to surrender. It did not seem possible that they were giving up the *Robert E. Lee* without a struggle. Bragg folded his arms in resignation. Lieutenant Rooks had a half contemptuous smile on his face. Knox put away his pistol and the engine crew relaxed.

The *Robert E. Lee* rolled listlessly in the quiet waters of the bay. Johnny saw an officer standing in the bow of the Union vessel, and he saw the name of the boat. It was the *James Adger*, a famous United States warship. Johnny could read the name plainly as the Yankee skipper brought his vessel about and maneuvered so that her heavy guns could fire a broadside. At the first signs of resistance the *Adger* was ready to sink the captured prize.

"Ahoy, *Robert E. Lee*," shouted a Yankee officer. "We are coming aboard."

It all seemed like a strange, weird nightmare to realize they were actually surrendering the blockade runner without a struggle. As Johnny thought of all her daring escapades of the past, a lump grew larger and larger in his throat.

The Yankee mate clambered aboard with a retinue of armed sailors. Captain Knox came forward to greet him. "I'm Captain Knox at your service. There's no need of any delay. We're a commercial ship and I'll be glad to have you look at our papers."

The United States naval officer smiled. "You're the *Robert E. Lee* and we've captured you at last. Long runs the fox, but the hounds catch him in the end. I admire your common sense in heaving to, Captain Knox. We would have blown you to the bottom of the sea."

Knox looked mollified. Besides, the crew was clearly on his side, but the British officer, Rooks, still wore a smile of open disgust.

Young Tabb stepped forward and confronted the United States officer. "I'm the ship's clerk here, sir, and I would like to say a word."

"Go ahead," responded the mate.

"If Captain Wilkinson had been left in command of the *Lee,* you would never have caught us. I am not a commercial sailor. I'm a member of the Confederate Navy, sir."

Magruder, Bragg, and Moncrief stepped up with him.

"We're Confederate Navy men and proud of it," spoke up Clay Bragg. "If we had our way we'd have gone down fighting."

The Yankee looked at him and back to Knox. "Evidently all your men don't share your opinion, Captain Knox."

"We're not his men," said the silent Moncrief. "I'd rather surrender to the enemy than fly under false colors."

"Well said, my man," said the mate. "My name is Gideon Mains from Eastport, Maine, and I admire your spirit, even though I regret that you and your friends will likely be sent to a Federal prison as captured enemies."

He turned to Knox. "Captain, we are taking over the *Lee* in the name of the United States government. I shall put a prize crew in charge. Meanwhile you will be transferred to the steamer *Newbern* for transportation to Fortress Monroe. These four men will be held as prisoners of war."

"I demand my rights as a citizen of Her Majesty's government," spoke up the Englishman. "I am Lieutenant Rooks."

"Your rights will be fully protected, Mr. Rooks. You will be sent to the provost marshal's office in New York, and when your claims are presented you will be given every consideration."

Johnny and his comrades were lowered down in one of their boats. The blocks and tackles creaked as the lifeboat swung down into the waves. The oars splashed in the rippling waters as they were rowed to the *James Adger*.

Johnny looked back, seeing through a mist of tears the long gray outline of the *Robert E. Lee*. She lay quietly in the water. He saw a flag being raised, saw it climb steadily, then unfurl in the gentle breeze. It was the Stars and Stripes.

He felt as though the end of the world had come and he stayed there gazing at the flag in melancholy meditation until a sailor nudged him. "Hurry up, Johnny Reb. Come out of your dreams."

They were ordered up the ladder and onto the deck of the *James Adger*, prisoners of war. Old Clay had been right. Johnny thought of Wilmington and his cousin, Captain Wilkinson, looking in vain for the return of the *Robert E. Lee*.

What Do You Think?

1. Describe the character of Captain Knox. Copy the sentences which illustrate the traits you enumerate.

2. How did the men feel about Captain Knox? Copy a sentence to prove your opinion.

3. From the few times that you met Ben Magruder, what would you say of his character? Copy a sentence to prove it.

4. Do you think the United States naval officer who boarded the *Robert E. Lee* was an honorable man? Why?

5. What two sides of Johnny's character are revealed in this story? Copy two sentences to prove your answer.

6. Which two incidents made the greatest impression on you?

Interpreting Sound Words

The author of this story used a number of words whose pronunciation imitates the sound he wishes to convey. Below is a list of these sound words, or *onomatopoetic words,* as they are called. Beside each word write what that word suggests to you. An example is given to show you what to do.

buzz—the sound of a carpenter's electric saw

boom	splash	rippling	shriek
bang	roar	scream	creak

What Do You Know about Ships?

Each of the words given below is related in some way to ships. Look up their meaning in your dictionary and be able to use them in sentences.

stern	powder magazine	deck
crow's-nest	cruiser	bow
rigging	helm	blocks and tackles

217

FRANCIS MILES FINCH

The Blue and the Gray

By the flow of the inland river,
　　Whence the fleets of iron have fled,
Where the blades of the grave-grass quiver,
　　Asleep are the ranks of the dead:
　　　　Under the sod and the dew,
　　　　　　Waiting the judgment day;
　　　　Under the one, the Blue,
　　　　　　Under the other, the Gray.

Sadly, but not with upbraiding,
　　The generous deed was done;
In the storm of the years that are fading
　　No braver battle was won:
　　　　Under the sod and the dew,
　　　　　　Waiting the judgment day;
　　　　Under the blossoms, the Blue,
　　　　　　Under the garlands, the Gray.

No more shall the war cry sever,
　　Or the winding rivers be red;
They banish our anger forever
　　When they laurel the graves of our dead!
　　　　Under the sod and the dew,
　　　　　　Waiting the judgment day;
　　　　Love and tears for the Blue,
　　　　　　Tears and love for the Gray.

The Starry Flag

ALL the way home from school Mary Russell raced the wild February wind. Faster and faster, as though the surge of the northeaster off Lake Michigan were a challenge to her spirit, she plunged along the high wooden sidewalks, past the armory, past the mayor's house, past St. Mary's Church. Faster and faster she sped, her strapped schoolbooks clutched in one hand and her bonnet pushed back on her head.

As she ran she counted over to herself the praises she had received when Sister Mary Gabriel had come into the seventh grade to distribute the monthly report cards. In geography, though Prussia and Muscovy and Barbary had seemed as far off as the moon, she had been given the mark of "Excellent."

In natural history, because she could tell of earthquakes and of thunderstorms, of tides and clouds and fire, her mark was equally high.

She had answered correctly all the answers to Bishop Duggan's questions on Christian Doctrine.

But the mark she had received in grammar sent her young heart soaring, for participles and prepositions and parsing and punctuation had long been the barrier in her work as a day student at St. Xavier's Academy. Now, though the hill had been hard to climb, she had conquered the rules of grammar laid down in the red-covered books.

As she skipped along, she made a song of the rules which had dismayed her:

> I did not know a suffix
> From an ordinary noun,
> But never will I let a verb
> Or adverb keep me down.

Her mother must be told at once of the victory she had won, and the thought gave still greater speed to her race against time. She was laughing to herself as she turned the corner of Washington Street.

It was then that she saw Abraham Lincoln.

His old plaid shawl slung loosely across his high, gaunt shoulders, he walked with solemn dignity as he

219

moved toward her, the mayor and the city councilmen behind him.

Mary stood still, all laughter gone.

Abraham Lincoln smiled at her, though there was sorrow in his gray eyes.

She curtsied, as she had been taught by the Sisters of Mercy, but her excited gaze never left the lined face of the man who alone held the destiny of the Union.

He moved on down the street toward the railroad station, where a train whistle shrieked its high, shrill warning that the hour had come for him to leave the tree-lined prairie streets for the heartbreaking journey to a war-shadowed White House. With her long bombazine skirt whipping around her slender ankles, Mary stood on the wintry Chicago corner until she could no longer see the high dark hat, the thin grim figure of the man who would soon be President.

Then, silently, as though afar she could hear the rumble of battle thunder, she stumbled up Washington Street to the little gray cottage across from the courthouse.

Somehow, because of the long shadow of the man she had seen, she expected home to look different from what it did on other days.

There was no change. The lone birch tree, stripped of its leaves, still held wintry pallor. The northern windows reflected only the grayness of the day. A few papers swirled across the brick walk, and the heavy, black type of a handbill caught her attention. For a brief moment she glanced at it, noting its plea for a meeting of all Abolitionists to be held that night in the opera house. She watched it blow away before she lifted the latch of the gate and moved toward the cottage door.

Her mother was sitting in front of the fire, her hands clasped in unaccustomed idleness, her eyes on the leaping flames. "Mary, darling," she greeted her daughter, but her voice was thick with tears.

The girl walked toward her. "I have just seen Mr. Lincoln," she said.

"I saw him, too," her mother's voice was low. "He came out of the courthouse and passed by this door."

Mary sat on a low stool near her mother's chair. "He looks like a brave man," she said.

Her mother did not stir. The clenched hands did not relax their nervous grip. "He'll need courage, all the courage he can muster,"

220

she said, although Mary could scarcely hear the words, "but, most of all, he'll need prayer."

"This is a terrible time, isn't it, Mother?" the girl asked.

"A terrible time," her mother repeated. "All wars are terrible, Mary, but a civil war seems the most terrible of all. North and South, we are the people of one nation; and yet it seems likely now that, in a little while, we shall be fighting one another."

"Will the North fight to free the slaves?" Mary asked.

"The North will fight to save the Union. Some of the Southern states declare that they are not bound to stay in the Union."

"Don't you think that Mr. Lincoln will free the slaves?" Mary persisted.

"I don't know." For the first time Margaret Russell looked toward her daughter. "Abraham Lincoln is a just man," she went on. "He will try to do what is right for the nation. Freeing the slaves may be part of that justice."

"Why have you been crying, Mother?" the girl asked.

For a moment there was no answer. Then Margaret Russell spoke. "I am thinking of the cost of war," she said, "for freedom is always bloodstained."

Silence settled in the little room.

After a while Mary arose and moved toward the window. Outside she could see the dusk of the evening settling upon the high bell tower and upon the gray walls of the courthouse across the street. She could see shadows, long as the fingers of time, spread across the wide courthouse yard. She placed her hands against the window casing, as though the better to see the coming of the night. A sense of the seriousness of the time came upon her. Consciousness of her own small role in such a mighty drama stirred her. This is Chicago, her brain whispered. This is Illinois. Out of this state, apart from all other states, has gone today the man who will be President.

He is taking with him his own courage and the courage of the men and women who crossed oceans and mountains and wildernesses to come to this frontier, not so long ago. My father came, my mother came, and all the rest of them came here because they had faith. They came in lake boats and in covered wagons, on horseback and on foot. They came with money and they came without money because freedom was in their souls. Abraham Lincoln must not fail them!

When darkness came she turned back to the room. Quietly Mary asked the question, "When war comes, will Father enlist?"

Quietly her mother answered her, "He will be among the first to go."

Down the street the girl heard the high laughter of children. It came nearer. "Stephen and Annie will soon be home," she said. "We shan't speak of war to them, shall we, Mother?"

"They will learn of it only too soon," Mrs. Russell answered, as she arose and moved slowly toward the unlighted kitchen.

After her mother had gone, Mary sat looking at her gay lavender bonnet, still in her hand. At last she turned from the window and very slowly took off her coat, with its carved ivory buttons. She carefully put away the bonnet and coat. Then she came to stand beside the walnut table as she unstrapped her schoolbooks. Slowly she lifted the catechism, and her geography, and arithmetic, and grammar and placed them in an orderly pile beside the still-dark oil lamp.

For a brief moment she held in her hand the monthly report card, and, scanning in the firelight the marks of which she had been so proud, she remembered her desire to share that pride with her mother. For all that she felt now, that joy might have been of yesterday or yesteryear.

Dimly she had known that great events were piling up over the nation. One night, as torchlights blazed, she had seen the Wigwam on the lake front crowded with men; in the next day's *Times* she had read that there Abraham Lincoln had been nominated for the Presidency. She had heard of Major Anderson and his stand at Fort Sumter; but it had all been a story apart from her own life until the day when Abraham Lincoln had passed her. Then, suddenly, she had become part of the world about her. Never again was she to feel apart from it.

Silently she slipped the report card between the pages of her grammar.

On this February night she had come into another world.

Detecting the Mood of a Story

1. What was the cause of Mary's happiness when the story opened? List the phrases which indicate that she was happy. Copy the sentence which changes the mood of the story.

2. Find two sentences in paragraph 6 on page 220 which set the mood of the latter part of the story. Find two color words in paragraph 6 which give the air of solemnity.

3. Find the sentence in paragraph 2 on page 222 which indicates that Mary has begun to comprehend the grave issues of the time.

4. Reread the last four paragraphs. In two or three sentences explain what caused Mary's change of mood.

5. What did Mrs. Russell mean when she said, ". . . freedom is always bloodstained"?

6. Did this story have any emotional effect on you? Explain.

O Captain! My Captain!

O CAPTAIN! my Captain! our fearful trip is done,
The ship has weather'd every rack, the prize we sought is won,
The port is near, the bells I hear, the people all exulting,
While follow eyes the steady keel, the vessel grim and daring;
But O heart! heart! heart!
O the bleeding drops of red,
Where on the deck my Captain lies,
Fallen cold and dead.

O Captain! my Captain! rise up and hear the bells;
Rise up—for you the flag is flung—for you the bugle trills,
For you bouquets and ribbon'd wreaths—for you the shores
a-crowding,
For you they call, the swaying mass, their eager faces turning;
Here Captain! dear father!
The arm beneath your head!
It is some dream that on the deck,
You've fallen cold and dead.

My Captain does not answer, his lips are pale and still,
My father does not feel my arm, he has no pulse nor will,
The ship is anchor'd safe and sound, its voyage closed and done,
From fearful trip the victor ship comes in with object won;
Exult O shores, and ring O bells!
But I with mournful tread,
Walk the deck my Captain lies,
Fallen cold and dead.

Angels of the Battlefields (1861-1865)

In the capital city of Washington, not very far away from the White House, stands a simple monument. Children, going home from school, play around it. Busy men and women hasten by it; but older men and women never pass it without a reverent glance upon its carved tablet.

For that tablet reminds them of stories their fathers and mothers told them when they were young, stories of the Catholic Sisters who served as nurses to both Federal and Confederate soldiers wounded in battles of the Civil War.

The tablet lists twelve communities of Catholic Sisters who served upon the battlefields:

Sisters of Charity of Nazareth
Daughters of Charity of Saint Vincent de Paul
Sisters of Charity of New York and Cincinnati
Sisters of Saint Dominic
Sisters of the Poor of Saint Francis
Sisters of the Holy Cross
Sisters of Saint Joseph
Sisters of Mercy
Sisters of Our Lady of Mercy
Sisters of Our Lady of Mount Carmel
Sisters of Providence
Sisters of Saint Ursula

No one can know the full record of the service of these Sisters. They themselves were far too busy caring for the wounded to set down the stories of their deeds. The memories of soldiers whom they served and saved have told the tales. Too many to mention, the accounts are alike in their themes of high courage and noble Christian charity.

Hundreds of Sisters nursed the wounded in the great military hospitals: the Satterlee in Philadelphia, the Douglas and the Stanton in Washington, and the Mt. St. Vincent in New York. In these hospitals thousands of Southern and of Northern soldiers were given the same care, often aiding one another under the direction of the nursing Sisters. In the Douglas young men of the Class of '61 of Georgetown University, that class which had divided at the Georgetown gate to go separate ways into the Confederate Army of Virginia and the Federal Army of the Potomac, held a sad reunion in the hospital wards. To the Stanton, in a winter twilight, came Abraham Lincoln, President of the United States, to see and give tribute to what the Sisters were doing for humanity.

Out beside the Ohio River, on a highway where armies passed and passed again, Mother de Chantal and her Sisters worked until they fell from exhaustion, sleeping in army blankets upon their chapel floor. Others of their group, going down the James River, met starving soldiers, gave them their own rations, and went hungry for days.

At another crossroads of war, Cairo, Illinois, stood the Brick Hospital, famed all down the Mississippi River as the cleanest, best equipped of all the Western military institutions. There Mother Angela directed her Sisters; and there one night Sister Josephine, standing guard alone, faced a mob of frenzied and mistaken soldiers and prevented a murder which would have been one of the most terrible tragedies of the war.

In Kentucky, again a dark and bloody ground, twelve weary Confederate soldiers came one night to the convent at Nazareth. They had marched many dangerous miles to ask the Sisters to go back with them to nurse the wounded of their army. Within the hour, late though it was, a group of Sisters went with them. For two nights and two days

they marched under a flag of truce to take up their task.

Down in the City Hospital of Memphis, Sister Alberta, who had seen an army ride through a peaceful valley in Kentucky, was one night called to assist a dying Northern soldier. As she walked through the ward, she saw her own brother, a Confederate, waiting for care. She lifted to her lips the crucifix of her Rosary, prayed to God for strength, and moved to the bedside of the other man.

In Vicksburg, so long under siege, Mother Mary de Sales turned the Sisters' convent and school into hospitals. There the Sisters nursed the wounded while bombs fell all around them. Was it any wonder that Jefferson Davis, President of the Confederate States of America, paid them a tribute as high as Abraham Lincoln had paid to other Sisters? When Vicksburg fell, the Sisters went with the army, suffering terrible privations. To keep sick men warm, Mother Mary de Sales herself cut wood in the forests and dragged it to the little inn which had been made into a hospital. Never once did the Sisters falter as they gave food to the hungry, drink to the thirsty, care to the wounded, consolation to the dying.

From the hospital ships at Shiloh went Mother Mary Teresa, that valiant soldier of the Cross whose only weapon was an armful of bandages as she moved over that bloody field on days and nights after the battle. Through soaking rain and driving hail she went, seeking the wounded among the dead and caring for them until they were taken to the ships.

The sound of the guns of Gettysburg carried to the wooded slope of the convent at Emmitsburg, ten miles away; and while cannon still roared over the Pennsylvania hills, the Sisters of Emmitsburg walked over rain-drenched, mud-clogged roads to care for the wounded. Hundreds of soldiers, slain or half-dead, lay upon the battlefield in ghastly heaps. With hardly a foot of ground to step on, the Sisters went among them. They picked up the wounded and bore them to farm wagons, which took them to the hospitals at Gettysburg; and there, for long months, they stayed and cared for those who needed them.

Everywhere through camps and hospitals Sisters died in the doing of their chosen duty, stricken by camp fevers, worn out by rigorous labor. They asked for nothing but

227

clothing, food, and hospital supplies for the men they nursed. They sought no honors, no fame. It was enough for them that Christ walked with them through the crowded wards of the hospitals and over the scarred and bloodstained earth of the battlefields.

Recalling Information

1. What is the purpose of the simple monument which is located near the White House in Washington?

2. How many communities of Sisters are listed on the tablet? Name three of them that you remember.

3. When did the Sisters serve their country by nursing the wounded on the battlefield?

4. Name four great military hospitals in which the Sisters served. Name the states in which they are located.

5. Name two instances, mentioned in "Angels of the Battlefields," in which the heroism of the Sisters impressed you.

6. Name two civic leaders who praised the work of the Sisters. What positions did these two men hold?

7. Name three corporal works of mercy mentioned in "Angels of the Battlefield."

8. What motive spurred the Sisters in their difficult work?

9. State in one sentence what impressed you most about "Angels of the Battlefield."

Supplying Homonyms

Below are twenty words taken from "Angels of the Battlefields." Copy them on your paper and beside each write a homonym.

too	days	capital	been
see	their	died	not
hour	road	one	no
through	inn	great	night
wood	bore	rain	told

228

JULIA WARD HOWE

Battle Hymn of the Republic

MINE eyes have seen the glory of the coming of the Lord;
He is trampling out the vintage where the grapes of wrath are stored;
He hath loosed the fateful lightning of His terrible swift sword;
 His truth is marching on.

> *Glory! glory! hallelujah!*
> *Glory! glory! hallelujah!*
> *Glory! glory! hallelujah!*
> *His truth is marching on!*

I have seen Him in the watch-fires of a hundred circling camps;
They have builded Him an altar in the evening dews and damps;
I can read His righteous sentence by the dim and flaring lamps;
 His day is marching on.

> *Glory! glory! hallelujah!*
> *Glory! glory! hallelujah!*
> *Glory! glory! hallelujah!*
> *His truth is marching on!*

In the beauty of the lilies Christ was born across the sea,
With a glory in His bosom that transfigures you and me;
As He died to make men holy, let us die to make men free,
 While God is marching on.

> *Glory! glory! hallelujah!*
> *Glory! glory! hallelujah!*
> *Glory! glory! hallelujah!*
> *His truth is marching on!*

Glory, Glory Hallelujah!

THE three Ward sisters—Julia and Louisa and little Annie—lived in New York when the town was young and gay. They were rich, well taught, and belles of the ball—Julia for her bright wit, Louisa for her beauty, little Annie for her charm.

In time they all married. Louisa married a famous sculptor and lived in a Roman palace. Little Annie married the grandson of a king and lived on a great estate near Philadelphia. Julia married a school teacher and lived, not too happily, in a comfortable but simple home in South Boston. All the Wards were what we would call today "front page." For different reasons their comings and goings appeared in print. But it was the story of one night in Julia's life that has kept alive the Ward fame for almost a hundred years.

Julia Ward had always wanted to write. As a little girl she had written verses which showed more spirit than style. As a young girl she wrote both poems and essays which won kind words from Henry Wadsworth Longfellow. But Longfellow was a dear old friend of the Ward family, and a very kind man. Julia was pleased, but not too trustful of his criticism. Only when she was able to sell work to a newspaper or magazine was she satisfied that the work was fairly good.

In New York she had known writers, but it was Boston which surrounded her with an understanding of the power of literature. For Boston, at that time, some years before the outbreak of the Civil War, was known as "the Athens of America." Longfellow, Lowell, Hawthorne, Emerson lived in its neighborhood. The *Atlantic Monthly*, already a magazine of literary authority, was published in Boston.

Boston was also the center of a great political controversy. The Abolitionists, inspired by William Lloyd Garrison and Charles Sumner, were strong in the town. Dr. Samuel Gridley Howe, Julia's husband, was one of the group. His wife, remembering the way of life she had seen in Georgia when she had visited her Southern cousins, the McAllisters, could not join wholeheartedly in her husband's strong opinions. She definitely believed that slavery must be abolished, but she was not convinced of the rightness of the means which some of her fellow-townsmen favored. She was not even deeply impressed when John Brown of Kansas came to her house to talk with Dr. Howe. She wrote of the justice of human freedom, but it was not inspired writing, at least not until the night in Washington which changed her.

Dr. Howe, who had won distinction by his work in the teaching of the blind, became associated with the Sanitary Commission, an organization for helping the victims of war, the sick, the wounded, and the dependents of Northern volunteers. In the course of the work he sometimes went to Washington. Because there were some women auxiliaries to the Commission, he took Julia with him, although his action was somewhat unwilling.

This was in November, 1861. It was Julia Ward Howe's first visit to Washington. The city was full of soldiers, and her first impression of the capital was the sight of men on picket duty along the railway tracks. The hotel, Willard's, was full of officers and office-seeking or contract-hunting civilians. Mrs. Howe was glad to get into work at the camps and hospitals, although what she saw often sickened her.

The governor of Massachusetts, coming to Washington with a party, arranged for the Howes to meet President Abraham Lincoln. Afterward, Julia Howe said that she best remembered from that meeting the sad expression of Lincoln's deepset eyes which were "the only feature of his face which could be called other than plain."

On November 18, 1861, a picnic was arranged for members of the governor's party, and Mrs. Howe was included in the invitation. The small group of women drove out from Washington with a coachman and a hamper basket of lunch. They crossed the Potomac River and drove into the territory from which Confederate troops had recently withdrawn. A review of the Union troops now on that ground was about to start, and many parties from Washington moved toward the scene. It was a gay panorama until the moment when Confederate troopers suddenly appeared. Then the carriages were whirled around, and driven post-haste back to Washington.

Because of the crowding, the carriages had to move slowly. They were overtaken by soldiers who had been ordered to retreat toward Washington. Some of them were singing, and Julia Howe joined in.

"John Brown's body lies a-mould'ring in the grave,
His soul is marching on."

Some of the boys in blue smiled at her. "Good for you ma'am," they called out, and swung ahead, shouting:

"Glory, glory hallelujah!"

Although she did not realize it at the moment, Julia Ward Howe was riding in a battle line.

Troops marched through the streets of Washington all day and all night. From her room in the hotel, after she had gone to bed, Mrs. Howe could hear the tramp of feet on the cobblestoned pavement. Remembering the wounded boys in the hospitals, she wept for the marchers. But underneath her sympathy ran a refrain, words which almost said themselves. They went to the swing of the song they had sung on the road, "John Brown's Body." But they were a different kind of words. There was nothing in them of hanging Jeff Davis to a sour apple tree. These were mighty words, flowing over the surface of her mind. Finally, she could stand the turmoil of her thoughts no longer. She arose from bed, lighted a lamp, and began to write.

"Mine eyes have seen the glory of the coming of the Lord," she set down. Then the pen flowed over paper for five stanzas. Later, she changed a few lines, but the song stands almost exactly as she wrote it that night in Willard's Hotel.

She did not call it a song. She thought it was a poem, "and a fairly good poem," and she sent it to the *Atlantic Monthly* for publication. The *Atlantic Monthly* accepted the verse—and paid Mrs. Howe six dollars for it.

It was published in January, 1862. Its effect amazed the author. The "Battle Hymn of the Republic" became the rallying cry of freedom from coast to coast, and from the Canadian border to the battle lines of the war. Soldiers sang it in the camps. Families of soldiers sang it at home. Men and women sang it at war rallies—all to the tune of "John Brown's Body." It was not a song now but a hymn; and it has stayed a people's hymn. Although Julia Ward Howe and her sisters are long since dead, Julia's *Glory Hallelujah* still goes ringing down the roads of fame.

Can You Correct the False Statements?

Some of these statements are true and some are false. Copy them on your paper, changing the word or phrase in the false statement to make it true.

1. All the Ward sisters were rich and attractive, but Julia was especially noted for her beauty.

2. Julia had always wanted to write, but after she had married and lived in New York, her opportunities for writing were less numerous.

3. Boston, shortly before the Civil War, was a literary center as well as a center of political controversy.

4. Dr. Samuel Howe, Julia's husband, was a fervent Abolitionist, but his wife did not favor some of the means which her fellow-townsmen favored.

5. On her visit to Washington, Julia worked at the camps and hospitals.

6. Through the influence of the Governor of Virginia, Dr. and Mrs. Howe met President Abraham Lincoln.

7. Mrs. Howe was paid six dollars for her poem by the *Atlantic Monthly*.

8. "The Battle Hymn of the Republic," sung to the tune of "John Brown's Body," became the rallying cry of freedom.

6. In Time of Need

WHAT should we do if our neighbor is in need?

A long, long time ago Christ answered that question. He told the people who heard His voice the story of the Good Samaritan. Through the centuries the Church has continued that teaching. Today, as always, she reminds us that, to follow Christ, we must practice justice and charity every day of our lives.

The stories which follow tell how this help was sometimes given: a Catholic attorney and a Protestant minister worked to win justice for a wrongly accused prisoner; a poor woman of New Orleans baked bread for the hungry; a pilot dared death to take food to an icebound town; the stepson of George Washington gave aid to Irish refugees who had sought freedom in a new land.

They lived, as we should live, by the word and deed of Christ, Who lived and died for all mankind.

MARJORIE MEDARY

A Prayer in Time of Need

IN THE beginning the Lord said:
"Let there be mountains."   And lo,
The mountains lifted up their heads.
And He robed them with forests,
And crowned them with diadems of snow;
And like unto kings in ermine
They wore glaciers upon their shoulders.
Lord of life, we praise Thee
For the majesty of mountains.

Give us, O Lord, we pray Thee,
A breed of men like mountains,
Who lift their foreheads freely to the sun;
Crown them with loving-kindness
And with gratitude that they are sons of Thine;
Robe them, we pray, with that true majesty
Which wears the ermine clean and undefiled,
Constant in service for the common good,
As glaciers feed the rivers and the soil.
Raise up, O Lord, we beg Thee,
A breed of mountain men.

One Saturday Morning

THE television in the living room of the house on Ivy Street was roaring out the story of the *Cripple Creek Cowboy*. *"I can whip my weight in wildcats,"* shouted the voice from the screen, *"and I'm here to stay!"*

Eileen Craven leaned against the wall beside the hall telephone. "I can't hear a word you're saying, Kathy," she told her best friend, with whom she had been talking for the last twenty minutes. "Jimmy and Bill have the television turned on full blast."

"I can hear it," said Kathy. "Are they deaf?"

"Kathy wants to know if you're deaf," Eileen called out above the din.

Jimmy and Bill were not deaf. They stretched at full length on the living-room floor where the pictured story of the dramatic meeting of Dick Dalton, the cowboy, and the gang of cattle raiders could roll over them in its full glory. "Tell Kathy to go read a good book," retorted Jimmy. Bill said nothing. Eileen sat down on the hall steps, a little weary from the length of her telephone conversation. Over the sound of televised canyon warfare, she took up the thread of her talk with Kathy. They spoke of many things, of the movie they expected to see that afternoon at the Tivoli, of the problem of pony-tail versus page-boy haircuts, of their hopes for the future, which included living, like Grace Kelly, in a castle at Monaco, or, robed in mink, in a penthouse above New York City.

"I guess you have to be a blonde," said Eileen. Her dark eyes clouded with sadness at the thought.

The televised thunder of life in the camp at Cripple Creek faded and died. The voice of the announcer of a commercial followed with the advice, *"And you get the mosta of the besta with Lesta pickles and preserves."* There was a change of program and Jimmy turned the knob. "Let's get out," he said to Bill.

It was then that Eileen, still at the telephone, saw the police car drawing up to the front of the house. "I'll call you later, Kathy," she cried, her voice lifting in sudden excitement. "Here come the police!"

"O.K.," said Kathy, in a resigned tone. "I suppose the neighbors complained about the noise."

"One policeman's carrying Rosemary," Eileen told her, and the telephone receiver slid toward the floor.

Jimmy and Bill and Eileen, in a frenzy of fear, dashed to the door to reach their five-year old sister. "The police are from Number Seven," Jimmy identified them. "What happened? And where's my mother?"

Less than a hour ago, Mrs. Craven and Rosemary had set out for the supermarket, across busy High Street, less than two blocks away. "Sometimes I think that you're all hollow inside," she had laughed, as she checked the grocery list. Now the policeman was carrying Rosemary through the front door and bearing her toward the living-room sofa. "Mommy was hit by a car! Mommy's hurt!" sobbed the little girl.

"She was coming out of the supermarket," the policeman told them. "She had a big bag of groceries in one arm and she was holding the child by the other hand as she started to cross High Street . . ."

"Is she dead?" Eileen was trembling.

"We called an ambulance and now she's at Immaculata Hospital." The officer's voice was soft with

sympathy. "Your mother was conscious and she gave us your father's business telephone number. We called him at once. He's on his way to see her."

"Mommy told the men to bring me home," said Rosemary, crying wildly, burying her head in the sofa cushions.

"Will she live?" Bill was gray with fear as he asked the question.

The policeman put his arm across the boy's shoulders. "I think she will," he comforted him, "but she'll get better faster if she knows you're all taking care of your little sister."

"Oh, we will! We will!" promised the three older Cravens.

"Who hit my mother?" asked Jimmy, his hands clenched in rage.

"A kid in a hot-rod car," said the policeman. "He ran through a red light and left the scene of the accident. They always do!"

"Didn't anybody get his license number?"

"I guess not," said the officer, "but two men say they could identify the driver and the car."

"I saw him, too," cried Rosemary.

"As he was coming toward you and your mother?" asked the policeman.

"After he hit her," said Rosemary.

"We'll catch him," said the officer as he turned toward the door.

"That won't help my mother very much," said Eileen.

"It'll keep him from violating the law another time and injuring another pedestrian."

As the officer left and the police car pulled away from the house, Eileen pushed herself into a galvanic burst of energy. "There's only one way we can help Mother," she told the boys and Rosemary as her anxiety burst forth into nervous activity. "We'll clean the house and the garage. You boys take the papers and trash out to the alley. I'll go at the living room."

She swept a handful of magazines off the top of a table onto a shelf below. She cleared the desk of Jimmy's unfinished homework, tossing the papers into a drawer. She kicked a pair of Bill's playshoes into the front closet. With the same rapid tempo, she snatched a picture from the wall and blew off a thin layer of dust. "We've got to work hard," she gasped.

For a while Rosemary rested quietly on the sofa. Then she announced, "I want to get dressed up and go to the hospital."

"You can't," said Eileen, plumping up the pillow of a chair. "We

239

can't see Mother until we hear from Father."

"I could have been hurt, too," said Rosemary.

"You weren't," said Eileen.

Rosemary arose from the sofa and went upstairs. When she came back, she was wearing her best dress.

"That dress is for Sundays, not Saturdays," said Eileen. "Take it off."

Bill, returning from the garage, called out, "The police car's back again."

Jimmy was only a few steps behind his brother. "Maybe they got the hot-rod driver," he gasped.

It was simpler than that. "We forgot to give you the groceries your mother was carrying when she was hit," said the officer. He bore a broken bag and an uncovered assortment of food packages.

The Craven children took the bundles from him. "Peanut butter," said Bill and, when the policeman left, added, "Let's eat."

"How can you think of food when your mother is hurt and in the hospital?" Eileen demanded.

"Mother would be fixing lunch for us now if she was here," said the boy. "I'll bet you don't know how to cook."

The challenge sped Eileen toward the kitchen. On her way she replaced the telephone receiver on its hook. She had gone but a few steps when the telephone rang. "It's Kathy again," she said. It wasn't. "No, thank you, we're not interested in buying a vacuum cleaner," she told an agent. She turned from the telephone to see Jimmy at the front door, engaged in conversation with Mrs. Oberg, who lived next door.

"I don't want to seem curious," Mrs. Oberg was saying, "but I just saw the police leaving the house."

"They came before to bring Rosemary home," said Jimmy.

Mrs. Oberg, appalled at the news, moved into the living room. Her gaze rested on Rosemary, resplendent in her best Sunday dress. "Did you run away and get lost?" she asked. Her reproach was dark as doom.

Rosemary faced her with outraged indignation. "I wasn't lost," she said. "Mommy was knocked down by a bad man in a noisy old hot-rod car. She's in the hospital. She's hurt. The policeman brought me home."

Quick to seize this neighborhood news item, Mrs. Oberg looked from one to another of the Craven chil-

240

dren. "Your mother hurt? Any bones broken? Any concussion? Any accident insurance? Who'll take care of all of you while she's in the hospital?"

The Cravens, suddenly united in a common cause, spoke as with one voice. "We'll do all the things we should do, just as if mother were here," said Eileen firmly and, as a loyal army, Jimmy and Bill and Rosemary echoed, "Oh, we will!"

Mrs. Oberg softened. "I'll do anything I can to help you," she promised.

"Thank you," said the children for, in spite of Mrs. Oberg's curiosity about the neighbors on Ivy Street, they knew she was generous and kind. They watched her leave, departing not to her own house, but to pass the news of Mrs. Craven's accident along the length and breadth of Ivy Street.

In the sudden quiet Eileen went out once more to the kitchen. She glanced nervously at the clock. A quarter to twelve. She shivered a little, for time was moving on and there was as yet no word from her father. Silently, earnestly, she began to pray, *"Hail, holy queen, mother of mercy, our life, our sweetness and our hope! To thee we cry. . . ."* She prayed the *Salve*

Regina as she lifted packages from the battered bag of groceries her mother had bought such a little while ago. She drew out bread, a bunch of carrots, green peppers, some lemons, lamb for stew and chicken for Sunday dinner. She found a can of coffee and a large carton of milk. She piled up butter and beans and a jar of marmalade, setting aside the peanut butter. As she worked, she prayed. "Oh, dear Blessed Mother, please watch over my mother and bring her home safely to all of us. We need her so. We love her so."

Only when Jimmy spoke did Eileen know that he was standing beside her. "I should have gone with mother," he said. "She should never have to carry a bag the size of this. I'm going to go with her the next time."

The next time! The full impact of the words hit Eileen with violent force. The next time? Who knew if there would ever be a next time for her mother? And what was ahead of them if the worst happened and her mother didn't get well? Suddenly the girl was trembling with terror. "I'm not afraid of today or tomorrow or next week or the week after," she told herself, "but what of the years to come?"

241

"You're crying," said Jimmy.

"So are you," said Eileen.

"What should we do?" asked Jimmy.

Eileen turned and walked back to the living room. "We can get our rosaries," she said.

They were kneeling, repeating the second decade of the Rosary, when the telephone rang.

"Let me get it," shouted Jimmy.

"Let me," yelled Bill.

"I want to talk," Rosemary insisted.

"I'm the eldest," said Eileen. "I'd better take it." Suddenly aged beyond her years, she sensed what the news meant to them. What was ahead of them if something happened to her mother? Respon-sibility that the girl was shouldering for a few hours might now descend upon her shoulders, a burden that she would bear for years to come. She was shaking with fright as she reached the phone. "Daddy!" she cried.

Jimmy and Bill and Rosemary crowded around her, their anxiety as great as her own. "Is Mother all right?" "Is she coming home?"

Eileen hung up the receiver. Her dark eyes were shining, her voice pitched high with happiness as she passed on the news. "The doctors have taken X rays," she said. "There's nothing broken. Mother will be all right."

Whooping with joy, the four Cravens trooped out to the kitchen. They made and devoured peanut-butter sandwiches. They drank

milk. They ate apples. "Let's make fudge," said Rosemary.

The doorbell rang. Mrs. Oberg, bearing gifts, brushed past Jimmy and headed for the back of the house. "I brought you a bakery cake," she said. "I'd have made one for you if I'd had time."

"It's chocolate," shouted Rosemary.

"I'll fix your dinner for you, too," said Mrs. Oberg. "What have you got in the icebox?"

"Just lamb and vegetables for stew," said Eileen.

"I'll have it ready for you at six o'clock," said Mrs. Oberg. She went off gaily with the lamb, the carrots, the onions, the green peppers.

The telephone rang again. "I'll take it!" Eileen stumbled into the hall, fell across the telephone table, lifted the instrument and dropped her weight upon the hall steps. "Oh, it's you, Kathy," she sighed, and rushed into a detailed account of the events of the morning.

The response came in sympathetic gasps. "Your mother? Is she badly hurt? Can I do anything to help you? Please tell me what I can do!"

Eileen paused. What was there to do? Lunch was over, the pea-nut-butter sandwiches and Mrs. Oberg's chocolate cake now gone. The lamb stew would soon be cooking on Mrs. Oberg's stove. In the relief that ended the anxiety of the morning, life once more seemed almost normal. Her mother would soon be home. Her father would come as fast as possible. The girl's face, which had been heavy with fear and sorrow, grew bright again. "You might come over, Kathy," she suggested.

"Can I bring anything?"

Eileen paused to think. "You could bring me that magazine that shows the pictures of the little princess of Monaco," she said. "We might be living in a castle someday. We'd better see what a castle is like."

The television in the living room was blaring once more. Again it was a Western film, a very old one that dimly showed an actor named Jack Holt as he conquered a villain. *"You pay me what you owe me, or you get out of town!"* a deep voice thundered from the screen. The sound vibrated through the house.

"I can hear that hollering all the way over here," said Kathy. "Are Jimmy and Bill deaf?"

"Kathy wants to know if you're deaf," Eileen called out.

This time there was no answer. Jimmy and Bill were too engrossed as Justice triumphed in the Old West.

There was little quiet in the house on Ivy Street, but peace and happiness and a strong sense of security had returned. Thoughtfully Eileen Craven hung up the receiver. Before she went back into the living room, she stopped for a moment and offered a silent prayer. "Thank you, Blessed Mother," she said, "for looking after all of us today."

There was a knock at the front door, then the sound of a familiar voice. "Does your mother put barley in the lamb stew?" asked Mrs. Oberg.

"She does," said Eileen, and walked toward the kitchen for the package of barley. "It's a nice world that's full of kind people," she mused, thinking of Mrs. Oberg and the policeman and the doctors at the hospital and of Kathy, who would soon be arriving with pictures of a royal palace that might well be a blueprint for the future.

Interpreting Story Ideas

Write the answers to the questions below.

1. Write a four-sentence description of the setting as the story opens.

2. Do you think this is a typical scene in a modern home? Why?

3. Do you think the Cravens were a happy family? Give reasons for your answers.

4. Make a statement about Eileen before she learns of her mother's accident and after it occurred.

5. What did you think of the policeman's character? Find two sentences to prove your answer.

6. Do you think you would have liked Mrs. Oberg? Give a reason for your answer.

7. Copy the sentence which states the moral of the story.

8. Did you enjoy this story? Give a reason for your answer.

DANIEL HENDERSON

Hymn for a Household

Lord Christ, beneath Thy starry dome
We light this flickering lamp of home,
And where bewildering shadows throng
Uplift our prayer and evensong.
Dost Thou, with heaven in Thy ken,
Seek still a dwelling place with men,
Wandering the world in ceaseless quest?
O Man of Nazareth, be our guest!

Lord Christ, the bird his nest has found,
The fox is sheltered in his ground,
But dost Thou still this dark earth tread
And have no place to lay Thy head?
Shepherd of mortals, here behold
A little flock, a wayside fold
That wait Thy presence to be blest—
O Man of Nazareth, be our guest!

Fair Trial

I. A JOURNEY FOR JUSTICE

THROUGH the thin walls of his room Benjamin Bard could hear the sound of voices, his father's, his mother's, and one which he finally knew was the voice of John Scott, their neighbor. The voices were low, then loud. Benjamin, lying in bed, paid no heed at first to what they were saying. Then, suddenly, a word flashed on his mind, and he turned over so that he could hear better the conversation in the kitchen.

"Then the sheriff arrested him," John Scott was saying. "He brought him in to the Washington County Jail, and there he is, at this very minute."

"Why did the sheriff arrest him?" Benjamin's mother asked.

"I have been telling you," John Scott said, a little impatiently. "He arrested him for what he said at the camp meeting."

"But it was a sermon," Mrs. Bard said. "This Jacob Gruber is a minister, to be correct, a Methodist Episcopal minister. He came here from Pennsylvania to preach at the meeting. He was only saying what he believed to be true."

"Maybe so," said John Scott, "but what he believes to be true is not what most of the white people around here believe. He talked against slavery."

"Why should he not talk against slavery?" Mrs. Bard demanded. "The law allows a man to speak his mind."

"There were quite a few slaves at the camp meeting," John Scott said. "They heard this Methodist minister talking against slavery. Now many people are afraid that perhaps the slaves will try to free themselves. That is why someone asked the sheriff to arrest this Jacob Gruber."

"What is the charge against him?" Benjamin's father asked. "What does the warrant for his arrest say that he has done?"

"The warrant says that he incited slaves to rebel against their masters."

"But the slaves have not done that," said Mr. Bard. "Nothing has happened here in Hagerstown since that sermon."

"It might happen," said John Scott.

"Who is Gruber's lawyer?" Mr. Bard inquired.

"He has none," Scott said. "There is not a lawyer in the town who will take his case."

"Is he getting a lawyer from his own town in Pennsylvania?"

"He has no money to send for one."

"What of the people who brought him for the camp meeting?" Mrs. Bard asked.

"They are afraid to do anything," Scott said, "afraid of their neighbors."

"That is unfair," Mrs. Bard declared. "We are Presbyterians, not Methodists. We had nothing to do with bringing Mr. Gruber here, but I feel that he should have a fair trial, with a good lawyer to defend him. Don't you?" she asked her husband.

"Yes," he said, "I do." There was a long silence, through which Benjamin could picture the three in the kitchen staring at one another. Then his father spoke again. "That young man who came here a month ago is a good lawyer. Do you remember his name?"

"His name is Taney," Mrs. Bard said. "T-a-n-e-y, you spell it; but you call it Tawney. He is the brother-in-law of Francis Scott Key, who wrote 'The Star-Spangled Banner.' He lives in Frederick."

"Perhaps he would consider taking Gruber's case," said Mr. Bard thoughtfully.

"Taney take that case?" John Scott laughed. "Why, he is one of the real aristocrats of Maryland. He comes from the fox-hunting crowd down in Calvert County. He goes to parties in Annapolis and Baltimore. He knows all the important men in Maryland."

"That is why I think he may take the case," said Benjamin's father. "Some of his acquaintances are the men who signed the Declaration of Independence and the Constitution. Anyhow, it seems to me that there would be no harm in asking him to take it."

"Mr. Taney is a Catholic," John Scott said.

"What of it?" said Benjamin's father.

"He may not want to defend a Methodist minister," Scott said.

"Don't be silly, John," said Benjamin's mother.

"Who'll go to ask him?" John Scott cried. "No man here can spare the time to go to Frederick in harvest season, even if he had the money for travel."

"A woman might do it," Benjamin's mother said.

"You?" John Scott laughed again.

"I," she said; and there was no laughter in her tone.

The voices fell low then, and Benjamin heard no more. After a little while a door slammed. John Scott, he thought, had gone. He turned over and slid into sleep.

Before dawn his father awakened him. "Get up, Benjamin," he said. "You have a long journey before you today."

"Journey? Where?" Benjamin asked sleepily. He tumbled out of bed, hurried into clothes, and went to the pump for his morning wash. Not until he saw that his mother was dressed in her Sunday best did he remember what he had heard during the night. "Where are we going?" he asked again.

"You are going with your mother on the stagecoach to Frederick," his father said. "Your mother has an errand there. I cannot leave the farm today; so you must go with her."

"To see Mr. Taney?" Benjamin started to ask, then thought better

248

of the question. "Yes, sir," he said. "Shall I wear my new suit?"

"It might be well," said his father, "on a journey like this."

"It may," said his mother, "be something to remember."

After his father had gone out into the fields, Benjamin and his mother hurried through the household tasks, then walked to the crossroad where the stagecoach to Frederick would stop on signal. They had a long wait, but at last the coach came whirling down the highroad, its red wheels gleaming in the Maryland sunlight. They climbed aboard, but could not find places together. The swaying of the coach body, the jumping of the springs delighted Benjamin almost as much as the looks of the passengers. He was the only lad aboard! He felt very much older than his years and very important as the coach rolled on over the hills. He was tired, however, by the time they came to Frederick, for twenty-seven miles by stagecoach was, after all, a long journey.

He wondered, as they got down from the coach, if his mother would stay at the hotel. To his delight she took him in and arranged for a room. When they had dined in the hotel dining-room, his mother said: "I must find a lawyer named Mr. Taney. Will you wait for me in the room upstairs until I come back?"

"I'd surely like to go with you," Benjamin said hopefully. "I want to see Mr. Taney."

"Why?" Mrs. Bard asked.

"I heard father say he's a good lawyer, and I want to be a lawyer, too."

His mother seemed to be thinking of her answer, and Benjamin's heart sank in fear that she would refuse him; but she said, "All right, Benjamin, come with me," and led him out into the street.

The town of Frederick, nestled among the mountains of Maryland, was less of a farm community than was Hagerstown. There were many small factories located in the town. Dry goods, groceries, and hardware filled many shops. There were even banks and office buildings.

Beyond the business streets stood handsome houses, many of them old, all of them well kept. Benjamin thought Frederick was a real city, with its schools and its churches. It was a city, he told himself, which was the right place for a great lawyer; and this Mr. Taney, to whom his mother had come, must really be a great lawyer. He would have to be, the lad decided, to win freedom for the man in the Hagerstown jail.

II. The Bards Call on Mr. Taney

Benjamin and his mother found Mr. Taney's office in a building on the main street of the town; but Mr. Taney was not there. His name, Roger Brooke Taney, was on the door, but the door was locked. After Mrs. Bard had knocked upon it, a man came from another office down the hall. "Mr. Taney has gone," he said.

"Will he be back this afternoon?" Mrs. Bard asked.

"No," said the man, "and he goes to Annapolis early in the morning."

"But how can I see him?" Benjamin's mother cried. "I have just come from Hagerstown."

"He lives over there," the man said. He led them to a window and pointed toward a house a little way from the heart of the town. "You may find him at home."

"Will it be all right for me to go to him there?"

"I think he will be willing to meet a client," the man said.

"I am not really a client," Mrs. Bard said, "but I wish to see him on something of importance."

"For someone else?"

Mrs. Bard frowned before she answered. "I think that it is important to everyone who knows anything about it," she said.

"What did you mean by that, Mother?" Benjamin asked her, as they went toward the white cottage which the man had pointed out as Mr. Taney's.

"It is like this, Benjamin," she said. "I have come here to ask a lawyer whom I do not know to take the case of a man whom I never saw. I have come because your father and I believe that everyone is entitled to a fair trial, and the only way Jacob Gruber can have one is by securing a good lawyer. It is important to him that he receive justice; but it is also important to every one of us to see that justice is given. For if justice is not done in one case, it may not be done in other cases. It is everyone's duty to do everything in his power to secure for every accused man the justice of a fair trial by jury."

"I see," Benjamin said. "Do you think Mr. Taney will see that?"

"If I did not think he would," Mrs. Bard said, "I would not have come here today."

She walked very straight as they turned into the little path from the

250

road to the white cottage. She sounded the shining brass knocker and motioned Benjamin to take off his hat as they heard footsteps coming through an inner hall. A pretty young girl opened the door and smiled at them. "Yes, Father is at home," she said, "but he is not meeting any clients this afternoon."

"I have come from Hagerstown," Mrs. Bard said.

"I'm sorry," said the pretty girl. "Is it something which must be done at once?"

"Unless something is done soon, a great injustice may be done to a man."

The young girl smiled. "I am afraid Father will break his own rule," she said, "when he hears that. I will tell him."

She led them into a parlor whose spinet and satin curtains made it seem the most beautiful room Benjamin had ever seen. He had not much time to admire the surroundings, for almost at once a slender, burning-eyed man came in.

"You wish to see me, madam?" he asked Benjamin's mother, and took a chair opposite her.

Quickly Mrs. Bard told him the story of Jacob Gruber. The minister had come from Pennsylvania to

preach at a camp meeting near Hagerstown. He had talked against slavery. There had been three or four hundred slaves at the meeting. None of them had done anything or threatened to do anything against their masters; but nearly all of the people in and around Hagerstown now feared what might happen. Jacob Gruber had been arrested and now was being held in jail. He had no money, no friends, no lawyer.

"We are not rich, my husband and I," Mrs. Bard said, "but we feel obliged to do what we can to make sure that this man has a fair trial. We can pay you something if you will take this case."

"You do not know this Jacob Gruber?" the man asked.

"No, we do not."

"And you do not belong to the congregation that asked him to speak?"

"No," said Mrs. Bard.

The man stared at her closely. His thin, sensitive mouth twitched a little and his eyes twinkled. "Why have you chosen me?" he asked.

"We think you are the best lawyer in Maryland," Mrs. Bard said.

The man flung back his head in laughter. "Come here, Anne," he cried, "and listen to this! A lady from Hagerstown says I am the best lawyer in Maryland.'

The pretty girl came back into the parlor. She stood behind Mr. Taney's chair and smiled down at him before she smiled at Mrs. Bard and Benjamin. "I think you are right," she said to Benjamin's mother, "but we don't tell Father that very often."

"This lady from Hagerstown is trying to persuade me to take the case of a man who she says has been arrested for something he has not done. The warrant says he incited slaves to riot—and there has been no riot. He needs a lawyer to defend him."

"The best lawyer possible," said Mrs. Bard.

"She and her husband do not know the arrested man," Mr. Taney went on, "but they want to pay me something to undertake his defense."

"Well?" asked the pretty girl. She smiled again. "You are going to take the case, aren't you, Father?"

"Of course I am going to take it —if I find out that it is what these people believe it to be. I will go back with them to Hagerstown on the morning coach."

"And the business in Annapolis?" Anne asked.

"That can wait."

Mrs. Bard stood up, and Benjamin came to stand beside her. "I do not know how to thank you," she said to Mr. Taney.

"I should be thanking you," he said, "for bringing me this kind of case. I'm a little tired of land disputes and family quarrels over estates. What are you going to be a few years from now?" he asked Benjamin.

"A lawyer," said Benjamin.

"Like me?"

"Oh, no," said Benjamin. "Not like you. But I'd like to be, sir."

Mr. Taney laughed again. He was still laughing as Benjamin and his mother looked back from the roadway. He was standing at the door of the white cottage, with his arm around Anne. "I'll meet you on the coach tomorrow," he called.

III. MR. TANEY GOES TO COURT

The trial of Jacob Gruber did not take place in Hagerstown, after all. Mr. Taney, returning with the Bards, stayed in the town long enough to study everything about the case. He found that feeling against the minister ran so high that there was very little chance that a trial in Hagerstown would be fair. It did not matter that Jacob Gruber had not really done what the accusation against him stated. Most men of the neighborhood thought he had done it, and that was enough for them. Mr. Taney, therefore, asked that the trial be transferred to Frederick; and so it happened that Benjamin Bard and his father and mother went by stagecoach to hear Mr. Taney defend the client whom they had wished upon him.

The Bards liked to think of Mr. Gruber as their particular charge, although Mr. Taney absolutely refused to accept from them any fee for his services. It was a privilege, Mr. Taney told Mr. Bard, to be able to show what the Constitution and its Bill of Rights meant to the plain citizen. It was a challenge to work in a case against public opinion when public opinion happened to be wrong.

The courtroom in Frederick was crowded when the Bards came in. People had traveled from as far as Pennsylvania to hear the trial. Farmers, tradesmen, and lawyers pushed against one another to see and hear all they could. For the trial of Jacob Gruber was no ordinary trial. Although it was forty

253

years before the Civil War, people seemed to realize that the question of slavery would some day become a great national question.

Maryland was one of the states where men held slaves, although a large number of Marylanders—Mr. Taney's family among them—had freed their slaves. Pennsylvania was not a state where slavery existed. Large numbers of people in Maryland who did not believe in slavery nevertheless felt that no man from another state had any right to come into their state and talk against slavery.

"Why does a man like Roger Brooke Taney take this case?" Benjamin heard one man ask another.

"I don't know," the other man said. "There's no money in it, either."

Between the courtroom crowd and the judge's bench were two tables. At one of them sat the district attorney and his assistants. It was their task to present the case against Jacob Gruber. At the other table sat Jacob Gruber, pale and nervous, between Mr. Taney and his law clerk. Mr. Taney was going over a big book. He looked tired, Benjamin thought, and almost as pale as the man he was defending.

Behind a rail at one side of the courtroom sat twelve men. They were, Benjamin knew, the jury, who would decide whether Jacob Gruber should go free or should be sent back to jail. Through Benjamin's mind ran the words *trial by jury*. That was something the Constitution promised every citizen. No matter how angry men might be at someone whom they thought had broken the law, they must give him a fair trial. That was why Mr. Taney was giving his

services free to a man he had never seen until he had gone with Benjamin and his mother to Hagerstown.

"It's a grand country we live in," the boy thought, as he looked around the courtroom.

Everyone stood up as the judge walked to the bench. Benjamin heard the court bailiff shout something about the honorable court's being in session. After twelve citizens had been chosen to serve as a jury, the trial began.

One after another, men went up to sit on a bench near the judge which the lawyers called the witness stand. First came men who

talked against the minister. The district attorney asked them questions, then Mr. Taney asked them other questions. Sometimes they changed their stories under the questions Mr. Taney asked. After them, came men who spoke for Jacob Gruber. But when all the stories had been told, there was doubt as to what the jury would think of Gruber's guilt.

At noon the judge left the bench, the jury was taken out, and the crowd went out from the courtroom. The Bards went to the hotel for dinner, but hurried back to the courthouse. After what seemed to Benjamin a long time, the judge, the jury, the lawyers, Jacob Gruber, and the crowd came back. The trial went on.

The district attorney made a very long speech. Benjamin dozed through most of it. Then Mr. Taney stood up, and the boy leaned forward to hear him. Mr. Taney spoke quietly, and said a great deal which Benjamin could not understand at all; but the boy saw that the men of the jury were watching the lawyer closely while they listened to his words.

Benjamin did his best to understand what the lawyer was saying that clearly was so important.

Mr. Taney was saying that, under the laws of the United States and the state of Maryland, the rights of conscience and freedom of speech were fully protected. No man could be prosecuted for preaching the articles of his religious creed unless his doctrine was immoral and meant to disturb public peace and order. Matters of national policy could be freely and fully discussed, in the pulpit or elsewhere, at all times.

Mr. Gruber, the lawyer went on, was a minister of a church which believed in the gradual and peaceable abolition of slavery. Everyone knew the doctrine he would preach. If any slaveholder believed this doctrine would disturb his slaves, he should have kept them from the camp meeting where the minister was to speak. Mr. Gruber did not go to the slaves. The slaves came to him. They could not have come if their masters had chosen to prevent them.

There was no law, Mr. Taney said, which forbids a citizen to speak of slavery as he thinks of it. "Here, in the temple of justice, we are prepared to maintain the same principles, and to use, if necessary, the same language which the minister used at the meeting.

"A hard necessity compels us," Mr. Taney said, "to endure the evil of slavery for a time. It cannot be easily or suddenly removed. Yet, while it continues, it is a blot on our national character; and every real lover of freedom confidently hopes that it will be finally wiped away."

Mr. Taney sat down. The judge spoke to the jury. The twelve men arose and filed out of the courtroom. The crowd settled back in their chairs with a sigh to await the decision.

"That jury will certainly bring in a verdict of guilty," Benjamin heard a man say. "Every man on the jury is a slaveowner."

"Do you really think the jury will convict Mr. Gruber?" Mrs. Bard asked Benjamin's father.

"I don't know," Mr. Bard said. "I only know that Mr. Taney has made a great argument for Mr. Gruber's freedom."

In a little while rumors began to run through the courtroom. The jury had voted a verdict, one said. It had found the defendant, Mr. Gruber, guilty and asked the judge to sentence him to five years of imprisonment. No, it was ten years of imprisonment, another rumor said. The jury could not decide at all, someone else declared.

Through all the time Mr. Gruber sat speechless beside Mr. Taney, who continued to look through his law books. Benjamin wondered if the pretty girl whom he had met at Mr. Taney's house was in court; but if she were, he could not see her. The afternoon grew late. Then, suddenly, the bailiff pounded his gavel again, the judge came back to the bench, and the jury filed back into the room.

"Have you found a verdict?" the judge asked the jury.

"We have, your Honor," one of the jurymen said.

"Read it," said the judge.

There was no other sound in the courtroom but that of the man's voice as he read, "We, the jury, find the defendant, Jacob Gruber,"—it seemed to Benjamin that everyone in the room watched the defendant and his lawyer until the words came,—"not guilty."

Instantly a cheer arose. Men pushed forward toward Mr. Taney. The bailiff's gavel came down heavily. "Order in the court!" he shouted; but a great cry went up from hundreds of throats, "Taney, Taney!" Mr. Taney put up his hand. "The victory is not mine!" he said. "It is the victory of justice in our land of the free."

Completing an Outline

Complete this outline of the story. You may refer to the story as often as necessary while you work.

I. ....

    A. Reason for the arrest

    B. Attitude of the people in Hagerstown

    C. Effect of sermon on the slaves

    D. Difficulty in securing a lawyer

II. The Bards' interest in the case

    A. ....

    B. ....

    C. ....

III. ....

    A. Benjamin makes ready

    B. A ride by stagecoach

    C. Arrival at Frederick Town

IV. Searching for the lawyer

    A. ....

    B. ....

V. ....

    A. Mrs. Bard explains the case

    B. Mr. Taney's reply

VI. The Trial

    A. ....

    B. ....

    C. ....

    D. ....

    E. ....

DENIS A. McCARTHY

The Land Where Hate Should Die

THIS is the land where hate should die—
      No feuds of faith, no spleen of race,
No darkly brooding fear should try
      Beneath our flag to find a place.
Lo! every people here has sent
      Its sons to answer freedom's call;
Their lifeblood is the strong cement
      That builds and binds the nation's wall.

This is the land where hate should die—
      Though dear to me my faith and shrine,
I serve my country well when I
      Respect beliefs that are not mine.
He little loves his land who'd cast
      Upon his neighbor's faith a doubt,
Or cite the wrongs of ages past,
      From present rights to bar him out.

This is the land where hate should die—
      This is the land where strife should cease,
Where dark, suspicious fear should fly
      Before our flag of love and peace.
Then let us purge of poisoned thought
      That service to the state we give,
And so be worthy, as we ought,
      Of the great land in which we live!

SISTER M. CATHARINE JOSEPH HAUGHEY, I.H.M.

The Story of Margaret Haughery:

The Bread Woman of New Orleans

IF you know New Orleans, you have passed the tiny green park where Camp Street meets Prytania. There you have seen the statue of an old woman, dressed in the style of another century, with a simple dress and a plain little bonnet, and her shawl tucked around her shoulders as she wore it long ago. Beside her stands the smaller statue of an orphan boy and on the base of the monument is inscribed but one word—MARGARET.

In New Orleans today they will tell you that this statue is the first erected in the United States to honor a woman, and they add that this city triangle is the first bit of public land dedicated to a woman; it is called "Margaret Park." Orphans from eleven institutions—Catholic, Protestant, and Jewish, of every race and color and creed, stood by in silent tribute when the statue was unveiled on July 9, 1884. The Archbishop of New Orleans and many priests were there. So was the Governor of Louisiana, who recounted the charitable deeds that had endeared the old woman in the black shawl to the people of the city she had loved.

If you know New Orleans, you know her name. It was Margaret Haughery. When she went to New Orleans as a bride, more than a hundred years ago, there were few who could pronounce her name. As the *Hyperion,* out from Baltimore, docked at the busy Louisiana port the girl saw a mass of strange races, brought to their new land by ships from the scores of ports that fringe the seven seas. French, Spanish, Portuguese, and a dozen even stranger tongues were heard above the clangor of ships' bells and shouts of the stevedores. "I'm Irish, and my husband is Irish, and our name is pronounced Hawry," Margaret told a sailor who directed them to a boarding house.

The future looked cloudless as they passed the old cathedral and the gleaming sunlight of Lafayette Square. Strangers smiled at them, and Margaret smiled back at them. "I've received more kindness in my life than I deserve," she told her young husband.

"You always repay it," he said.

"I hope I always will," she said. Although that was long ago, the memory of Margaret Haughery's kindness in this old southern city remains undimmed. Perhaps you know what she is called; it is "The Bread Woman of New Orleans." From the first steam bakery in the South, which she founded, went the great baskets of bread for the poor; with them went the determination of a noble woman that no one, if she could help it, would go hungry.

What had influenced Margaret Haughery? What was the story of her childhood, her youth, and her marriage, that inspired her ceaseless energy in the cause of humanity? The chain of events started in 1820 when times were hard in Ireland. Her parents, William and Margaret Gaffney, brought little Margaret with them to America. They came to Baltimore hopeful and happy, but in a few months, an epidemic of yellow fever broke out and the child was left an orphan. In Baltimore lived a Mrs. Richards, a Welsh Baptist, who had crossed the Atlantic on the same ship with the Gaffneys. Although her own husband had died in the epidemic, Mrs. Richards put aside her own grief to care for little seven-year-old Margaret. "I'm poor, but I love the child," Mrs. Richards told Father McElroy, the Jesuit priest who had grown deeply concerned about the girl's welfare. Then, under the spiritual guardianship of the Jesuit priest and in the house of the kindly woman from Wales, Margaret began to pattern her life of Christlike charity. The inspiring example of Mrs. Richards was a strong force in developing Margaret's deep love for humanity. Throughout her life, she never questioned in any way the nationality, the race, or the creed of the thousands of people she helped.

In 1834 she met and married Charles Haughery. He wasn't strong, but "a change of climate will make me well," he said, and they set sail for New Orleans. The southern sun could not cure him and the few short years of his life were numbered. The sadness of his early death was intensified by the passing of their infant daughter Frances. Though the sun still shone upon Spanish gardens and grilled French doorways in old

261

New Orleans, the way had grown dark for Margaret Haughery.

She didn't despair. Penniless, lonely, she went to work in the laundry of the St. Charles Hotel. There from her window she saw the Sisters of Charity as they went about their task of caring for the orphans. "I'll offer my services to them," she told herself, thinking of little Frances, the infant she had loved and lost. She was a woman of action. She asked questions, she followed suggestions, and she began the work that was to last for forty-six years as Apostle of Charity for the City of New Orleans.

For this work she needed money. With amazing initiative, she purchased two cows and started a dairy on a vacant lot behind an orphanage conducted by the Sisters of Charity. She borrowed a small cart, or wagonette, and began selling milk through the streets. At many places she begged food "for my poor." At this time Margaret met Sister Francis Regis Barrett. In later years, Margaret was heard to say, "Sister was all to me when my husband and child died." She assisted Sister Regis in many ventures and they remained close friends until Sister's death in the first years of the War Between the States. They suffered hardships together; they planned together. Both were dreamers of dreams; but, more than that, they were women who accomplished what they set out to do.

Did the Sisters of Charity need a new home? Margaret found it for them, though it was a tumbledown, abandoned place known as "Old Withers." The neighbors on New Levee Street protested to Margaret. "It's haunted," they told her. She laughed. "It needs cleaning," she said. Most of the work had to be done by flickering candlelight in the early evening. A group of boys, passing by, saw weird moving shadows cast on the windows by the movements of the Sisters of Charity. Terrified, the boys spread the alarm that they had seen the ghosts in "Old Withers." A crowd assembled, but Margaret, with pail and scrub brush in hand, came out and laughed at them.

Did the city need a new orphanage? Who but the dedicated young woman whose milk cart rattled daily through the streets could be the promoter? Margaret persuaded two of her rich acquaintances to donate land and on it the St. Theresa Asylum on Camp Street was built. Margaret's energy did not stop until she had raised money from her friends and contributed a large part of her own earnings.

In the meantime, she had established an independent dairy in the fast-growing "uptown part of New Orleans." Soon she owned thirty or forty cows and a thriving business, but a large part of her profits went into a third venture—the Louise Home, now an inexpensive residence for working girls.

The dairy had been a financial success, but Margaret's zeal to finance further charities led her into a new venture. In 1850 she took over a bakery and introduced the new steam methods. She then established bread delivery routes as she had formerly done with milk. Always, in the large baskets delivered free to orphanages and other institutions, there would be hidden small delicacies for the children and the aged.

The "Bread Woman of New Orleans" paid off the debt of the St. Theresa Home for Orphans and lifted the financial load from her other charities. Then, with high hope, she set the wheels in motion to attain her heart's desire. This would be an infant asylum. In each small child she saw her own little baby Frances, who had been hers for so short a time. Never thinking of her own needs, still wearing the simple black dress and the little black shawl and Quaker bonnet, she gave every penny she could earn toward the building of

263

the St. Vincent de Paul Infant Asylum at Race and Magazine Streets. This opened in 1862. Later a branch of the Asylum became known as St. Elizabeth's, an industrial school for girls, perhaps the first established in the South under Catholic auspices.

Margaret endeared herself to all New Orleans. Someone said of her that "she singled out the poor who needed her charity and the rich who needed her solicitude." To the rich and poor she was known only as "Margaret." When visitors asked what other name she possessed, her friends said, with the deference due to royalty, "She is just our Margaret!"

They tell you in New Orleans that Margaret never questioned those to whom she gave assistance, asking neither their race nor creed. That deference to others had probably been instilled in the childhood years when she had known the affectionate kindness of the Welsh Baptist, Mrs. Richards of Baltimore. The ladies from Protestant orphanages, amazed that Margaret would give them free bread for their orphans, would tell her, "We're Protestants." They would always receive the same answer, "The children are the children of God." Asked once why she did so much for so many, she said, "God has been good to me; I must be good to others."

A hundred years is a long time for the memory of a woman to survive in a swiftly moving civilization, but today, in New Orleans, you can still hear stories of the kindness of Margaret Haughery. They will tell you of the help she gave the homeless and the orphan, the deserted infants, and the penniless men and women. They will recall the terms of her will, which provided thousands of dollars for the Little Sisters of the Poor, the Sisters of the Good Shepherd, the Jewish Asylum, the Seventh Street Protestant Orphanage, and the Asylum for Widows and Orphans.

Cardinal Gibbons, who lived in New Orleans and, when a boy, had worked in a grocery store on Camp Street, remembered from his youth the old woman with the milk carts and the bread wagons. Who could forget her? "The sainted Margaret," the Cardinal called her, and saintly she was. Unable to read, she mastered the great book of love of her fellow men; unable to write, she left one of America's greatest biographies—the immortal record of her love of God and His poor.

What Do You Think?

Now that you have read the story, answer the following questions.

1. Why do you think the city of New Orleans dedicated a tract of public land to "The Bread Woman of New Orleans" and why do you think religious and civic officials alike honored her memory?

2. Do you think the fact that Margaret suffered herself influenced her in the relief she gave to others? Explain.

3. What do you think the author meant when she referred to Margaret as "a woman of action" and a "dreamer of dreams"?

4. What principle is proved by the fact that Margaret helped anyone and everyone who was in need?

Finding Synonyms

Choose a synonym for the first word in each row.

1. century	old	antiquated	ancient	100 years
2. inscribed	engraved	thought out	signed	oversee
3. erected	planned	built	studied	learned
4. recounted	told	revisited	revealed	renewed
5. clangor	tuba	noise	sorrow	vessel
6. stevedore	porter	ship leader	steward	sergeant
7. determination	spirit	exhilaration	firmness	dejection
8. epidemic	plague	starvation	typhoid	diseases
9. intensified	vivified	strengthened	exerted	stored
10. auspices	popularity	understanding	work	guidance
11. deference	age	respect	meekness	agility
12. instilled	imparted	silently	sought	unheard

ALINE KILMER

To Two Little Sisters of the Poor

SWEET and humble and gladly poor,
The grace of God came in at my door.

Sorrow and death were mine that day,
But the grace of God came in to stay;

The grace of God that spread its wings
Over all sad and pitiful things.

Sorrow turned to the touch of God,
Death became but His welcoming nod.

Gray-eyed, comforting, strong, and brave,
You came to ask but instead you gave.

Quickly you came and went, you two,
But the grace of God stayed after you.

RUTHERFORD G. MONTGOMERY

Storm Flight

THE Napier lurched and bounced as her low wings cracked the rough air that backwashed from Mount Kirby. Tommy wiped the usual smile from his lips and glanced at the flight bubble. Ahead lay trouble! It was written all over the spruce-choked side of the mountain. Gray-black clouds piled high in the notch toward which the Napier was heading. And there was no other crossing for a hundred miles along the divide, aside from the narrow pass. Heavily loaded, the Napier did not have ceiling enough to top the naked ridges towering above the storm.

Barrows, who sat beside Tommy, leaned over and shouted. His voice sounded like a whisper as it cut through the scream of the hurtling winds.

"Do you want to turn back?"

Tommy shook his head and gave the Napier all she had. Her powerful motor shook the sills inside her fuselage as it responded. Had the ship been loaded within her weight limit, the Napier would have taken clearance, and Tommy could have zoomed above the onrushing wall of storm that was rolling up out of the valley beyond the pass.

"People are starving across the hump! We must get this food through to them! We've got to!" shouted Barrows.

Tommy's eyes shifted to the gray mass that swirled down upon them. Barrow's face was expressionless. If Tommy cracked up the Napier, it would mean a loss of seven thousand dollars for Barrows, to say nothing of the danger to their lives. Barrows had picked Tommy to fly the load of rescue food into Happy Valley where a mountain community was stormlocked and starving.

Barrows was not a flier, himself. He had come along because he would not ask anyone to fly into a danger he would not face. He had picked Tommy from a recruit line because he was certain that the slender, steel-muscled boy with the curly hair and cold, blue eyes would not turn back.

The Napier shoved her slicing propeller into a swirling mass of powder-dry snow. The particles hurtled against the glass panes of the cabin. The Napier shifted suddenly, and one wing lifted with a sickening lurch. Tommy fought to keep her level and to hold his altitude.

Barrows settled back in his bucket seat and stared out of the little window at his side. In a flash the mountain walls were wiped out by the swirling mass of snow. No landmark showed the way to the pass. On both sides granite walls lurked in the white mists. Tommy would have to feel the Napier through the notch or crack up. Barrows looked across at his pilot and caught Tommy's eyes. He grinned and wrinkled his nose at the storm.

Tommy managed to level off and the Napier bore into the storm. Suddenly the white wall ahead scattered like a huge jig-saw puzzle that has been roughly shaken. A wall of granite, studded with scrub growth, came hurtling at them through the storm! Tommy laid the Napier over sharply and she lifted high into the air. The upward lift shot them into the storm again and blotted out all vision. Desperately Tommy put her nose down again. He must see where he was going! Again the clouds cleared and this time no

walls of granite loomed ahead. Tommy sent the ship roaring over the tall spruce toward the pass.

Flying close to the tops of tall spruce in a raging storm is a tough job, and Tommy felt a strange coldness in the region of his belt. Then he remembered the starving folks in Happy Valley and his lips set tight. Beside him Barrows was unmoved.

Tommy sucked in a breath of cold air. He could see the notch ahead, a low-lying valley curving down from high jagged ranges on either side. The Napier was bouncing and jerking as she hit the pass and roared through with less than five hundred feet of ceiling. Barrows reached over and slapped Tommy on the back. He bent close and roared into Tommy's ear.

"You get a regular job from now on!"

"Thanks!" Tommy shouted back. A regular job with Barrows would mean flying into almost inaccessible places, but Barrows paid top wages and had the best planes.

The Napier was almost clear of the mountain side when the updraft of the storm hit her. A howling demon of lashing air clutched at the ship, hurling it high into the air, turning it over on its side and

crashing Barrows against the little window at his side.

The Napier came out of the clutches of the storm with sickening suddenness. Her tail swept up and she spiraled dizzily, then she plunged downward and buried her nose in the white wall of storm that was sweeping up through the pass. Tommy fought to level off, but the wind was too powerful and he could not right the ship. For two or three sickening seconds they hurtled downward, then a rending crash shook them and a jarring impact jerked them sharply. Black lights flickered before his eyes.

When Tommy opened his eyes, he was numb with cold and icy particles were pelting his face. He sat up dizzily. A sharp pain shot through his left side. He shouted loudly: "Barrows! Barrows!"

Only the howling of the wind answered him. He staggered to his feet and looked around. Little could be seen through the driving storm. The Napier lay twisted and battered, her nose buried in a deep drift and her tail elevated. Tommy realized that he had been thrown through the window and side plates. He thanked his padded suit for being alive as he plowed to the ship and bent to look inside.

Barrows lay sprawled over the controls. Much of the packed food had fallen down on him. Tommy fought back the numbing pain in his side and began pulling Barrows free of the plane. Barrows groaned and opened his eyes as Tommy laid him in the snow beside the plane. A wavering smile came to his lips.

"Have to have a fire. Feet cold —cold—" Barrows slumped back and his eyes closed.

Tommy found plenty of logs in the snow. Hurriedly he swept clear a space and built a fire. He dug a heavy blanket from the wreck and fixed a shelter. Tommy guessed that Barrows was internally injured, but he had no way of knowing how seriously. Tommy watched and hoped that his boss would recover consciousness. But Barrows did not come to. His lips moved but he did not speak.

Tommy faced the danger coolly. He knew they could not be rescued for perhaps a week. The dwellers of Happy Valley did not know they were coming, so there was no hope of help from them, though the plane must be close to the settlement.

Tommy stood up. Night was beginning to darken the swirling storm. Grimly Tommy fixed the

shelter over his boss. He knew what Barrows would order if he were conscious, and he meant to follow that course. Hesitating only a moment, he plunged into the storm heading down the mountain. Their objective was still ahead, and Barrows would expect him to go on.

Through the first drift he wallowed, always going downhill. His side pained and weakened him, and he began to think he had acted the fool in braving the storm and leaving Barrows unconscious, possibly dying beside the fire. The storm raged about him, shutting out the world and piling up drifts.

But fate cares for those who dare greatly, and when their cause is mercy bound they are oftentimes lucky. Tommy fell into a drift. He raised himself wearily and wiped the snow from his face. Then he saw a light glimmering ahead. Eagerly he staggered forward and threw himself against the plank door of a snow-covered cabin.

Rough mountain men met him at the door. They were gaunt from hunger but they dragged him inside and placed him on a bunk. He had found the outmost cabin of the settlement. Tommy refused to rest until they backtracked to rescue Barrows. They were wildly joyous when they learned that the ship was loaded with food.

In a very short time Tommy and

the men of Happy Valley had rescued Barrows, unloaded the welcome supplies, and returned to the waiting community. All of Happy Valley was rounded up to share the food they so badly needed.

Late that night Barrows and Tommy sat beside a roaring fire and sipped tinned soup that was simmering hot. Barrows was bandaged and at rest. Tommy's side had ceased to pain.

"You have what it takes to fly for me," Barrows said.

"Thanks!" Tommy replied, and went on sipping his soup.

Recalling Details

Copy these sentences on your paper, completing them without referring to the story.

1. The name of the plane was . . . .
2. The purpose of the flight was . . . .
3. If the plane had cracked up it would have meant the loss of . . . . dollars and possibly the lives of two persons.
4. The starving mountain community was called . . . .
5. The pilot's name was . . . .
6. The plane crash was caused by . . . .
7. To have a regular job as pilot with Barrows meant . . . .
8. As a result of the crash Tommy was . . . .
9. Barrows was unconscious, and so Tommy decided . . . .
10. The story ends happily because (a) . . . ., (b) . . . . and (c) . . . . .

Knowing Synonyms and Antonyms

Mark S (synonym) or A (antonym) beside each pair of words.

1. lurched—swayed
2. elevated—lowered
3. rough—uncouth
4. altitude—height
5. desperately—hopefully
6. internally—externally
7. folks—people
8. pelting—beating
9. joyous—dejected
10. conscious—unaware

272

A Friend of St. Patrick

HIGH above the Potomac River, on wide quiet acres broken only by long rows of white monuments to America's heroic dead, lies Arlington Cemetery.

On the crest of one of its wooded hills that looks down upon the city of Washington, rises Arlington House. Few houses in America have known more history, few have known more sorrow. Owned first by John Parke Custis, Martha Washington's son, in 1802 it passed on to his son, George Washington Parke Custis.

There, in 1831, to the music of harps and violins and in the glow of candlelight, he gave in marriage his only child, Mary Ann Randolph Custis, to a young lieutenant of the United States Army, named Robert Edward Lee. As a military man, especially during the War with Mexico, Lee was often away from home, but Mrs. Lee and her seven children lived in the white house on the hill until the War Between the States began. Then, with her children, she was driven out, and never returned.

The years move quietly on the hills of Arlington. Today only the tread of tourists breaks the silence of the spacious rooms of the old mansion; only the dry magnolia leaves, rattling like sabres in the Virginia night, beat against the darkened windows.

Once a year, though, upon St. Patrick's Day, there comes a pilgrimage to Arlington House. A group of Irish-Americans, members of the George Washington Chapter of the Friendly Sons of St. Patrick, carry clusters of Irish shamrocks to place upon the grave of George Washington Parke Custis, for it

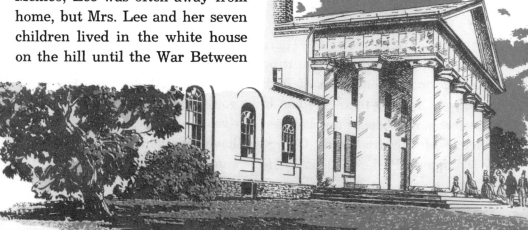

was the step-grandson of George Washington who rose up in 1826 to lead in America the protest against the mounting persecution of the people of Ireland.

Thousands of Irish were pouring into this country since Ireland was suffering from oppression. It had just been made an English law that Ireland should assume a large share of the English debt, obligations brought on by England's wars with France and the United States. The payment of the debt exhausted the Irish treasury.

When, in the year 1828, the price of crops fell, England seized Ireland's grain and sheep and swine, leaving to the impoverished tenants nothing but rotting potato fields. The right of Irish assembly was prohibited. Evictions became more frequent. Reform was needed desperately, and repeal of the union with England was the dream of every Irish patriot.

In the United States there arose a cry of outrage against the existing conditions in Ireland. There arose, also, the need of a reassuring welcome to the thousands of Irish who were seeking their freedom in the new land. One of the warmest friends of the Irish was George Washington Parke Custis. He voiced a demand for British reforms and, with a practical mind, he sponsored at once the Washington Benevolent Society to aid the immigrants. He contributed not only his name and financial help, but gave helpful advice on colonization and means of immediate livelihood. The purpose of the society, Custis stated, was "to express sympathy for the people of Ireland and an earnest desire and hope for speedy amelioration of their condition."

To the Irish of his time Custis became a national hero. George Washington before him had also been an honorary member of the Friendly Sons of St. Patrick, an organization which originated in Dublin in 1750 and flourished in eastern cities in the early days of the American Republic. His stepson, George Custis, became an active member of the Friendly Sons. Until his death in 1857 he seldom missed a St. Patrick's Day celebration in Washington, not only singing Irish melodies, but writing Irish lyrics.

Not long before he died Custis voiced a sentimental hope that "years after my mortal body shall have been laid in the bosom of our common mother, some honest Irish

274

heart may come and, dropping a shamrock on my grave, cry, 'God bless him.' "

The Irish in America have long memories. Each year, come St. Patrick's Day, the grave of George Washington Parke Custis, a true friend in time of need, is covered with green in the March sunlight. The Friendly Sons of St. Patrick of Virginia, remembering the man, remembering his deeds, stand together in the shadows of Arlington House and repeat "God bless him," as they drop Irish shamrocks upon his tomb.

True or False?

Copy these statements on your paper. Mark *True* or *False* before each one and then change the word or phrase to make the false ones true.

1. Arlington House was first owned by Martha Washington.

2. In 1802 Robert E. Lee and Mary Ann Randolph Custis were married in Arlington House.

3. Arlington Cemetery lies high above the Potomac River, the final resting place of American heroes.

4. Every year on St. Patrick's Day, Irish immigrants honor the grave and memory of George Washington Parke Custis, the step-grandson of George Washington.

5. England passed a law that Ireland must pay a large share of the debt which arose out of the long wars with France and the United States.

6. George Washington Parke Custis organized the Irish Benevolent Society to aid Irish immigrants.

7. The English seized the Irish crops and livestock, raised their rents, and denied the people the right of assembly.

8. The Friendly Sons of St. Patrick began in 1750 in New York.

9. George Washington Parke Custis, who died in 1846, was an active member of the Friendly Sons of St. Patrick.

10. To help the Irish immigrants he gave financial aid and sound advice on how to colonize and earn a living.

7. I'll Take the High Road

THE games of children do not change much through the years. Roman children played a form of hopscotch. "London Bridge" and "Farmer in the Dell" are more than a hundred years old. So is another game you have played—"Rich man, poor man, beggarman, chief . . ."

There are so many words to the game, so many ways of playing it, so many plans you could envision for the future as you danced and sang on city streets or country lanes on the long summer evenings.

Perhaps you did not decide then what you really wanted to be when you grew up; perhaps you have not yet decided. It's not as long a time ahead as you think before you must choose the road you shall follow. In these stories you will meet Martha who is thinking about her future; Steppin with his dancing feet; and Martin, with the knowledge that he is able to help the sick, who knows that he will be a doctor.

The high road of life is broad and bright. There will be thousands of opportunities for you. You'll travel fast and far if you carry with you the truths you are now learning at home, in church, in school.

DOROTHY BROWN THOMPSON

The City and the Trucks

THE city sleeps in its unconcern, but the highways are awake
With searching flashes and grinding gears and the hiss of air in a brake;
When darkness comes, like a roll of drums three million engines roar
Under throbbing hoods, and the nation's goods are out on the roads
    once more.

The city wakens to meet old needs and perhaps some new desires,
And finds the answer to all it asks brought in on the rubber tires:
There is coal and milk, there is rope and silk, there is shelter and food
    and dress
That lumbered in when the dawn was thin on the night highway
    express.

The city moves in its ordered round and never asks or knows
How drivers inch through the murky night as the fog bank comes and
    goes,
How they breast the beat of the blinding sleet and shift for the slippery
    climb,
How they stop a fire, or tinker a tire—and pull into town on time!

The city takes, and it goes its way, and the great dark hulks reload,
While mechanics grease, and test, and check, to make them safe for the
    road;
Then the crates are stacked and the boxes packed and the padding
    placed—and then
The tailboards slam, and the trailers ram—and the great trucks roll
    again!

Just-So[1]

THE little town of Plant City was asleep in the dark when Dave Ferris drove through in his truck with Martha in the front seat and Just-So in the rear. Martha was quieter than usual as they jolted along to the stockyard where the Fat Calf Show would take place. She knew how little money her big brother Johnny had left, and she also knew Johnny had to pay Dave for that ride.

It was cold for March. A bitter north wind blew strongly as they rumbled through town, numbing Martha's feet and even her hands in the pockets of her mackinaw. When they reached the Plant City stockyard, only one or two trucks were lined up ahead of them. A man rubbing his ears and stamping his feet stood there with a lantern. He helped unload. Just-So was finally persuaded to come to earth.

"Good luck to ya, Martha, good luck," said Dave, jumping hastily back to the front seat of his truck

and roaring off into the blackness. Now she was alone. Just-So leaned against her side. The heifer was lonely and frightened also.

"Right inside, sister. Get your calf weighed, first-off."

The man held open a large door into a big cavern. The Plant City stockyard on the outskirts of town was an enormous, long wooden building. On one side were the pens. They extended on Martha's right as far as she could see in the dim electric light. A wide passageway reached down the other side of the structure to the far end. It was bitterly cold in the drafty shed.

Just inside the door to the left was the weighing machine. The weights were in a small room with a glass window that opened onto the scales holding the animal to be weighed. Several farmers in overalls and jackets stood around an iron stove inside, blowing on their hands and talking in loud tones.

"Now then, young lady, all right with that heifer here."

Martha led Just-So onto the big scales and stepped away.

[1] From *Son of the Valley* by John R. Tunis, copyright 1949 by John R. Tunis, by permission of William Morrow and Company, Inc.

"Six fifty," said the voice from inside the room.

"Six fifty," chanted a voice at Martha's side. A man bent over the calf's halter with a tag. He asked her name. His fingers fumbled in the cold as he wrote.

"What class, girl? Senior?"

"No, sir." Her teeth chattered. "Junior heifer. She was dropped last June." Martha was a mountain girl and accustomed to cold weather, but this deep chill that penetrated her clothes was something she had seldom felt before.

"O.K." He scribbled on the tag. "Jake! Hey there, Jake. Show the little lady where her pen is; junior heifer."

They walked down the long passageway in the dim electric light, the frozen dirt hard as rock from the tramping of a million hoofs. Martha was almost the first contestant to appear. Once inside the pen she tied up Just-So. As soon as the man had closed the gate and vanished in the distance, Martha's arms went around the neck of the calf. The big Black Angus heifer turned her head. Her cold muzzle pushed affectionately against the girl. She felt lonely, too.

Soon the gate swung back and a boy slightly older than Martha entered, leading a Hereford. She looked the animal over carefully; it was a good calf.

There really was not much to do; yet to keep from freezing to death she was forced to do something. The wind came whistling through the spaces in the slats, penetrating Martha's thin mackinaw, chilling her feet and hands. Mechanically she started to work on Just-So's flanks with her brush.

The heifer was nervous and uneasy. Martha soon realized this and tried to steady her down. She walked around her, stroking her constantly, keeping up a steady stream of talk as she always did in the lean-to on the farm at home.

Before long the quietness of the vast cavern was shattered by shouts and yells. Up and down the enormous building echoed the sounds of the figures called out by the men on the weighing machine, the mooing of cattle, yells and cries as occasionally an animal got loose in the passageway. Outside the building a stream of trucks inched their way down, coming in to unload and then roared off. Every truck was full of calves. There was even one calf perched precariously on the rear seat of an ancient Model-T Ford sedan.

Noise and excitement everywhere! Over it all was the chatter of farmers arriving, the stamping of the cattle in their sawdust pens. The animals were pouring in now, Shorthorns and Herefords, several likely looking Black Angus calves, too. Yet to her eyes none could be compared with Just-So. She had been told that much would depend on the animal's appearance and behavior when the showing began. She hoped the heifer would obey as usual, that the noise and the people and the feverish atmosphere would not frighten her.

Now Martha was really cold. She tried to get some warmth from the heifer's body. Just-So was cold, too. She mooed in distress to the other calves around. Suddenly Mr. Sam, leader of the 4-H Club, appeared at Martha's side. He had brought her a paper cup full of hot coffee, so hot she could hardly hold it in her bare hands.

It was good to see an old friend. "Oh, thank you, Mr. Sam. I shore do thank you." She managed to get hold of the cup. The heat stung her frozen fingers, but she was grateful for it, happy also to be with someone she knew among all these strangers. Slowly she drank the hot liquid and gobbled one of the sandwiches Ma Heiskell had provided for her. Her feet were frozen stiff, it seemed; yet somehow she felt better as Mr. Sam looked over her calf with approval.

"She's really O.K., that heifer of yours!"

"What time is it, Mr. Sam?"

He glanced at his wrist watch. "Twenty till eight."

Twenty till eight. Why, she'd been there hours and hours and hours and still it was not even eight o'clock! The pen was nearly full now. It was daylight outside, a gray, cheerless morning.

Mr. Sam, who had many 4-H Club boys and girls to oversee, moved along, and Martha went to work again on Just-So's flanks, brushing, brushing, brushing. She brushed because the heifer liked her familiar touch and responded to it; besides, brushing Just-So helped to take her mind off the cold. After a while she stood off, surveying the calf with attention. The heifer was in excellent condition. That was certain. But what chance had Just-So with all those other animals?

Farmers came past with canes or sticks in their hands. They poked and whacked the calves. She heard several comments on Just-So.

"Number twelve. That's a choice animal, that is."

"She's 4-H, ain't she?"

"Yep, that's right."

Boys and girls from school poured into the stockyard. They all had mackinaws or jackets over their blue overalls, and either red peaked or corduroy caps.

Then three men entered the pen. They walked with authority and all wore badges. One was the little man who had spoken to her earlier that morning. Why, he *was* a judge after all! The youngsters in the pen began scraping and brushing furiously. This was the first test, the grading. Each calf must be graded first before the showing.

The chief judge stood surveying the crowded pen. He walked slowly up and down, turned and came back past the line of cattle, laying his hand here and there on a calf's flanks, poking another with his cane. The boys and girls, mostly older than Martha, watched nervously. Then the judge spoke a quiet word to the little man at his side, who had a long sheet of paper clipped to a board. The little man inspected a tag and wrote something down, and a third judge, with

282

paint brush in hand, slapped a mark on the calf's haunches.

One streak meant "Choice," two meant "Good," three, "Medium." The men scarcely looked at Just-So, and Martha's heart sank. Then the man with the paint brush was at her side. He drew one yellow mark across the calf's flanks.

"Take her outside, sister," he said.

Martha pushed her way to the exit with Just-So. Outside, a thin sun was shining; she felt warmer the moment she stepped into the open air. She was astonished to find that in the excitement of the grading she had lost some of the chill in her body.

Beside the exit stood an official. "Senior heifer? Junior? Junior. Line her up on that wire over there, young lady."

Martha noticed a long wire attached to two stakes set into the ground. Several heifers, all with one mark on their flanks, were tied to it. One of the boys she recognized as a contestant in her class. Leading Just-So over, she tied her to the wire. Soon they were joined by several others.

A few minutes later Kendall Butcher and the Johnson boy and several others from her class in school came along. They waved at her over the heads of the crowd. Their friendly gestures helped her.

Hours and hours later, or so it seemed, the three judges came out of the building and went to work. The chief judge, a well-dressed man with his gray felt hat shading his eyes, took command. He lined the cattle up with care, beckoning a boy here, nodding to a girl to move her calf, feeling a heifer there. The crowd pressed against the rope that restrained them and came closer.

The man nodded and motioned to Martha. She untied Just-So and went triumphantly to the head of the line. The boy with the Hereford who had come in shortly after Martha early in the morning and a girl with another Black Angus were both in the race, too. Any one of them could win.

Martha was not worried about Just-So's condition. The calf had been tended with intelligence and care and showed it. She seemed somehow to understand what was going on and to be anxious to show at her best. Her earlier nervousness had vanished. The greater the tension and crowd-excitement of the farmers and buyers around her, the better she behaved.

There were only four calves left

in the contest. Soon there were only three; then two—the Hereford and Just-So. Martha watched the judges, trying to guess what they wanted her to do as she led Just-So back and forth. Finally the chief judge stepped over. He spoke with unconcern. But his words were wonderful.

"Pull her out, sister," he said.

There was a murmur, a stir, a movement in the crowd as Martha went ahead with her heifer. She herself could hardly believe it. Just-So was a prize winner in her class. And now she was to be considered for Grand Champion.

This was the big moment. The crowd understood and pressed in closer. Martha could hear them talking all around her, farmers commenting shrewdly on the points of each animal, folks asking who the owner was. The name Burning Branch came now and then to her ears. Because of her youth and smallness she was the general favorite. Besides, her bearing impressed them all. She was alert and attentive. She moved quickly at the request of the judges.

"Yes, sir, fourteen years old, I am. Burning Branch School. Her name? Just-So's her name. Just-So. That's right. Six fifty. Yes,

sir, that's correct. Why now, she was dropped last June, late last June."

Faces in the crowd smiled at Martha encouragingly; she was the favorite. A little blonde girl in a saucy blue cap, a blue mackinaw, and blue jeans, she caught and held their attention. All around her Martha could hear voices, and the sound of her name and her father's. If only Pa were here! If only he could see her! For now they were being judged for Grand Champion, the last four—a Shorthorn, a Hereford, another Black Angus, and Just-So.

Following the instructions of the judges, she walked the heifer around in the narrowing circle. There was not much room. One of the judges turned to the crowd, half appealingly, half in command.

"Stand back there, folks, stand back, will ya please? Give the

little girl a chance." The crowd scattered back behind the ropes. With more room, Martha moved about easily, leading her heifer by the halter. She stopped, she went ahead. Just-So immediately stepped out with her. Their understanding was obvious. The girl loved the heifer and the heifer loved the girl. When she paused, the calf without a word from her stopped also, standing with her four feet planted securely, head up, a short-legged, deep-bodied, well-made animal.

The judge, with his hat pulled down over his eyes, stood concentrating, squinting first at one animal, then another. He stepped across to Just-So, felt the calf's haunches, her hocks, her shoulders. He was so absorbed in his job he could have been out there alone with the four calves and their owners. That was all he saw.

"Mighty nice heifer," said a farmer in the crowd.

"Yeah, shore, shore," replied someone else. "Only a calf's jest a rack to hang meat on."

Martha turned, annoyed. No, she isn't either! Just-So is my heifer. She's mine, she's no rack. She's perfect. You wait and see. Yet when she glanced at them from the corner of her eyes, she realized the other calves were just as good-looking.

Martha and Just-So had one advantage over the others. The other heifers did not obey their owners as well as Just-So. Occasionally one of them had to yank a calf, to speak sharply as they went round and round the narrowing circle. Martha never pulled, seldom spoke, and then always in an undertone. Those long hours of work, those days and days of practice, leading the calf across the pasture on a halter, those endless hours of fall and winter, when the show seemed far off and not very important, now began to pay. Round they went, the girl and the three boys, their hands close to their animals' heads. People broke through the rope once more, tightening the circle, pressing closer, commenting on the good points of each calf, admiring, criticizing.

The three judges stood at one side, with their heads together. Then, quite without warning, with no sign or signal, one of the judges left the group and walked across to Just-So.

He fastened a knot of fluttering blue ribbon to the heifer's halter. Grand Champion!

A spontaneous burst of applause broke from the tightly packed circle, from the crowd watching on the roadway leading to the street. People began running toward them from every direction. The farmers clapped loudly, agreeing with the choice. They were delighted. Nice calf. Nice little girl, too. Done a good job. Grand Champion!

In a moment Martha was surrounded. A man, two men, three, four crowded upon her, asking questions. A photographer quickly ran ahead, fell upon one knee, and began snapping the calf and its owner. Bang went a flash, bang-bang! Behind the circle of people she saw Kendall Butcher and the other boys from school shouting and throwing their caps in the air. Now the men were leading her back inside the building again, asking question after question.

She hesitated. The name of the farm? "Why now, we just haven't any name, our farm hasn't. The Heiskell place up Burning Branch a ways, that's all."

She went proudly into the shed,

286

folks making way for her, looking at her and at Just-So with admiring eyes, calling to her in friendly, warm tones. The calf followed obediently, the blue ribbon hanging from the halter.

FIRST PREMIUM

PLANT CITY FAT CALF SHOW

Now Martha was heading toward the ring filled with buyers, cattlemen and farmers. They turned, respect evident in their glances and their voices. This was the Grand Champion!

"Everyone clear out! Everyone clear out 'ceptin' only the buyers," a voice shouted.

It was the auctioneer, who stood in front of the microphone. The auction ring was in the center of the stockyard, a square place filled with sawdust, wooden stands on three sides jammed with spectators. Boys climbed and hauled themselves up onto the rafters overhead. The auctioneer was in the front row of the stands, in the center. Mr. Sam's friendly face was there in the front row beside him.

The auctioneer beckoned toward Martha with a smile. She found herself unable to smile back. Sell Just-So? she was thinking. Why, I dunno—I never thought of that.

I never figured to sell Just-So. No, that's impossible. I couldn't sell my best friend.

Martha realized that, as Grand Champion, Just-So would draw a fancy price. There would be stiff bidding. Cattle prices were high, and the heifer was worth a lot of money. Only Martha had never thought of Just-So as money. She had been a friend and companion.

Still and all, there might be enough from the sale to help carry the family along until the crops came in, maybe longer. Enough to buy that lime and fertilizer Johnny was always talking about, the phosphate he had set his heart on for the soil. But she couldn't sell Just-So. That would be selling someone you loved. Yet all the time Martha knew there was nothing else to do. She was a farm girl, and animals, she realized, were meant to be sold.

The auctioneer beckoned her to come over to the opposite stand. She saw that the program was being broadcast, and was prepared to answer as he held the microphone down and asked her some questions, the same questions. Then she went back again across the sawdust ring to Just-So. The calf rubbed her muzzle into Martha's arm. Tears came to the girl's eyes.

Then the auctioneer went into his chant, meaningless to Martha. She hardly heard his raucous tones shouting those peculiar noises or the bids from the stand or his entreaties as the price rose.

"Thirty-six bid . . . thirty-six . . . thirty-six coming up . . . anyone offer thirty-eight . . . who'll offer thirty-eight . . . thirty-eight! Forty coming up, folks . . ."

All she saw was Just-So and the blue ribbon on her halter as they walked around the ring. The heifer seemed unaware of her fate, only anxious to show at her best for Martha. Martha felt she had betrayed her.

Then, as quickly as it had begun, it was over. The sale had been made. She heard the voice of the auctioneer and the sharp rap of his hammer.

"Sold for forty to Mr. Jesse Carter of Plainville."

Someone grasped her arm, took the halter from her hand, and led her toward the passageway to the weighing room at the far end of the stockyard. Now Martha was crying openly.

A man who sat at a table took down her name and address, asking the same questions she had been asked all day long. He read the weight of the heifer from the tag, put down some figures. He glanced up and saw Martha's face.

"You kinda fond o' that calf, ain't ya, sister? Kinda hate to see her go. Don't worry; don't take on. You'll find your daddy'll be mighty proud of you. He'll buy you a-plenty o' new ones."

He began to figure out loud. "Lessee now! That's—why, that's over two hundred dollars. Two hundred and sixty dollars. Then there's the Valley Cattle Growers' prize of fifty bucks, and that National Steer Co-operative prize, that's fifty more. That's three hundred and sixty. There—sign your name where it says owner, please. There's a good girl. Just let me check those figgers a minute. Yes —three hundred and sixty dollars. You the owner, ain't ya? And your dad's name? Oh, I see. Well, your brother's then."

Martha had no purse with her. She had never expected anything like this, never imagined parting with Just-So. Wrapping the money in a roll, she stuffed it into the pocket of her mackinaw. Sobs came as she stepped from the stockyard door.

"Hey there, girl!"

The man opened the door and hurried after her. "Don't you want your blue ribbon?" He handed it to her.

She stood, unable to move. She hated the blue ribbon. She hated the man and the horrible gibbering, grinning auctioneer and the three judges and the crowd and the roll of bills in her pocket. Most of all, she hated herself.

Grasping at the ribbon, she snatched it from him, stuffed it into the other pocket of her mackinaw, and went up the path toward the highway.

Dark was over the farm when she finally turned in at the front gate after the ride and the long walk up from the bus stop. The family glanced at her from around the fire as she entered the room. Grandpappy was reading the newspaper. Johnny as usual was studying a booklet from the Agricultural College. Her mother was getting supper. Without a word Martha put the roll of bills on the table and the blue ribbon beside them. She flung her mackinaw half across the room. Without a word to anyone, she rushed into the other room and threw herself on the bed, crying.

Finally her mother entered and sat down on the bed beside her. "We've been talking it over Martha. We want to get that calf back for you. Do you happen to know who bought her?"

"Yes—yes, I do. Mr. Jesse Carter of Plainville."

Ma Heiskell rose and went to the door of the room. "Jesse Carter of Plainville," she called out.

Martha heard her Grandpappy's cracked tones. "Jesse Carter! Why, I know Jesse sence we was boys. Years ago him and me usta hunt together in the far woods t'other side of the mountain. C'mon, son! Let's go harness up them mules. We gotta see Jesse right away and get Just-So back."

Her mother returned and sat down again. "Don't you worry none, Martha; it'll be all right. They're going down to see Jesse Carter and get your heifer back again."

"But Ma, the money! We need that money terrible bad."

"Not like we did yesterday. Johnny's done sold six tons of that hay he grew on the upper pasture last summer for forty dollars a ton. We're all right for a while without the money from your heifer. Anyhow, Just-So's coming back to the farm."

Expressing Your Opinion

Do you think this story gives an example of a good family spirit? Give reasons for your answer.

List three ways in which the author made you feel that you were really present at the fair yourself. Copy sentences to illustrate your answer.

Understanding Dialect

You have noticed that John R. Tunis, the author of "Just-So," used dialect to make the story more realistic. Copy the list of words which appeared in the story and beside them write the correct spelling.

1. shore
2. ain't
3. 'ceptin'
4. dunno
5. usta
6. kinda
7. gotta
8. ya
9. c'mon
10. lessee
11. figgers
12. t'other

Noting Relationships

Complete these sentence-beginnings correctly by matching them with their proper endings.

Column I. Results

1. _____ Martha was more quiet than usual because
2. _____ Martha could scarcely hold the cup of hot coffee in her hand because
3. _____ Martha was delighted to see Mr. Sam because
4. _____ Martha was very nervous when
5. _____ Martha was a general favorite because
6. _____ Martha and Just-So had an advantage over the others because
7. _____ A photographer snapped pictures of the girl and the calf because
8. _____ Martha was upset when the auction began because
9. _____ Martha did not want the money or the blue ribbon because

Column II. Causes

a. she felt she had been untrue to her friend.
b. Just-So was named Grand Champion.
c. she was taking her heifer to the Fat Calf Show.
d. she hadn't thought of selling her calf.
e. it was bitterly cold and the raw wind was whistling through the shed.
f. the other heifers did not obey their owners.
g. he was her 4-H leader and friend.
h. the chief judge walked up and down surveying the cattle.
i. she was young and smart, alert, and attentive.

AMY LOWELL

Trades

I WANT to be a carpenter,
To work all day long in clean wood,
Shaving it into little thin slivers
Which screw up into curls behind my plane;
Pounding square, black nails into white boards,
With the claws of my hammer glistening
Like the tongue of a snake.
I want to shingle a house,
Sitting on a ridgepole, in a bright breeze.
I want to put the shingles on neatly,
Taking great care that each is directly between two others.
I want my hands to have the tang of wood:
Spruce, cedar, cypress.
I want to draw a line on a board with a flat pencil,
And then saw along that line,
With the sweet-smelling sawdust piling up in a yellow heap at my feet.
That is the life!

Heigh-ho!
It is much easier than to write this poem.

Steppin's First Public Appearance

To SEE Steppin Stebbins racing down the street one warm afternoon in June, no one would have believed that he was on his way to school. Every other school day in the whole year it had needed his mother's warning, "You'll be late," and his little sister Mary Ellis' constant scolding to get Steppin through his lunch and back to his desk before the tardy bell rang. But this day was different.

It was the last day of school. No more lessons, no more homework, no more scrambling out of bed in a hurry, nothing but fun for two blessed months! But it was not so much the thought of freedom to come as the great event of that very afternoon that made Steppin hurry. For he was to do a solo tap dance at the closing exercises of his class. "My first public appearance," he thought proudly as he ran down the street.

A changing traffic light on Eighth Avenue brought him to an abrupt halt. Hopping up and down on the curb, Steppin stared impatiently at the stream of automobiles, trucks and street cars roaring by. The thunder of the elevated trains overhead, the clank and clatter of street cars and honks of taxis went unnoticed. His ears were tuned to city din.

> School is out
> Hear me shout,

he crooned under his breath, while his feet beat out a tap in the same rhythm. Brush, brush, hop with his right foot, and brush, brush, hop with the left foot, over and over. As he danced Steppin kept an eye on the green signal light. Was it going to stay that way all day? Wouldn't it ever turn red?

At last it changed and Steppin darted across the street like a flash and scurried down the street. Out of habit he looked up at the street clock which generally told him he was in danger of being late. But today he saw that it had taken him only five minutes to come this far. As school was only two blocks away, Steppin slowed down to a walk and stopped before his favorite window, the pawn shop.

Treasures of all kinds were heaped together in the dusty shop window; tennis rackets, telescopes, banjos, roller skates, and shiny gold watches. Steppin usually played a game before that window. He picked out the thing he would most like to buy if he could have all the money he wanted. He often spent a long time over that choice, weighing values carefully. But this day he paid no attention to the wonderful display. He had caught sight of his reflection in the gilt mirror that stood at the back of the showcase.

He eyed himself proudly. "Boy, I sure do look like a professional," he murmured, strutting a little and grinning broadly. His coffee-brown face, shining with the good scrubbing he had given it, grinned back at him, showing all of his ivory white teeth. His hair under the tight skull cap he wore was slicked so close to his skull that it looked as if it was painted on. His big black eyes took in the navy blue coat of his Sunday suit, the stiffly starched white shirt with a little black bow tie, and the white duck trousers which his friend Charley Kee, the Chinese laundryman, had pressed for him in exchange for errands. Steppin sighed with satisfied approval.

Steppin had pored over pictures of many Negro celebrities who performed in night clubs and theatres, and this costume was the best imitation of his idols that he could manage. Except for one thing he was greatly pleased with the elegant entertainer he saw reflected in the mirror. His dancing shoes were all wrong. He had no soft flexible slippers with metal taps on their tips like a real dancer. He wore a pair of old sneakers and had stuck a cluster of thumbtacks in the tip of each sole to use for taps. They did pretty well, but Steppin was not satisfied with them.

"Oh, well, you can't have everything at once, I suppose," he consoled himself. "Anyway when I get to be a professional I'm going to have six dozen pairs of dancing shoes at a time, with solid silver taps on every single one of them. Even platinum, if I want to."

Steppin's dreams of the future carried him happily on to school. A few boys were playing ball in the playground. They called out to Steppin to play with them. "Not a chance," thought Steppin, not when he was about to make his first public appearance as a dancer. He must keep his clothes in order for an occasion like this. So he entered the large brick building and ran up the stairs to his classroom.

Steppin hardly recognized the familiar room, it looked so festive with garlands of evergreens on the walls and bowls of flowers on the window sills. Some of the girls, who were helping the teacher, Miss Blair, decorate the room, looked festive too, in their frilly dresses of pink and blue and white, their hair gay with bows of bright ribbons. Miss Blair herself, in a blue silk dress, with her blond hair fluffed out around her face, looked young as a girl, Steppin thought.

Miss Blair's desk had been taken away, and two big jars of lilacs stood one on each side of the platform. A bright poster painted by some of the children served as a backdrop. Steppin surveyed the room with approval. It looked almost like a stage.

But suddenly he thought of the moment when he would have to step up there before all the boys and girls. Cold shivers went up his spine. A strange sinking feeling gripped him in the stomach. He was scared! Steppin had never thought of that.

"Oh, my gosh, I've got to make good, and here I am as jumpy as a cat," he thought as he slid into his seat. His own name, Stephen A. Stebbins, seemed to jump at him from the neatly printed program on his desk. He stared at it and clenched his clammy hands under the desk.

While the other boys and girls, demure and solemn in their best clothes, took their seats, Steppin anxiously went over in his mind the dance routine he had so carefully worked out. He counted out the steps to the tune of *Marching through Georgia* which his sister, Mary Ellis, was to play for his accompaniment. Brush, brush, hop and brush, brush, hop; and heel and toe and break. "Gee, I wish I could have a tune with some snap to it," he thought. But the few selections which Mary Ellis could play by ear on their wheezy old organ at home did not include pieces with snap.

In a daze Steppin heard Miss Blair make her little opening speech and then announce: "Now we will have the first number on our program, a recitation of Kipling's poem *If*, by Martin Bruce, Junior." Martin had been speaking that piece on every school program since he was in the fourth grade and never yet had been able to get through all the "ifs" without help. Steppin had never before felt the slightest interest in his struggles, but now he found himself waiting in an agony of suspense every time Martin hesitated. When for the fourth time he began with "Eff you can" and stopped, open mouthed, with imploring eyes fixed on Miss Blair, Steppin knew how he felt. Suppose I forget my dance steps! But Miss Blair, with whispered prompting, urged Martin on to the final line which he knew by heart and which he spoke in ringing tones. "AND WHAT IS MORE, YOU'LL BE A MAN, MY SON."

Steppin's place was fifth on the program. It had seemed a long way down the list, but now the time was coming, quickly, surely, when he would have to get up on the platform and dance. He saw Mary Ellis come in quietly and take a seat. She had been excused early from her class so that she might play for him. Oh, if only something had happened to keep her from coming! But there she was, smiling at him as calmly as though he were not crazy with stage fright and about to be disgraced before the whole school.

The sweet, clear notes of a cornet recalled Steppin from his miserable thoughts. That was David Harmon and he was playing the Schubert *Serenade*. David was a member of their school orchestra and was an old hand at public appearances. Watching him standing there so easy and calm, Steppin felt sick with envy and fright. "Oh, my gosh, why didn't I practice more on cartwheels, so I could do a cart-wheel, then go into a split to finish the act? I could try, maybe, but like as not I'd land on my head and a fine finale that would be."

The last soft note of the *Serenade* died away. David bowed grace-fully to the class and returned to his seat. "That was lovely, David." Miss Blair rose and beamed on him, then, still smiling, she looked over at Steppin. "Next on our program will be a tap dance by Stephen A. Stebbins, and"—she smiled at Mary Ellis—"his little sister will play his accompaniment."

Like one in a dream Steppin found himself getting to his feet, while before him the big yellow bow on Mary Ellis' hair bobbed up as she rose and went to the piano. His knees trembled and his legs felt like cooked noodles, thought Steppin miserably, but somehow he mounted the platform and bowed gravely. This wasn't a bit the way he had dreamed it—this horrible nightmare. Mary Ellis struck the first chord. To his surprise his feet responded, al-though they felt like solid blocks of wood. Mechanically he went through the simple steps of his dance. In a few moments he forgot the staring boys and girls in front of him and began to dance as though his life depended on it. He thought of nothing but the rhythm and the beat of his dancing feet. He varied his few steps with pantomime, making himself very tall, then letting his arms hang perfectly limp from his shoulders so that they flapped queerly with every step. Someone giggled. Then a wave of chuckles swept over the classroom. That did it. It was all fun now. Joyously he hopped and whirled. No longer afraid, he varied his pantomime, now grin-ning at his audience, now looking very solemn.

He had just completed a quick whirl on one foot and was finishing with a split when he felt a stinging in the soles of his feet. Steppin knew very well what that meant. The thumbtacks were working up through the soles of his sneakers! Every time he hopped the pain grew sharper. Brush, brush, tap; brush, brush, tap, ouch! Steppin nearly yelled out with pain. "I can't give up, the show has got to go on," he reminded himself, like

an old trouper. And all the while his feet tapped and his face wore a stiff frozen smile.

Then one of the boys began clapping in time to the music. Soon others joined in, marking the beat. "Boy, they're with me. I got to go on if it kills me." Steppin flashed his white teeth in a bright agonized grin and spread out his hands in an inviting gesture to his friends. The whole room broke into clapping. Almost over now, thought Steppin gratefully. Mary Ellis was loudly pounding out the last chorus —"Hurrah, hurrah, the flag that makes us free."

Suddenly Steppin tripped! The thumbtacks in his shoes had caught on a rough spot of the floor. Quick as a flash, even as he stumbled, Steppin knew there was only one thing to do. He threw out his arms, and, hurling himself forward with all his might, tried to turn his fall into a cartwheel. He felt himself flying through space and in the next instant he was teetering on his feet, gasping for breath as he slid to the floor in a fast split.

In a daze he heard the loud applause and suddenly he realized that in his cartwheel he had flung himself right off the platform. A pleased grin spread from ear to ear. "Well, tie my shoes! I didn't know I had it in me."

Just then Mary Ellis, who had gone placidly on with her piece, struck the last chord with a resounding thump. Steppin scrambled to his feet, bowed politely as Miss Blair had taught him, and limped to his seat. The continued clapping was music in his ears. He looked over at Miss Blair who smiled and nodded encouragingly. Steppin rose and bowed again with a flourish, glowing with pride and happiness.

The program continued, but Steppin hardly heard or saw what was going on, though he clapped heartily for each performer. He was lost in a haze of glory and triumph. "Boy, applause sure is jam on my bread," he chuckled while he slyly removed the torturing thumbtacks from his shoes. "From now on, nothing is going to stop me. I'm going to be a first-class dancer or bust."

Proving Statements

Here are some statements about characters and events in the story. Read them and then write a fact which you remember to prove the statement.

1. Steppin was a regular boy and Mary Ellis was a typical sister.

2. Steppin was unusually happy on this particular day.

3. Steppin was quite proud of himself.

4. Only one thing kept Steppin from being pleased with his outfit.

5. Steppin was clever at making things "do."

6. Steppin didn't enjoy the first four numbers on the program very much.

7. David Harmon didn't mind appearing with his cornet before the class.

8. Steppin's feet began to trouble him.

9. Steppin covered up his error and the audience did not detect it.

10. The children enjoyed Steppin's performance.

JOYCE KILMER

Main Street

I LIKE to look at the blossomy track of the moon upon the sea,
But it isn't half so fine a sight as Main Street used to be
When it all was covered over with a couple of feet of snow,
And over the crisp and radiant road the ringing sleighs would go.

Now, Main Street bordered with autumn leaves, it was a pleasant thing,
And its gutters were gay with dandelions early in the spring;
I like to think of it white with frost or dusty in the heat,
Because I think it is humaner than any other street.

A city street that is busy and wide is ground by a thousand wheels,
And a burden of traffic on its breast is all it ever feels;
It is dully conscious of weight and speed and of work that never ends,
But it cannot be human like Main Street, and recognize its friends.

There were only about a hundred teams on Main Street in a day,
And twenty or thirty people, I guess, and some children out to play.
And there wasn't a wagon or buggy, or a man or a girl or boy
That Main Street didn't remember, and somehow seem to enjoy.

The truck and the motor and trolley car and the elevated train,
They make the weary city street reverberate with pain:
But there is yet an echo left deep down within my heart
Of the music the Main Street cobblestones made beneath a butcher's
    cart.

God be thanked for the Milky Way that runs across the sky,
That's the path that my feet would tread whenever I have to die.
Some folks call it a Silver Sword, and some a Pearly Crown,
But the only thing I think it is, is Main Street, Heaventown.

Little Leaguer

STEVE DONOVAN is a pitcher for a Little League baseball team that is known in the town of Longview as the Cherokees. He is twelve years old, weighs one hundred and twenty pounds, lives at the corner of Gilmore and Oakley, and is in the seventh grade at St. Mary's School. He is proud of two things—his crew haircut and his Cherokee uniform.

Steve is no Johnnie-come-lately to baseball. When he was eight the Cherokees accepted him as bat boy for their midget team, not because of his speed or his skill, but because he was under their feet all the time and they decided to put him to work. All went well until he tripped on the bat one day and hurt his jaw. He didn't cry. "It's a good thing I didn't break my pitching arm," he said, as he picked himself up from the dusty diamond.

"You never pitched a ball in your life," a Cherokee taunted him.

"Wait and see," said Steve. "I will someday."

When he was ten the Cherokees gave him a tryout. He came home bursting with pride. "I'm an athlete now," he told his mother.

It didn't take long for his mother to notice the change in Steve. She smiled, but said nothing when he began to watch his diet, as was suggested in the Little League's manual. Steve now drank milk without protest and even avoided the between-meal snacks he had once consumed, such as potato chips, peanut-butter sandwiches, doughnuts, cold drinks, ice-cream cones, candy bars, popcorn, cupcakes, and large and hard portions of overcooked fudge made by his sister Betsy.

Steve became a pitcher when he was twelve. "We'll win the Little League world championship this year," he boasted to his father, for the boy had set his goal on the day when the Cherokees would clinch the local pennant and get a chance to compete in the Little League's national competition at Williamsport, Pennsylvania.

"That's the spirit," said his

301

father, but he kept watching the team at practice.

"How am I doing, Dad?" Steve asked him one day.

A former semi-pro player himself, Steve's father had seen at once the boy's weakness. "You're a pretty good righthander," he told him, "but you'll have to learn to field your position."

"I'll keep at it," Steve assured him.

In Steve's bedroom there hung a clipping from a magazine story about the Little Leagues that had been written by Bob Feller when he was pitching for the Cleveland Indians. The clipping read:

TO THE PLAYERS

Know the rules. Read and study as many books as you can on baseball fundamentals.

Concentrate on one position, but be prepared to play another when necessary.

Work to overcome your playing weakness rather than practice your strong points.

Steve knew these instructions by heart. He repeated them to his father. "That's good advice, isn't it, Dad?"

"It's fine advice," said his father, "but add one more line to it."

"What's that?"

"Play without fear; lose without anger," said his father. "That's a bit of wisdom that is older than I am."

"I don't want to lose," Steve protested.

His father put his arm across the boy's shoulders. "Steve," he said, "the moment you lose a game may be the greatest test of your character."

Steve stiffened in resentment. "I don't want to fail the Cherokees," he said.

His father swung the boy around so that they faced each other. "Fear is the worst handicap you can have in life," he said, "and you're afraid you'll lose, aren't you?"

"Of course I'm scared," Steve admitted. "I heard one of the umpires call me a choke-up guy. I know what that means. It's a player who fails in the clutch."

"What does that matter, if a boy has given his best?" There was anger in the man's voice. "Baseball is a game, not a matter of life or death."

"Don't you want me to play?" Steve stormed. "Are you going to act like Butch Barry's father? He won't let Butch stay on the team anymore."

"Why?"

"Aw, Butch cried himself sick one night when he lost the game for us."

"Then Butch shouldn't be playing. There are more important things in life than winning a ball game, and the greatest of these is a sense of values."

"What d'ya mean, Dad?"

The man looked up at the clipping on the wall. "I am sure that Bob Feller wanted every boy to know that for most of us baseball is just a form of recreation. He'd tell you, if he were here, that no one should be punished for losing a fly in the sun or be rewarded for hitting a home run. He would—"

"Bob Feller really said that," Steve cut in. "I read it somewhere. The Little League says so, too."

"That's good," said his father, "but some of you lads get so cocky about being the heroes of the diamond that you can't take defeat."

Steve shuffled his right foot nervously. "Dad, were you ever scared when you played ball?" he asked.

His father laughed. "Scared? I was scared stiff!" he admitted.

303

"Did you ever lose?"

"More times than I won, boy."

"Did you quit playing?"

"I stayed with the game."

Steve smiled. "Then I'll stick with your motto," he said, and repeated, "Play without fear; lose without anger."

"It's a good slogan, Steve."

"Can I say it in my own words?"

"What are they?"

The boy hesitated for a minute, then said, "Grin when you win; grin when you lose."

His father patted him on the back. "No matter which way the chips fall, you'll be a winner if you live up to that slogan," he said.

On the day that Steve Donovan pitched for the Cherokees all of Longview seemed to be at the local field at the edge of the town. Cars, bicycles and baby carriages crowded nearby streets and vacant lots, for the Little League team was a community project, sponsored by the members of the Longview Merchant's Association.

"The kids are nothing but walking ads for the Kwality Shoe Store and the Valley Barber Shop," a neighbor of the Donovans had protested to Steve's mother.

Mrs. Donovan rose swiftly to defend the merchants. "You should be as happy as we are," she told the woman, "that the men of this town have enough interest in the boys to pay for their uniforms."

On the Cherokee team were a Jewish catcher, several Protestant boys, and three Catholics, including Steve Donovan. Among the players of different races and creeds were the Longview banker's son, the plumber's boy, a fireman's younger brother, and a boy whose father was no longer able to work. "This is democracy at its grass roots," the mayor of Longview once said.

"I wouldn't miss this game," Steve's sister Betsy confided to her dearest friend Margie as they followed Steve's father through the crowd.

"It's out of this world," gasped Margie, who always spoke in superlatives.

A shouting crowd greeted the Cherokees as they came out of the dugout. A thinner cry came forth in tribute to the Grizzlies, who had come from nearby Catesville. Everyone watched as Coach Jerry Murphy of the Cherokees set the line-up and gave last minute instructions. Betsy eyed the rival nine. "Take a look at the Grizzly who's getting up to bat," she directed Margie. "He's making like Carl Furillo, clamping a wad of gum on the button of his cap."

Margie giggled. "Take a look at Steve," she said. "He makes like Mickey Mantle; he's chewing bubble gum!"

They watched Steve go out to the mound to throw the first ball. The Cherokee catcher, Bennie Herman, waited for the pitch.

"Bennie's good," said Steve's father.

Betsy caught a troubled note in her father's voice. "Isn't Steve?" she asked.

"Steve's good, too," he assured her quietly, "but he isn't seasoned. Don't expect too much of him yet."

The late afternoon game went on. Lights came on in the town, shining from the box factory and the telephone company's exchange and from the tall antennae of the radio station. As they went into the next to the last inning, the score was 1–0 in favor of the Cherokees. Slowly, surely, Steve's arm again came down in an arc. The ball leaped to the plate.

"Strike one!"

The batter set himself, expecting more speed, but Steve's ball wasn't speeding. It floated, drifted, and the batter swung in vain.

"Strike two!"

Slowly, with the appearance of great ease, Steve pitched. This time the batter, waiting for a moment too long, let it go by.

"You're out!"

The Longview crowd began to cheer. The noise grew in volume as the second batter, hitting under a fast ball, fouled out the catcher. "'Atta boy, Donovan!" roared the Cherokee fans.

"Steve's a living doll," shrieked Margie.

"He's a choke-up guy," jeered a Grizzly fan standing in front of her. "I've watched the kid in practice. There's no speed in him, and his pace is always the same."

Another pitch and the third batter swung. He topped the ball and it struck in front of the plate and dribbled toward the mound. Steve, coming in fast, made a stab at the ball, but he fumbled. The ball slipped away. A runner was on first.

The fourth batter came up and, like the first two, went down.

The crowd roared. Steve left the mound and sat in the dugout, watching tensely as the Cherokees failed to score on the last half of the inning.

In the first half of the final inning

305

Steve was still holding his ground. He let go a fast ball. The batter swung and got only a piece of it, so that it fell in front of the plate and rolled slowly inside the third-base line. Steve grabbed it and hurled it wildly over the head of the stretching first baseman. The runner went on down to second.

Now Steve was back on the mound. He kept the ball high and close. As the ball left his hand, he saw the slight shift of the batter's hands. "He's going to bunt," he told himself and was off the mound before the ball hit the ground.

"That's an easy bunt to field," said Steve's father to Betsy. "The bunt rolled almost halfway to the mound." However, he watched the boy closely, tensely, knowing that split-second action would be required. But Steve wasn't quick enough, and runners were now on first and third.

In his effort to keep the ball high, Steve walked the next batter. The bases were loaded with nobody out.

The next batter came up and Steve let fly another fast ball. The batter bunted. With unsteady hand Steve reached for the ball. Then suddenly, clumsily, tripping over his right foot, clutching at thin air, the boy sprawled on the ground. Two runs came in.

"Donovan's blowing the game!" rose the bitter cry from the Cherokee fans. "Take him out!"

Another pitcher, Don Crandall, came out of the bull pen and walked toward the mound. Steve handed him the ball and then, head up and shoulders high as if he did not hear the jeers of the crowd, walked toward the dugout.

Betsy Donovan was crying.

"Now stop that!" said her father sternly. "You're not too young to learn that you'll always find ups and downs in life."

"What happened to Stevie?" murmured Margie.

No one explained.

"He lost, didn't he?" she whispered to Betsy.

"So what?" Betsy challenged her.

In their half of the last inning the Cherokees got one man on base but failed to score. The final score was posted: Grizzlies 2, Cherokees 1.

Pushing through the homegoing crowd, Steve's father walked toward the dugout. There was no sign of Steve. Other players, back in blue jeans and sweaters, drifted past him. The Grizzlies, elated by unexpected triumph, whooped by like conquering heroes. Umpires came out. Then came the coach, Jerry Murphy. "Take it easy on the boy," he urged Steve's father. "He'll learn the tricks of the game in time. One body blow doesn't kill a fighter. It just takes the wind out of him."

Steve's father was about to turn away when he saw his son coming toward him.

"Hi, Dad," said Steve. He was smiling!

"Hi, Steve," said his father.

Steve came closer. "I've got a lot to learn, haven't I?"

"You've plenty of time," his father comforted him.

"Guess I'm no Herb Score," said the Little Leaguer, "or a Sal Maglie or a Whitey Ford. The Grizzlies sure beat me today."

"There'll be other days—"

Steve clutched his father's arm. "I'll be back again," he said. "The fellows were swell to me, and the coach told me to report tomorrow. He wasn't mad. I told him I'd promised you to grin if I won and grin if I lost."

"That's the ticket, Steve," said his father.

The street lights were shining all over Longview as they left the baseball field. Betsy and Margie were waiting for them. "How about stopping at the Hamburger Corner?" asked Betsy. "Mom doesn't expect us home for supper."

"We'll celebrate," said Steve Donovan's father. "This boy won his toughest victory today."

"I lost," Steve reminded him.

His father corrected him. "No, you didn't lose, Steve," he said. "You'll always be the winner if you can smile when the odds are against you."

Steve grinned. "Let's eat," he said.

Proving Statements

Some of the statements given below are true and others are false. Copy on your papers those you think are true and then find the sentence in the story which proves it. Beside the true statements write the page and paragraph numbers of the sentence which proves the statements.

1. Steve Donovan, a twelve-year-old seventh grader at St. Mary's school, was a pitcher for the Grizzlies.

2. His mother noticed that after he made the team a change came over Steve.

3. Steve was a "hero-worshipper" of Bob Feller, who once pitched for the New York Giants.

4. Dad told Steve that baseball is merely a form of recreation.

5. The Cherokee team was made up of boys of all races and creeds.

6. Bennie Herman was the coach of the Cherokee team.

7. At the eighth inning the Cherokees were leading with a score of 1–0.

8. The Cherokees won the game with a score of 2–1.

9. Dad told Steve that one is always a winner if he can smile when he is losing.

ERNEST L. THAYER

Casey at the Bat

THE outlook wasn't brilliant for the Mudville nine that day;
The score stood four to two with but one inning more to play;
And so, when Cooney died at first, and Barrows did the same,
A sickly silence fell upon the patrons of the game.

A straggling few got up to go in deep despair. The rest
Clung to the hope which springs eternal in the human breast;
They thought, if only Casey could but get a whack, at that,
They'd put up even money now, with Casey at the bat.

But Flynn preceded Casey, as did also Jimmy Blake,
And the former was a pudding, and the latter was a fake;
So upon that stricken multitude grim melancholy sat,
For there seemed but little chance of Casey's getting to the bat.

But Flynn let drive a single, to the wonderment of all,
And Blake, the much despised, tore the cover off the ball;
And when the dust had lifted, and they saw what had occurred,
There was Jimmy safe on second, and Flynn a-hugging third.

Then from the gladdened multitude went up a joyous yell,
It bounded from the mountaintop, and rattled in the dell;
It struck upon the hillside and recoiled upon the flat;
For Casey, mighty Casey, was advancing to the bat.

There was ease in Casey's manner as he stepped into his place;
There was pride in Casey's bearing, and a smile on Casey's face;
And when, responding to the cheers, he lightly doffed his hat,
No stranger in the crowd could doubt 'twas Casey at the bat.

Ten thousand eyes were on him as he rubbed his hands with dirt,
Five thousand tongues applauded when he wiped them on his shirt;
Then while the writhing pitcher ground the ball into his hip,
Defiance gleamed in Casey's eye, a sneer curled Casey's lip.

And now the leather-covered sphere came hurtling through the air,
And Casey stood a-watching it in haughty grandeur there;
Close by the sturdy batsman the ball unheeded sped.
"That ain't my style," said Casey. "Strike one," the umpire said.

From the benches, black with people, there went up a muffled roar,
Like the beating of the storm waves on a stern and distant shore;
"Kill him! Kill the umpire!" shouted someone on the stand.
And it's likely they'd have killed him had not Casey raised his hand.

With a smile of Christian charity great Casey's visage shone;
He stilled the rising tumult; he bade the game go on;
He signaled to the pitcher, and once more the spheroid flew,
But Casey still ignored it, and the umpire said, "Strike two."

"Fraud!" cried the maddened thousands, and the echo answered,
    "Fraud!"
But a scornful look from Casey, and the audience was awed;
They saw his face grow stern and cold; they saw his muscles strain,
And they knew that Casey wouldn't let that ball go by again.

The sneer is gone from Casey's lips, his teeth are clenched in hate,
He pounds with cruel violence his bat upon the plate;
And now the pitcher holds the ball, and now he lets it go,
And now the air is shattered by the force of Casey's blow.

Oh! somewhere in this favored land the sun is shining bright,
The band is playing somewhere, and somewhere hearts are light;
And somewhere men are laughing, and somewhere children shout,
But there is no joy in Mudville—mighty Casey has struck out.

Emergency

In the days when automobiles were new and rare, there lived three lively children in a Midwestern village called Warsaw Junction. Martin and Henry were brothers; Ardeth Howard was the village doctor's daughter. Their days were filled with good intentions, which too often were misunderstood by their families and neighbors. When the children tried to give away some newly born puppies, it became a village project.

IT was Dr. Howard who finally solved the problem of what to do with two extra puppies.

"I have to make another visit on the mountain," he said. "I'll be only a few miles from Davey's cabin, and, if you wish, you can go along and we'll drive over to Davey's and see if he wants them."

Martin and Henry and Ardeth were wild with delight—not only to find such an ideal home for the dogs, but to have another day in the country with the doctor and a visit to Wild Davey in the bargain! Wild Davey was a hermit who loved animals.

They washed the taffy out of one puppy's coat and put iodine on the other one's nose, and packed them in a large covered basket. Henry wanted to put the lunch in the same basket to save space, but Martin and Ardeth feared there might be nothing left for themselves if they did.

It was cloudy this morning as they started, and the meadowlarks did not sing.

"The first cool day we've had in weeks," remarked the doctor. "Fall is not so far away now."

"And school, too," added Ardeth gloomily.

"Oh, school isn't so bad," said Martin. "I get lots of bright ideas for having fun in school."

Long before they reached Wild Davey's cabin they could hear his dogs. They were howling and whining very lamentably, and, in the darkness of the tall green pines on a cloudy day, the sound was most dismal.

311

"That's queer," said Dr. Howard. "Davey's dogs are usually very well behaved."

There was something in the air that made them frightened.

"What if Davey was hurt?" asked Ardeth.

"Just what I was thinking," said her father. "He cuts and handles logs that are far too big for one old man alone."

Some of the dogs ran out to bark at them; others continued to howl, with mouths open and muzzles pointed toward the sky. No figure of man with gun appeared in the open doorway.

Dr. Howard hastily tied the horse and, taking his medical kit with him, went into the house.

The children followed with the basket of puppies and the lunch.

The cabin, which had been so neat in appearance at their last visit, was now completely untidy. There were dark stains on the floor, the gun was propped carelessly against a chair, and on the homemade bed lay Wild Davey, his face as white as the long hair that fell about his shoulders. One of his feet was roughly bound in a bloodstained bandage, and there was a dark pool of blood beside the bed.

Dr. Howard spoke quietly to Davey. "You have had an accident. Can you tell me about it and let me examine your foot?"

The old man stirred and opened his eyes. He moved his lips several times before he could make the sounds come through.

"Och, Doctor," he said, "I don't know if ye've come in time. I'm a mighty bleeder."

The three children stood huddled beside the door, looking on with frightened eyes, while Dr. Howard bent over the old man's foot, working at the stiffened bandage with quick, sure fingers.

"Martin," said Dr. Howard briskly, "you and Henry build up a fire in the stove, and, Ardeth, see if there is water in the kettle. I want you to work fast now. We have no time to waste. I need boiling water."

They dropped their baskets and ran to obey orders, glad to be able to help. In a few moments a fire was roaring up the chimney and a kettle was beginning to sing.

"Get my other case, Ardeth. The one with the bandages in, you know."

"I was choppin' a tree," said Davey faintly. "I dinna ken wha' went wrong. I chopped my foot square open."

"All right, Davey," said Doctor Howard. "Don't talk now. You're a brave fellow, and we'll try to not let it hurt you. Clear the table children, and you'll have to help me lift him up there. The bed's too low to work on."

"Daddy, what are you going to do?" asked Ardeth fearfully.

"I'll have to take some stitches, Ardeth," said her father. "I'm sorry it had to happen like this when we were on an excursion, but a doctor's duties don't wait on his pleasures. This is an emergency and we only just came in time."

"I'm strong, Dr. Howard," said Martin. "I can help you lift him." The doctor looked at Martin appraisingly.

"Yes, you are," he said, "and you've got good nerves, too, haven't you, boy? I wonder if you could give the anesthetic for me?"

"I don't know what that is," said Martin, "but I could try."

Dr. Howard continued to look at him as if he were seeing him for the first time.

"It's giving chloroform," he said in a low voice. "A few drops on a sponge held over his nose, while I attend to his foot. It will keep him from feeling pain and struggling. But you would have to count the drops and keep a steady hand. I won't have time to watch you, and, if you get excited and pour too much, it might put him to sleep forever. Do you understand that?"

Martin stood straight and returned the doctor's gaze steadily. "Yes sir," he said in a firm voice. "I understand that."

Just then the kettle boiled over.

"You think you could do it, Martin?"

"Yes, sir, if you'll show me how."

Wild Davey weighed very little, they discovered, when they came to lift him. Dr. Howard could almost have managed to lift him alone, but it hurt him less to have the four of them do it. They put him on the long table, which he had hewn out of logs himself. But, even with all their care, the old man groaned and cried with the pain of moving his foot.

The doctor sterilized his instruments in the boiling water and laid them on a clean towel on a chair beside the table.

"Ardeth, can you help me, too?" asked her father gravely.

"I think I can, Daddy," said Ardeth a bit uncertainly, "but I wouldn't like to have to hold the sponge."

"All I want you to do is to pass me my instruments very quickly when I ask you for them. Are your hands clean?"

"I washed them with soap," said Ardeth.

"I guess I'll go outside and wait," said Henry. "I haven't got my lucky ring."

"You can see to the horse, Henry," said Dr. Howard. "Now, Martin, a drop at a time, on the sponge like this, and stop when-

ever I tell you to. It's a big responsibility, but I trust you. Are you ready?"

"Yes, sir," said Martin steadily.

His hand did not falter, tilting the bottle just enough to let the liquid drop on the sponge as the doctor told him. His eyes counted the drops. The heavy, sweetish odor rose up about them. Dr. Howard's skillful hands moved quickly, cutting away the ragged flesh, cleaning the deep gash with antiseptic, closing the wound with deft stitches. White as the bandage, Ardeth stood by and passed him the things he called for.

In twenty minutes' time Wild Davey's foot was cleaned and sewed together and wrapped in a sterilized bandage. They lifted Davey carefully back in bed, and then Ardeth lay quietly down on the floor and fainted.

"Tut-tut!" said Dr. Howard. "Throw some cold water on her face, Martin. It's the smell of the chloroform and the sight of blood. Poor child! I never should have let her do it, but I don't know how I could have managed without the two of you. I'm afraid she'll never make a trained nurse."

Sprinkling water in Ardeth's face, Martin looked up eagerly at Dr. Howard. "Do you think I'll ever make a doctor?" he asked.

"Yes," said Dr. Howard, "I think that you will make a very good one."

When Ardeth sat up a moment later, she saw them shaking hands.

The children stayed with Davey while Dr. Howard drove a few miles to a near-by homestead to get one of the older girls of the family to come to cook and care for Davey until he was better. She promised to care for the puppies, too, until Davey was up and around again.

"I'll be back tomorrow to dress Davey's foot," said the doctor, "and I'll bring all the old bones the butcher can spare for the dogs."

Ardeth and Henry chattered all the way home, for, now that the ordeal of being a surgical nurse was over, Ardeth felt quite gay and talkative. But Martin rode quietly beside Dr. Howard, sunk in his own dreams. The vision, which he had long cherished, of himself in smart cowboy attire, riding a spirited horse, roping cattle on the range, chasing wild horses, and perhaps holding up a train and distributing what he took from the rich among the needy poor—all of this had suddenly vanished. Now he saw himself driving his horse and buggy along winding country roads, and people ran out to him, holding up bleeding hands or feet, or called him inside to save the lives of little children who were very ill. He saw himself carrying a little black bag just like Dr. Howard's, and in it was all the magic of healing.

It would be a good many years before he was a man, but Martin knew now without a doubt what he was going to be. He looked at Dr. Howard out of the corner of his eye. The doctor was not a heroic figure like a cowboy. He was a little stooped and shabby, and now he looked tired as he let the horse take its own way home, the reins held slackly in the hands which had been so quick and sure with Davey's foot.

Martin breathed a long sigh and turned his head again to the front, where between the horse's ears the dusty white road was unrolling before him, a road that went over hills and through valleys and into the future.

Personal Experience

1. Martin, Henry, and Ardeth helped Dr. Howard during an emergency. Which of their jobs would you have chosen? Why?

2. Can you tell of a personal experience when you were required to help? Were you as capable and calm as Martin?

3. Tell what Christian principle you think this story especially portrays.

Word Meanings

Write interesting sentences, using each of the words listed below.

lamentably	appraisingly
dismal	anesthetic
sterilized	deft
antiseptic	cherished

316

T. S. ELIOT

Prelude I

THE winter evening settles down
With smell of steaks in passageways.
Six o'clock.
The burnt-out ends of smoky days.
And now a gusty shower wraps
The grimy scraps
Of withered leaves about your feet
And newspapers from vacant lots;
The showers beat
On broken blinds and chimney-pots,
And at the corner of the street
A lonely cab-horse steams and stamps.
And then the lighting of the lamps.

The Pastor of Sainte Anne's

UPON the front of the City Hall of Detroit the City Council has placed statues of four men who had, in earlier times, done more than any others for that settlement. The council named them in the order of their coming: Marquette, the missionary; LaSalle, the explorer; Cadillac, the founder of the city; and Father Gabriel Richard. Three of them died, as they had lived, citizens of France. Father Richard, born in France, came to the United States soon after our nation was established and became one of the most useful American citizens of his dangerous and daring time.

Father Richard, a Sulpician priest, was the pastor of the parish of Sainte Anne which covered the entire state of Michigan. Its pastor traveled every year as far east as Lake Erie, as far north as the Sault Sainte Marie, and as far west as the neighborhood of Chicago. He went on foot, in canoes, on trading schooners.

His first concern for his parish was education. He established a parish school, then an academy for young women and a seminary for young men, and, in 1817, was one of the founders of the University of Michigan. There were no Sisters in the Detroit of that time, and Father Richard himself taught the parish school.

And what he taught!

He taught his students to read and write in both French and English, to do arithmetic, to locate on maps the countries of the world and to know something of their histories.· Deciding that the boys and girls needed more training for the daily work of living, he taught them trades and handicraft arts. He brought a printing press from Baltimore—perhaps the first west of the Alleghenies—and used it to teach his students printing as he put out the first Catholic newspaper in the United States.

Before the end of the eighteenth century Detroit was one of the wildest towns of the frontier, a place where, at certain times of the year, Indians and whites, hunters and traders, came to buy or sell furs and firearms. One of Father Richard's first activities was the betterment of conditions in these camps. His success in this one-man campaign won for him the admiration of all law-abiding citizens of the town.

The opening of the Erie Canal poured great numbers of immigrants into Detroit. There, in the narrow bottleneck of traffic, thieves and tricksters robbed the strangers. Father Richard realized that the only way to combat this condition was to get the immigrants out to the farms they sought. To do this, roads must be built westward and northward. The pastor of Sainte Anne's worked early and late to get these roads under way. Meantime, he found food and shelter for the immigrants. He advised them whom to trust. He took them into court to claim their rights. Through the crucial years Father Richard was a tall, gaunt figure of justice, guarding the western crossroads.

Every Sunday afternoon Father Richard lectured in the Council House to people of all creeds. He spoke of Christian principles and their relation to good citizenship. He taught that every man who knew the truth must do everything in his power to spread the truth. Thanking God for the right of freedom of speech, he never used speech, either public or private, for anything but good.

Then someone in Detroit had the idea that a man who did so much for his community at home should be the representative of that community in Congress. In 1823 he was elected as representative from the Territory of Michigan. His campaign was one of the most hotly fought which that territory had ever seen; and it was noteworthy that he was elected largely by the votes of his non-Catholic neighbors.

In the Congress of the United States, in the years 1823 and 1824, Father Richard, the only priest ever elected to Congress, served upon Capitol Hill with some of the giants of American statesmanship—Henry Clay, James Buchanan, Sam Houston, and Daniel Webster. Always he moved among them with quiet dignity; but he sometimes broke the quiet by a speech which rang out his demands for justice, not only for his own people in Michigan, but for all the nation.

"Build roads!" was his cry. Build a road, a military road, between Detroit and Chicago. Build a road to Lake Michigan. Cut a wagon trail to the Grand River Valley. Build a road up to Lake Huron. Build, build that men and women may find new homes, that through these homes the nation may grow wide in size, as it is great in its foundation. Because the men in Congress heard and heeded him, they voted for the roads; and the course of the republic moved westward, not sluggishly now, but fast, with the Conestoga wagons racing where once the little Canadian ponies had made their difficult way.

Father Richard died as he had lived—in the service of his fellow men. When Asiatic cholera, one of the most terrible of all plagues, came to Detroit in the summer of 1832, Father Richard devoted himself to the sick and dying. For two months he allowed himself no real rest. He turned one of the church buildings into a hospital. There he nursed everyone brought to him. Day and night, he went through the streets on his way to the bedsides of those who summoned him. He scorned caution, ran all risks. "Who am I," he once asked, "to deny the call of anyone for whom my Savior died?" He himself died as he would have wished, helping others in the name of Christ, Who helps all men.

The parish of Sainte Anne still stands in the city of Detroit. Its boundaries now are measured by city blocks, not by the Great Lakes which Father Richard sailed to visit his parishioners. Great factories have risen within it. Tens of thousands of men and women go to work every day through streets which were only trails in the old days. A new civilization, a civilization of wheels and engines and motors, has replaced the old ways of canoes and sailboats and blossoming pear trees in the French gardens; but the Cross of Christ still glistens high above the Detroit River that was once the waterway of the *voyageurs.*

Classifying Facts

Prepare three columns on your paper. Mark one *Priest,* the second *Teacher,* the third *Citizen.* List the facts you learned about Father Gabriel Richard under these three main headings

Drawing Conclusions

Choose the two *best* answers to complete this statement:

From this account of the life of Father Richard, I learned that
a. Detroit was one of the wildest towns of the frontier;
b. religion and education are both powerful influences in producing a good citizen;
c. there were no Sisters in Detroit at this time;
d. Father Richard was devoted to his duties;
e. love of God and service of one's neighbor go hand in hand.

8. Long May Our Land Be Bright

EVERY one of us has heard and thrilled to the Air Force song, "Here we go into the wild blue yonder."

It has been the theme song of our time, the era of high adventure, and of our nation, the land of high adventurers. For just as their forefathers used their freedom to ride covered wagons over prairie grass and desert plains, Americans today have widened that freedom by sailing ships over faraway seas and by lifting planes into distant skies.

The spirit of American freedom has moved far beyond the towns where it was born. It has gone up to the Arctic, down to the Antarctic, far down in the Pacific. It has not interfered with the lives and ways of other peoples, but it has vastly enlarged the American mind. Tahiti and Fairbanks are as near to Chicago now, as Philadelphia was to Boston in 1776.

Stories of American adventure have written great names in the record of American achievement; but no one has given greater service to God and country than have those supreme adventurers, the American missionary priests and Sisters who have carried the Cross to the people of distant lands.

WILLIAM CULLEN BRYANT

America

Oh mother of a mighty race,
Yet lovely in thy youthful grace!
The elder dames, thy haughty peers,
Admire and hate thy blooming years.
    With words of shame
And taunts of scorn they join thy name.

What cordial welcomes greet the guest
By thy lone rivers of the West;
How faith is kept, and truth revered,
And man is loved, and God is feared,
    In woodland homes,
And where the ocean border foams.

There's freedom at thy gates and rest
For Earth's down-trodden and oppressed,
A shelter for the hunted head,
For the starved laborer toil and bread.
    Power, at thy bounds,
Stops and calls back his baffled hounds.

Thine eye, with every coming hour,
Shall brighten, and thy form shall tower;
And when thy sisters, elder born,
Would brand thy name with words of scorn,
    Before thine eye,
Upon their lips the taunt shall die.

NEIL BOYTON, S.J.

A River for Mary Immaculate

DOWN that broad, undiscovered river which was to be known as the Wisconsin, crept two canoes carrying seven white men. Five of these bronze-skinned paddlers wore the fringed coats and skin trousers, the pudding-bag caps and gay red sashes that proclaimed the woodsmen. But he who plied the bow paddle of the first canoe was dressed differently. The faded black gown that covered his lean figure was frayed. Long and dark brown was the hair that the wide-brimmed hat hid. He did not look his thirty-six years. At his girdle hung the crucifix of his Savior. And with every dip of his paddle, the breviary, suspended by a cord from his neck, swayed and threatened to pitch into the quiet water.

A smile of expectancy lit up this Blackrobe's features as the canoe glided by the next pine-wooded point. This smile faded away as another stretch of the unknown river unfolded before his gaze. He called over his shoulder, "Still the Great Water eludes us, Louis."

The man in blanket coat and jaunty cap of beaverskins, whom he addressed, ceased his exertions, while the gentle current carried the canoe onward.

"I never believed half the old-squaws' tales those Fox and Mascouten Indians told us. It is a month since we left the beach at Mackinac. We have already come weary leagues beyond our calculations and always, good Father Marquette, this river opens up another stretch. It seems—"

The Blackrobe interrupted the man. Undaunted certainty shone in his eyes.

"Louis—Louis Joliet! Where is your faith? Neither of us must lose sight of our purpose on this voyage into the unknown. You paddle toward the South Sea to seek new nations of these red children and win them for the King. I, to teach them to know our great God, of Whom they have hitherto been pitifully ignorant. Neither of us shall fail, with Mary Immaculate's aid."

There came into Father Marquette's face the tender expression

325

of one who has heard a well-beloved name.

"And I'll be satisfied," mumbled the stern paddler in that canoe, "if I ever see the Mission at Mackinac again, with this still attached to my scalp." He touched affectionately the long black hair that curled out under his beaverskin cap.

"Ah, Jean, I heard that," cried Father Marquette gayly. "Never fear; those precious locks of yours will grow to turn white."

"It's a wonder they haven't yet, my Father," retorted the woodsman, and he grinned.

Again the three took up their paddles and Joliet signaled the four woodsmen in the second canoe that he was crossing the current towards the other still shore.

The look of filial devotion that Mary Immaculate's name had kindled in Marquette's eyes yet lingered, and his thoughts, as he plied his paddle, turned back to that last Mass he had said a month ago in the little birchbark chapel of the Mission of Saint Ignace when this expedition had started to seek fuller knowledge of the Great Water. The Blackrobe murmured again the petition he had begged that May morning of 1673.

"You know, Mary Immaculate, I do not seek the Great Water for fame. I desire that honor to be yours. But I do wish to bring those other sheep, who live along its banks, into your Son's fold. And you know, Mary Immaculate, my promise to you—when my eyes fall on this river, I shall name it in honor of your Immaculate Conception."

This thought led to another consoling one. For Father Marquette recalled that it was on December 8 last, the very Feast of the Immaculate Conception, that Louis Joliet, his companion-explorer, had come paddling through the ice to the Mackinac shore with the long-expected permission from Superiors in distant Quebec, to sail and seek the unknown river.

The two had spent the long winter gathering from the stray bands of Indians, who came to the bleak mission, every scrap of information and rumor about the mighty stream that flowed through the unknown lands to the west.

Comforted and strengthened in the knowledge of Mary Immaculate's aid, the Blackrobe bent to his paddle, and the canoe sped down these waters, which no white man had ever yet seen.

An hour later, the woodsmen's canoe had forged ahead, and now Joliet's keen eye noted they had stopped, with dripping paddles across the bark sides and listened intently. He saw Peter, the bow paddle, reach back for his flint-lock musket that lay atop a bundle of gift beads.

"Look! Our men are on guard ahead," warned Joliet. "Dip your paddles in deeper, my Father—Jean."

Under the added urge, the light birchbark canoe was lifted through the still waters till it slid alongside its mate.

As all lay on their oars, there came from beyond the curtain of dark green pines that covered the low-cliffed bank, a strange uncanny moan, such as an animal in its agony might utter.

It was very quiet in the canoes, and when a fish broke the surface nearby with a silver flash, several of the woodsmen crossed themselves devoutly. Then on the clear air broke the quavering opening notes of a most mournful song. The notes rose and fell, and their sound was utter sorrow.

Suddenly Father Marquette's hand went up. "I have heard that song before, my children. I have heard it when I was stationed at the abandoned Mission of the Holy Spirit on Lake Superior. It is the one the Illinois call 'The Song to Go Above.'"

He turned to his fellow-explorer and said, "Louis, let us leave the men on guard here and go ashore. Some poor Illinois is far along the way when he sings his Death Chant. I am needed."

Jean, the woodsman, propelled the canoe into the quiet water under the low bank. Father Marquette and Louis Joliet leaped lightly to the shore. The two light crafts were backed out into the stream, while the woodsmen laid their powder where they could reach it in a hurry.

The Blackrobe, followed by his companion, disappeared into the shadows cast by the thickly growing pines. Those on guard in the canoes heard a twig snap—a cone fall. Then silence settled on the waters once more. Again the wailing notes of that Death Song came to the alert ears of the woodsmen. It wailed away as though strength had deserted the singer.

In the meantime, after breaking through the underbrush, the two moccasined voyagers had come upon a scene that made the soul-hunger gnaw at the breast of the Blackrobe.

There was a small clearing, maybe a hundred steps behind the bank of the river, and here, on the southern pine wall, the new green growths of mid-June were all burnt away to black, snarled wires. Marquette and Joliet halted as though struck. For there on the ground in twisted, grotesque positions, mute witnesses to the agony in which they had expired, lay three—no, four terribly seared corpses. On the charred branches of a tall scorched pine, hurled as one might cast mud on a wall, sprawled the blackened trunk of another Indian. The charred legs and arms were outspread in a pathetic, supplicating attitude.

"In the Name of God!" exclaimed Joliet in an awed whisper, "what new sort of deviltry of this benighted wilderness have we now stumbled on, good Father Marquette?"

Before the Blackrobe could reply, from the further edge of the scorched clearing came again the high quivering notes of the Death Song.

Noiselessly the two stepped across the charred area, around the dreadful dead, and entered the green undergrowth beyond. A few steps, and they were gazing down upon the powder-blackened body of an old Indian. Seated on his haunches by his master's side,

328

with head upturned, was a lean brownish-yellow hound. Seeing the two, the hound tilted his head to a steeper angle and gave a lingering howl.

The Death Song stopped in the middle of a quavering note, and the hand of the lone singer sought and closed on a charred warclub. He lifted himself feebly to brandish the weapon in the direction of the Blackrobe.

Then it was that Joliet, with pity in his tone, whispered, "See, my Father, the Indian's sight has been blasted away."

"On guard, No Flesh!" the Indian commanded in the Illinois tongue. "Wolves! Wolves! At last!"

The lean hound ceased howling and, standing with one paw on the Indian's breast and every tooth showing, faced the two men.

"No, brother," spoke Marquette, "not wolves, but a shepherd. What dreadful thing has happened to you and your party?"

The Indian turned to the face he could not see. "Who is the white man that speaks to Long Fox with Illinois words?" he demanded.

Marquette smiled, "Long Fox, I am the one who prays and instructs."

The burnt hand dropped the warclub and, with sightless eyes, the Illinois searched the face of the Blackrobe. "You are a Blackrobe. It is good," replied Long Fox. "Now I know your voice. Moons ago I sat in your Prayer Cabin on the shores of the Lake of Copper (Lake Superior) and listened to your words of wisdom. I kept them in my breast. Since I lay here I have asked the Manitou, Who made heaven and earth, that the road I follow after death be the same as yours."

"What's he saying? What has happened?" exclaimed Joliet.

"Wait, Louis. I will tell you shortly." Easing the burnt Illinois, Marquette asked questions and listened as Long Fox told his tale.

When the old Illinois had finished, the Blackrobe translated for his companion. "Long Fox says there were six Illinois in his party. They stole a powder keg from some trappers who have a cabin that, I think, must have been some leagues south of the large village where five days ago we got the two guides to show us the portage to this river.

"Long Fox and his party were on their way to the Illinois country to the south. The day before yesterday they camped here, and his grandson rolled the keg too close to the campfire. Long Fox says suddenly the devil of the trappers came out of the keg in scorching flames. Then he was hurled many feet. Of his companions, only his grandson moaned for many hours. Then he also was silent.

"Long Fox says it has been night since. He thought of the Prayer he had heard taught the Ottawas in the chapel at Holy Spirit Mission, and he prayed Our Blessed Lord—"

Tears had come to Marquette's eyes and he added huskily, "Louis, tell Jean and some of the woodsmen to come ashore, and you bring me fresh water."

When Joliet was gone, the Blackrobe bent lower and instructed: "Long Fox, the Good Manitou, Who made heaven and earth, has surely sent me to your side. Listen, you have been through many fights with the Sioux and you realize— for you had started your Death Chant—that the rest of the journey is short. What must one do, to go to the land of delights where death and disease are forever banished?"

"Blackrobe, one must believe in the Prayer; so I heard you teach the Ottawas."

"Well, then?"

"Then I believe, Blackrobe."

"And one must pray."

"Very well, I wish to pray, but I have not the sense to do so. Teach me, Blackrobe."

Quickly Marquette gave instruction to this well-disposed soul.

There was a crunching of burnt pine cones, and Joliet and several of the woodsmen came into view. Joliet carried water in a dripping birchbark dish. This he gave to Father Marquette and knelt at the priest's side. Repeating the formula of the Sacrament, the Blackrobe poured the saving waters on the blistered brow of the old Illinois.

"It is good," said Long Fox. "Now I am ready to go along the right trail." He turned to the hound, who had been sitting on his haunches, watching the party. "No Flesh, come here." The hound crept closer and buried his muzzle in Long Fox's hand. "This dog, Blackrobe, is faithful. He brought me a squirrel and kept me alive. He would have died with me. He lives and I give him to you." Long Fox patted the brown head. "No Flesh, Blackrobe is your master now. Go to him."

Obediently the lean hound walked over to Father Marquette and sat looking up into his new owner's face. The tail wagged as if asking, "What orders, master?"

Soon the woodsmen carried the ndian as gently as they could, cross the charred clearing and into he gloomy pine forest. Before hey reached the canoes at the ank, Long Fox struggled in their rms and they halted. They lowred the poor burnt body to the round. Again the Death Song of he Illinois came high and clear. here was a note of triumph in it ow. Then it quivered and broke ff sharply. The hound, No Flesh, quatted back on his haunches and owled.

Marquette observed to his comanion, "I gave Long Fox the name f Mary in baptism. And if I never ut the waters of salvation on another head this voyage, I feel that ur expedition has been successful.

Surely, this was a predestined one. Louis, we were almost visibly led to his side before the end. Not in vain have I invoked Mary Immaculate. She is the leader of this expedition, and she claims her own on the way. And did you notice how she has given me a fine, faithful hound?"

The Blackrobe bent low. "Come here, No Flesh." He petted the brownish-yellow head. "You have served your Indian master well and faithfully. There is a place for you in my canoe and at my fireside."

The dog walked beside him as they left the pine woods behind. They took with them the body of Long Fox, who had gone to God while yet the baptismal drops glistened on his forehead. Once more on the broad, still bosom of the river, they weighted the body and in midcurrent consigned it to the waters.

As the canoes were paddled along the river that was to be known as the Wisconsin, the two in Marquette's canoe were silent, till the Blackrobe exclaimed: "I recall the old Illinois now! Long Fox came often to my cabin at Holy Spirit Mission to look at the religious paintings I showed and listen to the instructions I gave about them. Then one day he disappeared. I thought in my ignorance that the seed had fallen on hard soil. How blind even the keenest-sighted of us are! Ah, Louis, my friend, we have been witnesses to the happy death of one who tried to follow Our Master."

"Happy, yet, my Father," exclaimed Joliet, "if I had my choice of a death, it would be fighting—to go down gloriously for King—"

"Or Kingdom," said Father Marquette, "as did our blessed martyred brothers—good Father Jogues and Brébeuf twenty odd years ago on the Iroquois and the Huron Missions."

The Blackrobe sighed. "But a martyr's death is granted only to chosen souls. For us weaker ones,

are left lonely deaths. Like our good Father Menard, who wore out seeking the scattered red children of His Master to the north of us, twelve years ago, or, better yet, glorious Francis Xavier on that desolate Chinese island." The brown eyes glistened as he went on: "These deaths are my models. To wear out as a shepherd should and then to die alone and abandoned, this is my ideal! And it has been, ever since I was a wee lad and the good God first put into my curly head the desire of serving Him here in the mid-American wilderness. But how I chatter, and you paddle!"

Jean, the woodsman, drove his paddle into the water murmuring, "They can have their going down gloriously for the King in France and their lonely deaths, but if I had my way, I'd like, please God, to die in my bed. Heavens help us! If half the tales of those two feather-stuck and paint-daubed scouts, who showed us the portage to this river and then refused to go any further, are true, it's doubtful if I will ever see an honest bed again. Going— going—only God knows where—in search of a great river, whose banks are lined with skulking Sioux, or worse savages. My poor scalp lock! Soon you and I are liable to say good-by forever!"

"That's shameful, Jean," chided Marquette. "We paddle under the protection of her who is more powerful than all the red warriors in the New World. Is not that correct, No Flesh?" The Blackrobe looked down upon his dog, lying on a reed mat in the bottom of the canoe. The brownish-yellow hound wagged his tail contentedly.

The next morning, gray fog clouds covered parts of the river as Father Marquette and Louis Joliet stood in the shore willows of an island and looked toward the unknown stretches ahead. Vaguely through the mist downstream appeared another island, thickly overgrown with trees. Opposite, wooded points on the banks loomed up. Beyond, the fog cut off the view. Something of the fascination of gazing upon stretches of this veiled world yet to be explored, held the two men.

The woodsmen, concealed in the willows, were busy overhauling the two canoes, and the commanders were about to give the signal to embark, when No Flesh, who was foraging in the underbrush, came up and began to growl.

At the same moment, through a break in the misty horizon, Joliet saw something that made him pull the Blackrobe to the ground. He uttered a warning to the woodsmen, and all movement behind the willow screen ceased. As a precaution against barking, Marquette held No Flesh's jaws.

Out of the gray cloud wall along the flats on the southern shore skimmed a small bark canoe. It carried two plumed Indians, their faces daubed with red. Another bark glided into sight and then three more came out of the mists.

"This is no hunting party. Our brothers are painted for war," observed Marquette, "and from the manner in which they paddle, they are Sioux. The Ottawas and Illinois paddle differently."

The Indians were kneeling in their small canoes. Each bonneted warrior took three or four dips of his paddle to the right and then the same number of strokes to the left, and the birchbark canoes seemed to fly over the smooth waters. As silently as they had come out of the mists of the lower river, the war party glided along the further shore and disappeared into a foggy cloud upstream.

"But for that leak Francis and René discovered in the woodsmen's

canoe," said Joliet, as the last of the hostile Sioux was swallowed up in the gray fog, "we would have paddled into the midst of them. It is not a pleasant thought." Joliet smiled ruefully, but he continued, "Yet we must go on to seek fuller knowledge of the Great Water; whether it flows into the South Sea, or the Western Ocean below the British Colony of Virginia, or the Mexican gulf where the Spanish are."

"As always Mary Immaculate shields her own," Marquette's face was glowing. "I feel such confidence, Louis, my friend, that we shall in all safety visit the nations dwelling along the great river. Mary Immaculate will permit this. Unworthy client as I am, she will let me open the passage to such of our Fathers as have awaited this good fortune for so long a time."

When no more Sioux appeared, the order was given to resume the voyage. Again, Marquette, Joliet, and Jean paddled in the first canoe. No Flesh picked out a comfortable spot between bags of supplies and watched the still shores slip by. He showed interest when the canoe breasted a point and came upon a doe and her fawn, drinking at the waterside.

The morning sun was burning up the mists on the river valley, and before the canoes had added a

league to their journey, the clear blue sky of a June day opened above the party.

Hot high noon blazed down upon them, and the twisting river widened. Oaks and walnuts and basswood crowded either shore. More islands, thick-wooded with willows and aspens, rose ahead, drew near, and dropped astern of the tireless paddlers. The scallops of green-clad hills beyond the flood plains of this river unbent and straightened away. A group of woody delta islands surrounded the canoes. It was mid-afternoon of the seventeenth of June, 1673.

The little expedition paddled on, keeping full in the current, close to the green northern shore. There came into the mind of Joliet fragments of the warnings the elder of the guides had given as they bade the voyagers good-by at the Wisconsin portage. "White men, strange monsters lie in wait for such venturesome ones as you . . . evil spirits of air and water will plot your disaster. We will not see you again. We go no further."

The canoe swept around a willow point, and Joliet was about to speak when Marquette turned back from his bow position. At once Louis Joliet noted the rapture that shone on the tanned face of the Blackrobe. Marquette pointed ahead at the new world of water that was being revealed to them. "We have reached the Great Water! Oh! Louis, my friend, I cannot express to you the joy that floods my breast. So long have I prayed the aid of Mary Immaculate that it might be permitted to me, all unworthy as I am, to behold this river of rivers and to bring the Prayer to her Son's red-skinned children who dwell along its banks." Tears were in Marquette's eyes and, unashamed, he let them flow down his cheeks.

The two canoes were paddled side by side, and as they floated along, the vastness of this mighty stream awed into silence the first of white men to behold its upper reaches.

At Marquette's command the prows of the canoes were turned into the northern shore and a landing was made on the sunlit point. Here he and Joliet turned scientists and, unpacking their instruments, took the sun.

When their calculations were finished, Marquette announced: "If my figures are correct, it is near 42½° where this river we are leaving pours its waters into the—" The Blackrobe checked himself. "I was almost forgetting a promise I made to Mary Immaculate long ago."

Marquette stooped where the swifter current ran and cupping his hands, lifted some of the water. He poured the bright drops back, saying: "O greatest of streams, I christen you henceforth with the name of Mary's unique prerogative —I christen you the River of the Conception."

As Father Marquette began to speak, Louis Joliet and the other woodsmen hastily tossed off their caps and, standing erect and bareheaded in the sun, they uttered a loud and fervent "Amen" as the Blackrobe finished.

The Blackrobe stood there a long time, his eyes fixed longingly on the wide waters that flowed ever southward between the towering bluffs. Then he lifted his gaze on high and his companions heard him pray: "O Mary Immaculate, Mother of God and Mediatrix of All Graces, aid me to carry the knowledge of your Son to these nations that dwell in darkness along these lower shores."

336

Recalling Details

How well can you recall details? Write your answers in complete sentences.

1. How old was Father Marquette when this story took place?
2. In what year did the expedition take place?
3. What was the name of the mournful song which attracted the party to the shore?
4. What was the baptismal name of Long Fox?
5. What was the name of Long Fox's dog?
6. How did Father Marquette wish to die?
7. What caused Long Fox's death?
8. What saved the expedition from an encounter with the hostile Sioux?
9. In what month did Father Marquette and Louis Joliet reach their destination?
10. How did they determine where they were?

Building New Words

Copy these words on your paper. Then, by adding prefixes and suffixes, make three more words using the underlined word as the root.

1. cover _____ _____ _____
2. dress _____ _____ _____
3. perfect _____ _____ _____
4. promise _____ _____ _____
5. claim _____ _____ _____
6. appear _____ _____ _____
7. turn _____ _____ _____
8. intend _____ _____ _____
9. figure _____ _____ _____
10. notice _____ _____ _____

EDNA ST. VINCENT MILLAY

Renascence

THE world stands out on either side
No wider than the heart is wide;
Above the world is stretched the sky,—
No higher than the soul is high.
The heart can push the sea and land
Farther away on either hand;
The soul can split the sky in two,
And let the face of God shine through.

MARY MAXTONE

Skywriting

No feathered bird can weave
Pattern more perfect, pure,
Nor smoldering comet leave
A lovelier signature
Than they who in the sun
The vandal winds defy
And posters paste upon
The billboards of the sky.

Point Barrow

"Dɪᴛ-darr-darr, darr-dit-dit-darr, darr-dit-dit-dit." WXB — WXB — WXB — de (from) — KHCAL." The blurred buzz of my own radio-sending rang harshly in my ears. Through the cockpit cover I could see fog on the water ahead, motionless piles of light gray cotton wool with dark gray patches here and there. Out to sea the white wall of fog stood impassable and still as the ice packs from which it rose. Inland under floating islands of fog stretched the barren Arctic land. We were turning toward it as our only chance of reaching Point Barrow, the bleak northern tip of Alaska. Could we get through that night? If the weather ahead was not worse. I must get my message to the Barrow operator.

"WXB — WXB — WXB," I called to him.

"Dit-darr-dit!" A sharp clean note came through my receiver. There he was! Right on the watch, though I had called him off schedule. Then there really was a man waiting for us, I thought with relief. There really was a Point Barrow. We weren't jumping off into space. Somewhere ahead in that white wilderness a man was listening for us, guiding us in.

Now, my message: "Flying—thru — fog — and — rain — going — inland — wea (weather) — pse (please)?"

His notes came back clearly. I wrote rapidly not to miss a word, "Low — fog — bank — rolling — off — ice — now — clearing — fog — expected — soon — pass — over — ground — vis (visibility) — one — mile." I poked the pad forward to my husband in the front cockpit. He glanced at it and nodded. That meant "Ok. That's what I wanted to know. We'll push on."

On for hours through the unreal shifting world of soft mist. Here a cloud and there a drizzle; here a wall and there, fast melting, a hole through which gleamed the hard metallic scales of the sea. There was no mirage. That rippling steel below us was real. If one flew into it blindly it might as well be steel. At times we seemed to be riding on its scaly back and then, with a roar, up we climbed into white blankness. No sight of land; no sight of sea or sky; only our instruments to show the position of the plane. Circling down again, my husband motioned me to reel in the antenna. We were flying too near the water. The ball-weight on the end might be snapped off. Perhaps we might even be forced to land unexpectedly on open sea and have both weight and wire torn off at the impact. His gesture was a danger signal for me and I waited, tense, for the nod and second gesture, "All right now—reel out again." At times we would come out of the fog, not into daylight but into the strange gray night. The Arctic sun just under the horizon still lit the sky with a light that did not belong to dawn or dusk. A cold gray light seemed to grow off the ice pack.

We should be very near by now. Would we be able to get through or would we have to turn back? The fog was closing in behind us. It might be impossible to return to Aklavik. A note from the front cockpit—"Weather at Barrow?" We were flying under the fog again, too low to trail a long antenna. I reeled out a few feet of wire, which would not allow me to transmit messages but was sufficient for receiving. It all depended on the man at Barrow. If only he would go on sending in spite of our silence. We were powerless to let him know.

"Weather, weather, weather—send us weather," I pleaded mentally and put on my ear-phones. Silence. Wisps of fog scudded past us. No, there he was, "Darr-dit-darr, dit-dit-dit-dit," calling us. Twice, three times, four times—then silence again, waiting for us to answer. I held my breath, "Weather, weather." There he goes again. "Do—u (you)—hear—me?" came the message. Silence again. He was waiting for my call. "Yes, yes," I answered silently, "but I can't send—go ahead—weather!"

"Darr-dit-darr; dit-dit-dit-dit." There he was again. My pencil took down the letters, slowly spelling out the message, "Fog—lifting—fast (Good man! He did it!)—visibility—two—miles (He did it! Good for him!)—don't—think—u — have — any — trouble — find —lagoon." There it was—just what we wanted. I poked my husband excitedly with the pad. That operator at Barrow—he did it—we'd get through all right now. "Fog lifting, visibility two miles." Oh, what a grand man!

We could see the gray flat coast line now and watched it closely for Barrow. That might be it—a stretch of whitish irregular blocks —houses? No, as we came nearer, they were the strange pushed-up blocks of the ice pack crushed against a little harbor. Well, these were houses. We had come on a small low spit of land squeezed between two seas of ice blocks. Yes, there were houses. We peered down at them eagerly, four tipsy weather-beaten shacks and a few tents, the color of the ice blocks. Can this be Barrow? I almost cried with disappointment looking at that deserted group. No sign of a person, no sign of smoke, no sign of life. It can't be Barrow. Childishly, my first thought ran on, "Why, I thought they'd have a regular Thanksgiving dinner for us.

There couldn't be any dinner down there—no smoke." I felt very hungry. We circled again. "No!" I realized with relief. "No radio mast! It isn't Barrow." We followed the shore line until we found a larger and newer group of houses between the ice pack and an open lagoon. This was Barrow, ten or twelve red roofs, numerous shacks and tents, a church steeple and— yes, there they were—the radio masts.

We were landing on the lagoon. I pulled off two bulky pairs of warm

flying socks and put on some rubber-soled shoes for walking. Although it was not freezing weather, my feet became numb before we reached the small crowd of people on shore. A strange group huddled together in the half-light of the Arctic night. I looked at them—pointed hoods, fur parkas, sealskin boots—and thought at first, "They're all Eskimos." No, that must be the radio man in the khaki mackinaw. I felt a glow of gratitude and waved at him. As we climbed up the bank the crowd of Eskimos drew back, an attitude of respect and wonder never seen in the usual crowd. As they moved a great cry arose—not a shout, but a slow deep cry of welcome. Something in it was akin to the bleak land and the ice pack.

Can You Write a Story Ending?

Reread the first eight paragraphs of this account. Presume that since the Lindberghs were unable to transmit messages, the operator at Barrow ceased sending messages to them. Write a brief ending for the story in view of that fact.

Matching Words and Definitions

From the words in Column II, choose a word that means the same or nearly the same as each of the words in Column I.

Column I	Column II
1. ____ impassable	a. dreary, dismal
2. ____ bleak	b. similar, related
3. ____ gleamed	c. flashed, appeared
4. ____ metallic	d. move swiftly
5. ____ mirage	e. unable to penetrate
6. ____ impact	f. send out, send through
7. ____ transmit	g. pond, small lake
8. ____ scudded	h. illusion
9. ____ lagoon	i. containing metal
10. ____ akin	j. a striking, collision

342

The Shell

AND then I pressed the shell
Close to my ear
And listened well,
And straightway like a bell
Came low and clear
The slow, sad murmur of the distant seas,
Whipped by an icy breeze
Upon a shore
Wind-swept and desolate.
It was a sunless strand that never bore
The footprint of a man,
Nor felt the weight
Since time began
Of any human quality or stir
Save what the dreary winds and waves incur.
And in the hush of waters was the sound
Of pebbles rolling round,
Forever rolling with a hollow sound.
And bubbling sea-weeds as the waters go,
Swish to and fro
Their long, cold tentacles of slimy gray.
There was no day,
Nor ever came a night
Setting the stars alight
To wonder at the moon:
Was twilight only and the frightened croon,
Smitten to whispers, of the dreary wind
And waves that journeyed blind—
And then I loosed my ear. . . . O, it was sweet
To hear a cart go jolting down the street.

PAUL SIPLE

Caught in a Blizzard

Richard Evelyn Byrd, honored officer of the United States Navy, first to fly over the North Pole, set out upon an even harder task: the exploration of the Antarctic Continent. He was to fly over the bottom of the world, not once only in a single spectacular flight but in a series of scientific expeditions which were to furnish accurate knowledge of that unknown icebound continent.

In the summer of 1929 (winter, "down under") the expedition steamed out of New York and headed south. On the staff were famous scientists, cameramen, radio operators, flyers, and Boy Scout Paul Siple, who had been selected by the National Council Office of the Boy Scouts of America as their member best qualified by training and experience to accompany the expedition.

Upon Paul Siple's return from the frozen land that surrounds the South Pole, he wrote a book entitled *A Boy Scout with Byrd*. The record is a tribute to Commander Byrd and his band of specialists who set up camp on the edge of the Ross Barrier, the shelf of ice which juts northward from the desolate Antarctic continent. It is also a tribute to the friendships formed in the sunless winter on Little America, and it honors Commander Byrd, his geologist, and his pilots, who overcame all hazards and dropped the American flag on the jagged shelf of ice that is the South Pole.

Paul Siple, assigned to the task of driving a dog team, described many incidents in the lives of the men who went with Commander Byrd. One he called "Caught in a Blizzard."

IN less than a month the sun, that had been circling about in the sky continuously for twenty-four hours of the day since our arrival, would sink below the horizon and leave us for four months. For the past month it had been dipping more and more to the south, but before it would disappear entirely there was a great deal of work to be done.

The mechanics and pilots started to dismantle the planes and put

344

them away for the winter. They folded back the wings of the Fairchild and built a snow-block wall about it, covering it with tarpaulins. The giant Ford plane, which had been moved about the camp several times by aid of man power and as many as sixty dogs at one time, was still minus its wings, and in this condition it was inclosed in a huge snow-block wall and covered over. Storehouses were built to take care of food supplies and our spare equipment. The last cache of material, left by the *Eleanor Bolling*, was being brought into camp, that is, all that we could find of it.

Severe blizzards had covered over the cache many times and in spite of the fact that nearly every member of the camp helped in the digging, many valuable articles were destined never to come to light. Many times, when we dog drivers were hauling loads from this cache, during this late season of the year, blizzards would come up with very little warning. We were often caught in them and had many anxious minutes before we would get back into camp. On one occasion, when blizzards had been holding up for several days our work of hauling materials from the Barrier cache, there was a great deal of consternation aroused as to whether we would ever get any of these valuable supplies into camp before they were snowed under and lost track of.

So early one morning, even though the weather looked very thick, the dog teams were ordered to make a trip to the cache. Only three teams were available this day for regular freighting, including Quin Blackburn's, Mike Thorne's, and my own. The other teams were preparing to lay some food depots to the south that would facilitate the trail work next spring. As we started out, a biting wind from the east was cutting across our trail at almost right angles. It was picking up little scurries of snow, and occasionally stronger gusts would throw the stinging little crystals up into our faces. Gradually the visibility became poorer and poorer, and fresh snow added body to the driving wind.

We were almost at our destination or we would have turned back at once, but we felt that a quarter of a mile more would make very little difference. However, when we arrived at the Barrier cache the wind velocity had risen so greatly that it was picking up the surface

snow and sending it swirling about through the air like a great cloud rising from the surface twenty or thirty feet above us. We estimated the velocity of the wind to be fifty or sixty miles an hour. Our dogs began to cower, from the ferocity of the roaring blast, and turn down wind to seek relief. We tried to hide our faces from the stinging little pellets and the biting air.

We worked as rapidly as we could, loading fifty-pound boxes of gasoline onto our sleds. We agreed to make our loads light; for we knew we would have a great deal of difficulty traveling as it was. After having lashed about fifteen cases apiece securely to our sleds we made ready to start, but we found our dogs to be very unwilling to move from their comfortable positions. They were all curled up in the snow and as we yelled at them they raised their heads with their pleading eyes begging for

Before us lay five miles of torture. At every hundred yards along the trail orange flags had been placed for just such an emergency, but the storm was so severe and thick that we could not make out their dim outlines within less than fifty feet. It meant that as we found one of these flags, we would have to go in a straight line as well as we could judge towards the next flag. The trail itself was obliterated, except that it was harder packed than the general surface about it, and as we would get off it, we could notice some difference in the way the sled ran. The greatest difficulty in doing this blind driving from one flag to another was that our dogs would constantly swing down wind and leave the trail completely. We had to be continuously on the alert to keep the team headed straight in the direction of the next flag.

Mike Thorne took the lead and most of the time had practically to keep his hand on the collar of his lead dog to keep him headed right. Quin went second and I brought up the rear. We were all to keep in sight of each other so that if one of us had to stop, the rest would not go on and leave him.

We forced our way along for about half an hour, and as the icy

mercy. Their fur was full of snow, their eyes and faces nearly covered over with an icy mask. Little drifts were building around them, and as the blast struck them more fully, they recoiled like a person snuggling back into bed upon his first contact with the frosty early morning air. We had to threaten them with the use of our whips to remind them that they must obey us. Slowly and painfully they rose to their feet, whining and cowering behind one another for shelter.

torture became harder to bear and my dogs seemed to be following the other teams very well, I would occasionally duck my head away from the wind and pull it inside my windproof clothing in order to warm up a bit, before facing that driving fury.

Suddenly, on one of these occasions when I had not been watching the team for a few seconds, I felt the sled pulling harder on soft snow. I came to my senses with a startled feeling. One glance ahead showed me that I was off the trail and there was no sign, in any direction, of the other two teams. My dogs had swung down wind, I saw at once, and it took all my strength to pull them back up wind and make them face directly into it. Within a few feet my back trail was entirely obliterated. For an instant a pang of excitement ran through me. I realized that if I did not call every aid of my senses to me, I would be hopelessly lost in my milky white surroundings.

A few minutes before, I had been shuddering with the cold; now I broke out into a sweat with the excitement and the exertion of making my dogs pull the load up into the wind. The poor creatures whined and cowered as the biting sandlike particles of snow dashed into their faces and hurt their eyes.

I knew that if I was down wind, the trail had to be some place up wind and running at almost right angles. At last I struck a harder spot in the surface, and hoping it to be the trail, I struck to it as well as I could. At last I found one of the trail flags. My instincts told me to turn to the left. However, after thinking over every factor that could lead me to choose the route, I decided that the camp must lie to the right, as the wind direction indicated.

As long as I was beside my lead dog Pete and kept encouraging him, he managed to stick fairly well to the trail, but occasionally I would have to lead him by the collar to keep him on it. We forced our way along and sighted the next flag. We knew, at least, that we were headed either for the camp or back to the Barrier cache, where we could construct some kind of shelter and perhaps find food. But after we had conquered the distance of two or three more flags I thought I could begin to hear uncertainly, through the roar of the wind, the barking of dogs and voices calling. A few moments later the dim outline of two huddled teams appeared before me on the trail, and as I joined them there was a mutual feeling of relief, for Mike and Quin had been almost as worried at my disappearance as I had.

Now, realizing how easy it was to stray away, we redoubled our efforts to keep together. We plugged on, encouraging our dogs, even though the pain of progress brought tears from our eyes that froze on our cheeks. We felt the inclination of giving up at times when the trail became too uncertain, and of trying to dig ourselves into the snow and wait for the blizzard to ease up. It was only the thought of how Commander Byrd and the men back in camp might be worrying that kept us plugging on.

It seemed to take hours as we painfully struggled along from flag to flag, but at last we saw our first goal: the gasoline cache on the brow of the hill, a little over half a mile away from Little America.

Writing a Newspaper Story

Journalists are always interested in the briefest way to give an account of a happening to the public. They follow what they call the "5-W formula," *who, when, where, what, why.* Frequently they include an "H" (*how*) in the formula. These points they present in their first paragraph, called "the summary lead." This lead they develop more fully in the paragraphs which follow. To attract attention to the story they try to get an unusual, attractive way of expressing their idea, which they refer to as "putting a WOW in the lead."

Using "Caught in a Blizzard" as your source of information, write a summary lead to tell your readers what happened. Use the "5-W and H formula" and put a WOW in the lead.

What Is Your Opinion?

What do you think is the purpose of the first four paragraphs in this story?

Do you think it is good or bad to take such risks? Give reasons for your answers.

349

LOUISE DRISCOLL

Hold Fast Your Dreams

WITHIN your heart
Keep one still, secret spot
Where dreams may go,
And sheltered so,
May thrive and grow—
Where doubt and fear are not.
Oh, keep a place apart
Within your heart,
For little dreams to go.

JOHN MASEFIELD

Adventure On

THOUGH you have conquered earth and charted sea
And planned the courses of all stars that be,
Adventure on, more wonders are in thee.

Adventure on, for from the littlest clue
Has come whatever worth man ever knew;
The next to lighten all men may be you.

Think, though you thunder on in might, in pride,
Others may follow fainting, without guide,
Burn out a trackway for them; blaze it wide.

What though the gleam may be a feeble one,
Go on, the man behind you may have none;
Even the dimmest gleam is from the sun.

A Mystery of the Sea

THE brigantine *Dei Gratia*, outward bound from Nova Scotia, was sailing steadily before a good wind. She was about seven hundred miles west of Gibraltar. It was the afternoon of December 4, in the year 1872. Captain Morehouse was on the deck, making a routine inspection of the horizon, when his eye was caught by another ship in the distance. He lifted his telescope to survey the stranger more closely. As his eye focused on the ship, an exclamation of surprise broke from him. He knew he was gazing upon the brigantine *Mary Celeste* under command of his old friend Captain Benjamin S. Briggs.

Captain Morehouse knew that the *Mary Celeste* had left Staten Island

in New York harbor about a month before, and that she had been bound across the Atlantic for Genoa with a cargo of alcohol. He was therefore astonished to discover her in these waters and apparently sailing northwest. He lowered the telescope and called to his first mate. When the man had joined his captain, Morehouse handed him the telescope.

"Take a look at yonder ship and tell me what you see," he commanded.

The mate raised the glass to his eye, took a long look, and lowering it said, "It's the *Mary Celeste,* sir, but her foresail and upper topsail are missing."

"I thought I couldn't mistake the *Mary Celeste,*" said Captain Morehouse. "But she has no business in these waters. She was bound for Genoa. Do you think we may be wrong?"

The mate shook his head. "I'd take an oath on it, sir. That's the *Mary Celeste,* or I never saw her before."

Captain Morehouse looked again at the distant ship and noted, in addition to the missing sails, that her lower topsail, jib, and foretopmast staysail were securely set.

"But why is she sailing northwest away from Europe instead of toward it?" he asked. Then he spoke in a tone, hurried and sharp. "Something is wrong. Alter our course to come up with her."

The mate sprang to carry out his captain's orders, and the *Dei Gratia* was soon heading toward the *Mary Celeste.*

As they drew near the ship, they could see that the main staysail was lying loose on top of the forward house. Captain Morehouse now called out, "Ahoy, *Mary Celeste!*" He waited anxiously, his eyes sweeping the empty decks. "Captain Briggs! Ahoy, there!"

No answering shout came from the *Mary Celeste.* Greatly wondering, Captain Morehouse now ordered three of his men to board her. A boat was lowered and the men rowed across toward the path of the quietly sailing brigantine, and when she was abeam of them, they swung aboard her.

On their return shortly to the *Dei Gratia,* the three seamen had a strange report to give.

Except for the sails and some water below decks, everything aboard the *Mary Celeste* seemed normal. There was no sign of violence or damage other than might be expected after sailing for some days without a crew. The cargo was undisturbed. The clothing and personal belongings of the officers and men were in their proper places. Even the pipes of the seamen were still in their quarters. Dresses, coats, and other clothing of a woman and a small child were found in the cabin. But the ship's papers were missing, the ship's only lifeboat was gone, and there was not a soul, living or dead, anywhere to be seen.

Captain Morehouse knew that the captain of the *Mary Celeste* had taken his wife and his two-year old daughter with him on this voyage. In addition to her captain, the *Mary Celeste* carried two officers, a steward, and four seamen. What had happened to all these people? Had

pirates overwhelmed them? Captain Morehouse dismissed the idea, since nothing on the *Mary Celeste* had been disturbed. Pirates would have ransacked her hold and stripped her of all they could lay hands on. Had there been a mutiny? If so, where were the signs of struggle? And why had the victors abandoned the ship?

With the questions whirling unanswered in his brain, Captain Morehouse ordered his mate and two seamen aboard the *Mary Celeste* to sail her to Gibraltar. There an inquiry was conducted. No evidence of mutiny, piracy, or disaster was found. Everything aboard was too orderly for that. The last entry

in the log book was dated November 24, and the last entry on the log slate was November 25, at 8.00 o'clock in the morning, ten days before the ship was found. The absence of her papers and the lifeboat pointed to one thing: apparently the ship had been deserted by all hands. But why would a captain with a wife and a small child deliberately leave a ship in midocean when she was not in trouble?

The case has never been solved. No trace of Captain Briggs or his wife and child or any of the crew was ever found.

SEVERAL studies of the *Mary Celeste* mystery have been published, and several theories about what happened to the ship have been advanced. Some are ridiculous and none is very convincing. I have a theory, too, and marine historians have told me that it makes more sense than any so far advanced. It is based on a strange experience I had on May 11, 1936, in the Arguin Banks off the coast of French West Africa.

The waters in that area along the west coast of Africa are largely unsurveyed. I was sailing south from Port Etienne, a fishing village in French West Africa, to Dakar. For reasons of my own (being then in the British naval intelligence service) I was taking my chances in uncharted waters. My boat, the *Girl Pat*, sixty-eight feet long and diesel-powered, with a crew of four, was making close to fourteen knots with the engine going and the sails up.

About ten o'clock that night I was standing on the afterdeck when I noticed the boat listing slightly to windward. I called to the man at the wheel, "How's her head?"

"Dead on south by west, skipper."

I looked for the sounding lead. As I threw it over the side, I noticed that the boat was not moving. The sounding showed that we were in only eight feet of water. The ship's draft was ten feet. I yelled to the man at the wheel to stop the engine and went at once to the cabin hatch to call the others.

"All hands on deck! We're ashore!"

They came up running. They were frightened and wanted to take to the lifeboat immediately. But there seemed to be no danger. Although the water was leaving her sides quickly, the ship remained on an even keel. In thirty minutes the *Girl Pat* was high and dry. Even then she stayed on nearly an even keel, as straight and as steady as if she were in dry dock. It seemed as if a giant hand had grasped the bottom of the boat and lifted her firmly, but very carefully, out of the water.

"Let me go over the side, skipper," said one of the crew. "I'll walk around her and have a look."

"No," I said, "we might be on quicksand."

There was nothing we could do until daylight; so we made coffee and waited. In the excitement no one had thought to stow the sails!

When the daylight came we found that the ship was sitting in the middle of an island of sand, about a mile in circumference and three feet above sea level. We threw some things over the side; the sand appeared to be firm. Then one of the crew climbed over with a rope tied under his armpits so that he could be pulled back if he began to sink. He walked away from the ship in the four directions of the compass and reported that the island was solid to the water's edge. At that the rest of us climbed down and walked about, gathering sea shells to pass the time.

All day we stayed there high and dry, and the next morning we saw another island to the north of us, which had risen from the sea during the night. That afternoon I saw surf breaking to the west of us. Through my binocular I saw the surface of the water there becoming calm and then the gradual appearance of a third island above the water. Before dark the island to the north sank and disappeared completely into the ocean.

The disappearance of that island gave hope to the crew of the *Girl Pat*. We held a conference to discuss our situation. Some were for leaving the ship and striking out in the small dinghy that served as our lifeboat. But I pointed out to them that the nearest land on the African coast was nearly one hundred miles to the east. If we rowed there in the dinghy, we should still have to go ashore and walk in the desert either one hundred and twenty miles north to Port Etienne or two hundred and forty miles south to Saint Louis. Undoubtedly we should die of thirst in the desert. Or we might be captured and killed by the cruel tribesmen who live in that part of French West Africa.

"There's a good chance this island may sink," I told them. "It may sink in a few weeks or in a few days, as that island to the north sank a while ago. I say let's remain here

until our food runs out. Then if we're still stranded, let's row ashore and take a chance in the desert."

The men agreed with me. That night we slept on the deck. About nine o'clock I dozed off. When I awoke, I felt the boat rocking from side to side. I thought I was dreaming. I looked at my watch and saw that it was three in the morning. Then I realized that I was awake and the boat was actually swaying. I yelled to the boys to get the sounding lead. They were already awake and taking soundings with great excitement.

It was discovered that there was already eight feet of water amidships. In twenty minutes we had fourteen feet of water below us, and I started the engine. Very cautiously we began to move, taking soundings continuously. At times the water was thirty-six feet deep and at other times we scraped the bottom. An hour and a half later we ran aground again in eight feet of water.

When daylight broke we saw that we were stuck on the northeast shore of another island. On the far side the rusted ribs of a steamship's bow stuck out of the sand. But we were sure that deeper water lay directly ahead of our bow. We put the anchor in the dinghy and rowed out to the end of the anchor line and dropped it. By winching a few feet at a time on the anchor line and running the engine at full speed, we managed to pull the boat off the sand and had her afloat again at noon.

Our engine pumps were by this time clogged with sand churned up by the propeller. We worked on them, put the engine into commission, and set our sails, drifting slowly north and northwest for thirty minutes. Then to our great relief, we found that our sounding line, one hundred and twenty fathoms in length, was unable to touch bottom. We were back in the deep Atlantic once more.

Since by now our supplies were rather low, I decided to return to Port Etienne and replenish them before resuming the voyage to Dakar. There an officer of the Foreign Legion, when he head of the *Girl Pat's* weird experience, informed me that the rising and sinking sand islands are well known in that part of Africa. The natives call them the Phantom Islands. The officer said that some French scientists attribute the islands to a great river that flows under the Sahara Desert and empties somewhere on the floor of the Atlantic, sixty to one hundred miles from the coast. These scientists believe that sand gathers in the outlet of this underground river and, at intervals, the sand

clogs the outlet completely. Then the dammed-up river, increasing its pressure, finally succeeds in flinging the tremendous barrier of sand into the ocean. These sudden upheavals of sand form islands that rise to the surface, later settling and sinking below again.

It is quite possible that the *Mary Celeste* could have been lifted from the ocean by one of the Phantom Islands. To be sure, the *Mary Celeste,* when found, was more than six hundred miles north of where the *Girl Pat* ran aground. But the Phantom Islands may extend much farther north than the *Girl Pat's* position. And it is not only possible but probable that the *Mary Celeste* could have sailed farther south than her recorded positions.

In those days most sailing-ship officers estimated their positions by dead reckoning and not by instrument. Modern steamships—which hold to a course more accurately than a sailing ship—are often twenty miles off their mark on a run of eighty miles between two British Isles ports when the navigation is done by dead reckoning. If a steamship can err twenty miles in an eighty-mile trip, it would be easy for a sailing ship to err six hundred miles in a three-thousand mile crossing of the Atlantic—and such ships frequently did. The missing sails would also point to the fact that the *Mary Celeste* was blown off her course.

Presuming that the *Mary Celeste* was south of her course to begin with—and the best trade winds at that time of the year are farther south—and presuming that the northerly gales of a storm drove her even more to the south, it is possible to picture Captain Brigg's ship running aground on one of the Phantom Islands. The *Mary Celeste* weighed only 282 tons; she could have rested high, dry, and on even keel without breaking, just like the *Girl Pat.*

The rest is easy to imagine; the captain and his wife and child and the crew crowding into the lifeboat and rowing away from the island, as the crew of the *Girl Pat* wanted to do; the journey to the mainland and the terrible final ordeal on the hot sands of the desert. Their chances of survival in the desert in 1872 were smaller than ours would have been in 1936. There was no French Foreign Legion in West Africa then, and the tribesmen were untroubled by higher authorities.

And finally, after the storm had subsided, the *Mary Celeste*, left alone and undamaged on the island, floated off when the sand beneath her submerged. The prevailing winds there under normal conditions are from the southeast. The ship would have sailed away to the north or northwest, as the *Girl Pat* would have done had we left her. That was the direction that the *Mary Celeste* was sailing when she was sighted so many years ago by the astonished Nova Scotian sailors on the deck of the *Dei Gratia.*

It may well be that the *Girl Pat's* adventure solved one of the greatest mysteries of the sea.

Comparing Stories

This selection tells two connected stories, one happening in 1872, one in 1936. Use these dates to head two columns on a sheet of paper and list in correct order the incidents in each story, keeping similar incidents opposite each other.

A Story of the South Seas

More than twenty-five years ago the children's librarians of the United States awarded their first medal to the author of the most distinguished book of that year for children. The award, presented every year since then, is called "The John Newbery Medal" in honor of a jolly English bookseller who, as long ago as 1745, set up a bookshop at St. Paul's Churchyard in London and chose an utterly untried trade, the business of publishing books for children.

Children owe a great debt of gratitude to John Newbery, and they owe one to modern writers like Armstrong Sperry, who has been a winner of the Newbery Medal. Armstrong Sperry is a modest man; when he received the national award he talked little about himself. His own childhood, he admitted, had been influenced by family stories of the South Seas but, after this brief explanation, he told the story about a little band of Polynesians who faced the destruction of their world and then rebuilt it. It is a record of high adventure and courage.

In a farmhouse set among the rocky hills of Connecticut a small boy listened to tales of hair-raising adventures with bold pirates in the China Sea, of cannibals, and of islands rich with pearls. The boy was Armstrong Sperry, the storyteller his great-grandfather, Captain Sereno Armstrong. Many of the tales were about one island— Bora Bora. "Prettiest island I ever did see," said the captain. "I'd like *you* to see it some day, young'un!"

While at school, young Armstrong Sperry read stories of the South Seas that fired his imagination. He longed to stow away on the first ship that was sailing south. But it was not until years later, after finishing art school and work as an illustrator in an advertising agency, that he finally visited Bora Bora.

He sailed from Tahiti on a small copra schooner. The paint had long blistered and peeled from her hull; her rigging was a frayed patchwork of rope, wire, and bits of string. Every inch of space in the hold was crammed with cases of cargo, and her decks were crowded with pigs, chickens, and lumber. But the bunches of red bananas swinging from her rails and the crowds of friendly natives swarming her decks lent color and romance to the shabby vessel. The ship's name meant Flower of the Lime Tree, and her captain wore black mustachios that looked like handlebars, and a red sash around his waist.

A crowd had gathered on shore to wish the travelers *bon voyage*. They played concertinas and wept as they broke into the measures of their singing dance. A rusty cannon was fired, the ship set sail, and the song of parting was lost in the distance.

The schooner stopped at many islands to land cargo and passengers, and to take on the vanilla pods and copra that the natives had gathered. Weeks passed and Bora Bora was still just over the horizon. And then one morning the captain called out from the wheel, "There is Bora Bora!"

"That's only a large cloud," said Sperry. But as the schooner sailed down upon it, the cloud became a single peak that towered two thousand feet straight up from the plane of the sea. The peak was of volcanic rock that glistened in the sun

like amethyst. Waterfalls seemed to spill from the clouds, and wild goats leaped from crag to crag. Sperry felt that Bora Bora was everything a South Sea island ought to be.

The island's entire population was on the beach to welcome the ship. As Sperry stepped ashore, a huge white-haired giant of a man came forward to meet him. The tall man, who wore a crown of banana leaves, was the great chief of Bora Bora. When Sperry asked where he might find a house to live in, the chief said, "You shall have my house." And picking up Sperry's baggage, he led him down a path under the breadfruit trees to a house that stood on the edge of a lagoon.

The chief's house was perched high on stilts. All day long the wind from the sea blew in and out through the bamboo walls, and at night rats and lizards fought together in the roof thatch. The chief moved his wife and four children to one end of the single long room and gave the other end to Armstrong Sperry. Here he settled down to live, the only white man on the island.

Sperry went into the mountains with the people to hunt the wild pig and to bring back great bunches of golden bananas and sacks of oranges. At night, by the light of torches, he fished with them on the barrier reef. Back at the bamboo house the chief told endless tales of daring, and the people came to sing

361

their ancient chants. Because Armstrong Sperry was interested in their legends, they patiently sang songs over and over until he had caught every shade of meaning.

Life on Bora Bora seemed to Armstrong Sperry too good to be true. But something happened which changed everything.

A blight killed the vanilla vines on all the islands—*except* Bora Bora. Overnight the price of vanilla jumped so high that the people found themselves in the position of millionaires. Trading schooners and merchants with luxuries of many kinds arrived at the island. All the old ways of working were forgotten, for why should a man spend hours at sea fishing, when he could buy a whole case of canned sardines with one sack of vanilla pods?

The people became soft with easy living. Only the old chief remained unchanged. "My people are forgetting the old ways," he said sadly. "That is not good. We were a great people. We crossed this ocean in our sailing canoes when the world was young. We were without fear. But who spears the octopus or stabs the shark today?"

But the easy riches did not last. New vanilla vines grew to replace those destroyed by blight on other islands. The price of vanilla fell sharply and great sacks of vanilla piled up in the sheds of Bora Bora.

And then one afternoon a hurricane struck. As the sea climbed higher and higher into the village, people retreated to caves in the mountains. Many were drowned.

For a day and a night the hurricane continued. When at last the wind decreased, and the survivors could return to their villages, the scene of destruction was nearly beyond belief. Their homes, canoes, and weapons were gone. Their wells and springs were filled with salt water. The banana and orange trees and the breadfruits, upon which they depended for most of their food, were ruined.

The people were filled with despair. Only the old chief was undaunted. He rose to the crisis like one of the hero-gods of his legends. He gathered his people around him and recalled to them the courage of their forefathers, who had crossed and recrossed the Pacific in their sailing canoes. The fire of his spirit put courage into the faltering and strengthened the weak. Slowly the people took up the old life where they had left off and rebuilt their world.

Definite or Indefinite?

Copy the phrases below and beside each write *definite* or *indefinite,* according to the idea which the phrase conveys.

some day	overnight
years later	one sack of vanilla pods
weeks passed	four children
two thousand feet	a single room
a giant of a man	a day and a night

Drawing Conclusions

Choose the two *best* answers to complete this statement:

"A Story of the South Seas" illustrates

a. the effect that one good, strong character can have on a group;
b. that Armstrong Sperry was a daring adventurer;
c. that the South Sea Islands are lovely and exciting;
d. that wealth does not of necessity make people happy.

Using Homonyms

Write a homonym for each of the words listed below.

tales	sail	great	whole
heir	red	might	buy
some	straight	blew	scene

Using Your Glossary

Using the glossary or the dictionary, find the meanings of the words listed below and write a sentence for each one.

copra	volcanic	legends	luxuries	undaunted
concertinas	ancient	blight	decreased	crisis

SIDNEY LANIER

Dear Land of All My Love

LONG as thine art shall love true love,
Long as thy science truth shall know,
Long as thine eagle harms no dove,
Long as thy law by law shall grow,
Long as thy God is God above,
Thy brother every man below,
So long, dear land of all my love,
Thy name shall shine, thy fame shall grow.

BISHOP JOHN LANCASTER SPALDING

God of All the Free

AND Thou, O God, of Whom we hold
Our country and our freedom fair,
Within Thy tender love enfold
This land; for all Thy people care.
Uplift our hearts above our fortunes high;
Let not the good we have make us forget
The better things that in Thy Heavens lie!
Keep, still, amid the fever and the fret
Of all this eager life, our thoughts on Thee,
The hope, the strength, the God of all the free.

FRAY ANGELICO CHAVEZ, O.F.M.

Our Lady of the Conquest[1]

I AM a small wooden statue of the Blessed Virgin Mary, dressed in real clothes of silk and gold braid like a Spanish queen of old, and I have been in this country for more than three hundred and twenty-five years. My name for centuries has been "La Conquistadora." You may as well call me, as you would spell it, "La Con-kees-tah-do-rah."

If ever you should come to Santa Fe, you will find me in my same old Conquistadora Chapel in the Cathedral of St. Francis of Assisi. The venerable adobe walls and the carved brown ceiling are rich with memories. The dust beneath the flooring is all that remains of many who centuries ago paid me living tribute and in death keep me faithful company. From the living you will find tokens of humble remembrance, like a burning candle or a bunch of home-grown flowers, the quiet presence of an aged woman

or a young man praying. If there are bouquets of more costly blooms about, you can be sure that some happy bride left me the flowers from her wedding that morning . . .

My expression is somewhat sad. Almost all Spanish Madonnas are sad. I might well reflect the many sorrows that many of my people have bravely undergone these many long centuries. I might also appear as though I am still thinking of my loving knights and courtiers who are no more. At the same time I manage to keep the triumphant air of that Lady conceived without sin being borne aloft into eternal glory. Age has not erased the dignity and poise that belong to a Conquistadora, a Lady who has conquered.

Beneath my feet may also be seen a small, gold-painted pedestal, which replaces one sawn off and lost long ago. Though it is covered with antique molding to go with my ancient self and the style of my garments, it is really a modern work of precision underneath; it is an eight-sided block of white pine that was cut and fitted together in

[1]From *La Conquistadora: The Biography of an Ancient Statue*, by Fray Angelico Chavez, O.F.M., published by St. Anthony Guild Press, Paterson, N. J., 1954.

the humming shops of the atomic city of Los Alamos, not long after the first bombs went off at Alamogordo, then at Hiroshima and Nagasaki. For, as I am myself a prayer to her who crushed the infernal serpent's head, so this pedestal under my feet represents a continual prayer that Mary may hold vanquished underfoot whatever there may be of evil in atomic power.

Every year now, on a late Sunday afternoon in June, as my procession wind slowly through the narrow streets of Santa Fe to my chapel at Rosario, I can make out the atomic city against the blue mountain flank, a thin white blur that turns into a sparkling necklace of lights as darkness falls. And the soft Spanish syllables of the Ave Maria ascend to heaven pleading softly in a haunting old Spanish melody: "Santa Maria . . . pray for us sinners . . ."

Of course, I know that I, a statue, am not immortal. The day will come when all the stars will fall. Nevertheless, I shall live on in the memories of those, my courtiers, who may see God face to face and behold His Mother's real beauty forever, for having fulfilled her prophecy in the Gospel by calling her blessed in every generation until the end of time.

Which Will You Do?

Choose one of the following projects.

1. Study your favorite picture of the Blessed Virgin, and using Fray Angelico Chavez's work as a model, write about that picture.

2. Draw and color the statue of Our Lady of the Conquest as described in this selection.

3. Compose a short prayer to Our Lady of the Conquest.

4. Look up some information about the author of the story and share it with the class.

Word Meanings

In each of the groups select the word which does not belong with the others and write it on your paper.

1. venerable	revered	old	infirm
2. adobe	zinc	stone	brick
3. tribute	praise	reverence	money
4. reflect	meditate	ponder	shine
5. triumphant	victorious	solemn	glorious
6. aloft	within	above	on high
7. antique	ancient	unusable	aged
8. precision	force	accuracy	exactitude
9. infernal	diabolical	devilish	lasting
10. immortal	perishable	undying	eternal

Glossary

This glossary, or little dictionary, on the following pages will help you to pronounce and understand the meanings of the new or unusual words used in *These Are Our Freedoms*.

The following list shows you how each marked letter is pronounced by giving as an example the same sound in a word that you know. This is called a *pronunciation key*.

ā *as in* lāte

å *as in* al'wåys

ă *as in* ăm

ă *as in* ăp·pear'

ä *as in* ärm

à *as in* àsk

â *as in* câre

ē *as in* hē

ê *as in* ê·nough'

ĕ *as in* nĕt

ĕ *as in* si'lĕnt

ē *as in* mak'ēr

ẹ *as in* hẹre

ī *as in* rīde

ĭ *as in* ĭn

ĭ *as in* pos'sĭ·ble

ō *as in* ōld

ô *as in* ô·bey'

ŏ *as in* nŏt

ŏ *as in* cŏn·nect'

ô *as in* sôft

ô *as in* hôrse

ū *as in* ūse

û *as in* û·nite'

ŭ *as in* ŭs

ŭ *as in* cir'cŭs

û *as in* bûrn

ōō *as in* mōōn

ŏŏ *as in* tŏŏk

oi *as in* oil

ou *as in* out

~~th~~ *as in* ~~th~~at

th *as in* thin

tụ *as in* natụre

dụ *as in* verdụre

N *as in* boN

a·beam' (à·bēm'), *adv*. Off to one side of a ship and at a line at right angles to her keel.

ab'o·li'tion (ăb'ô·lĭsh'ŭn), *n*. A complete destroying or ending of something.

ab'o·li'tion·ist (ăb'ô·lĭsh'ŭn·ĭst), *n*. A person who believed in and who worked for the complete destruction, or abolition, of slavery.

ab'sen·tee' (ăb'sĕn·tē'), *n*. A person who is absent, as, an *absentee landlord* is one who lives in another country or district than that where his property is situated.

A·dèle' (à·dĕl').

ad'ju·tant gen'er·al (ăj'ŏŏ·tănt jĕn'ēr·ăl), *n*. A military officer having administrative charge of the militia of a State or Territory.

aide (ād), *n*. An army or navy officer who acts as an assistant to a superior officer.

a·kin' (à·kĭn'), *adj*. Of the same kind; alike.

A·kla'vik (à·klä'vĭk). A trading post, north of the Arctic Circle, in northwestern Canada.

Al'a·mo·gor'do (ăl'à·mô·gôr'dō). A town in southern New Mexico, north of which is Alamogordo Air Base, the scene of the first man-made atomic explosion.

A·las'ka (à·lăs'kà) **Highway**. A military and commercial road built by U. S. Army engineers. It runs 1523 miles from Dawson Creek, British Columbia, to Fairbanks.

Al'be·marle (ăl'bê·märl). A county in central Virginia.

Al·ber'ta (ăl·bûr'tà). A province in western Canada.

al'ka·li (ăl'kà·lĭ), *n*. A mineral salt sometimes found in the soil of dry regions.

Al'le·ghe'ny (ăl'ê·gā'nĭ). **Mountains**. Mountain ranges in Pennsylvania, Maryland, and West Virginia.

Al'len, E'than (ăl'ĕn, ē'thăn). An American Revolutionary soldier; commander of the Green Mountain Boys in the capture of Fort Ticonderoga.

al·lude' (ă·lūd'), *v*. To refer to something indirectly or without actually describing it.

am'bus·cade' (ăm'bŭs·kād'), *n*. A concealed trap for catching or attacking an enemy by surprise. Sometimes called an **am'bush** (ăm'bŏŏsh).

a·mel'io·ra'tion (à·mēl'yô·rā'shŭn), *n*. The act of improving or making better.

369

An′chor·age (ăng′kĕr·ĭj). A seaport city in south central Alaska. It is now an important Army post and airport.

an′es·thet′ic (ăn′ĕs·thĕt′ĭk), *n.* A liquid, a gas, etc., which causes numbness or loss of feeling.

An′ge·la (ăn′jĕ·là), **Mother.** A Sister of the Holy Cross, from the Motherhouse at Notre Dame, Indiana.

An′gli·can (ăng′glĭ·kăn), *adj.* Having to do with the Church of England.

an′guish (ăng′gwĭsh), *n.* Extreme pain, either of body or mind.

An·nap′o·lis (à·năp′ŏ·lĭs). The capital of Maryland. The United States Naval Academy is located there. Frequently the Academy is referred to as *Annapolis.*

Ant′werp (ănt′wûrp). A city in northern Belgium.

Ap′po·mat′tox (ăp′ŏ·măt′ŭks). A town in Virginia where General Lee surrendered to General Grant, thus ending the War Between the States.

ap·praise′ (à·prāz′), *v.* To judge or estimate the value, worth, or qualities.

ap′pre·hen′sive (ăp′rê·hĕn′sĭv), *adj.* Fearful of what may be coming.

ap·pren′tice (à·prĕn′tĭs), *n.* A person who is learning his trade under a skilled worker. An **apprentice seaman** is one who has completed his boot training.

Arc′tic (ärk′tĭk) **Circle.** A parallel of latitude (66° 30′ N. latitude), 1650 miles from the North Pole.

Ar′gen·tine (är′jĕn·tēn), **The.** A South American republic, also called *Argentina.* Cattle raising is an important industry.

Ar·gu·in′ (är·gŏŏ·ēn′) **Banks.** Sandy shoals off the west coast of Africa.

Ar′nold (är′năld), **Benedict.** An American general in the Revolutionary War. In the early years of the War he served his country well, but in 1779 he sold military secrets to the enemy.

as·suage′ (à·swāj′), *v.* To quiet, calm, or soothe.

As·to′ri·a (ăs·tōr′ĭ·à). A city in Oregon, founded as a trading post in 1811.

Ath′ens (ăth′ĕnz). A city in Greece, famed as a center of learning and culture. During the nineteenth century, Boston was called the *Athens of America* because of its leadership in learning, arts, and letters.

aux·il′ia·ries (ôg·zĭl′yà·rĭz), *n. pl.* Groups, often of women, organized to give aid or assistance to official committees, etc.

a·weigh′ (à·wā′), *adj.* A sea term, applied to an anchor, meaning just clear of the ground, so that a vessel can make headway.

back′wash′ (băk′wŏsh′), *n.* A surge of air and other gas that moves backward, especially that caused by a propeller or jet stream.

baf′fle (băf′′l), *v.* To confuse.

bail′iff (bāl′ĭf), *n.* An officer in court, used as a messenger or usher. He also has charge of prisoners when they are brought into court to stand trial.

Ban′croft (băn′krŏft) **Hall.** A large building at the United States Naval Academy.

Ba′ra·ta′ri·a (bä′rà·tä′rê·à). An island in the Gulf of Mexico, not far from New Orleans. Formerly it was the haunt of pirates.

Bar′ba·ry (bär′bà·rĭ). A region in northern Africa, extending from Egypt to the Atlantic Ocean.

Bar′ce·lo′na (bär′sĕ·lō′nà). A city in Spain, where Columbus was welcomed by Ferdinand and Isabella on his return from the New World.

bar′low (bär′lō) **knife,** *n.* A type of jackknife with only one blade.

bass (bās) **drum,** *n.* The largest kind of drum, giving a deep, low sound.

be·guile′ (bê·gīl′), *v.* To cheat or to deceive.

be·hoove′ (bê·hŏŏv′), *v.* To be necessary or, proper as a matter of duty.

Bel′ter (bĕl′tĕr), **John Henry.** A cabinetmaker active in New York City between 1844 and 1865. His elaborately carved furniture of rosewood and walnut was very popular in the '50's.

be·night′ed (bê·nīt′ĕd), *adj.* Involved in or due to moral darkness or ignorance.

Ben·ni′no (bà·nē′nŏ).

be·reave′ment (bê·rēv′mĕnt), *n.* The sorrow caused by the death of some dearly loved person.

Bill of Rights. The first ten amendments to the Constitution of the United States, stating the rights and privileges of the people.

Black An′gus (ăng′gŭs). A common name for *Aberdeen-Angus,* a kind of hornless black beef cattle native to Aberdeen, Scotland.

Black Hills (blăk hĭlz). A mountain group in South Dakota and Wyoming.

Black′robe′ (blăk′rōb′). The Indian name for *priest.*

block and tack′le (blŏk ănd tăk′′l), *n.* Grooved pulleys, with ropes, etc., for hoisting or hauling.

block·ade′ (blŏk·ād′), *n.* The act of shutting up a place by troops, warships, etc., to prevent coming in or going out. A **blockade-runner** is a vessel or person that runs through a blockade.

bom′ba·zine′ (bŏm′bà·zēn′), *n.* A dress material made of wool combined with silk or cotton and having the appearance of stripes, or ribs, running through it.

bon′vo′yage′ (bôN′vwà′yàzh′). A French expression of farewell, meaning *a good voyage.*

Bo'ra Bo'ra (bō'rȧ bō'rȧ). One of the Society Islands about two hundred miles northwest of Tahiti in the South Pacific Ocean.

bow'ie (bō'ĭ; bōō'ĭ) **knife,** *n.* A knife with a long, strong blade.

box (bŏks), *n.* The driver's seat on a carriage or coach.

Bran'dy·wine' (brăn'dĭ·wĭn'). A creek in Pennsylvania and Delaware, near which the British defeated the Americans in a Revolutionary War battle.

bread'fruit' (brĕd'frōōt'), *n.* The large round fruit of a Polynesian tree which, when baked, somewhat resembles bread.

Bré'beuf', Jean (brā'bûf', zhäN). A French Jesuit missionary, martyred by the Iroquois.

breed (brēd), *n.* A kind or variety; race; as, men of courageous *breed.*

Bridg'er, James. (brĭj'ẽr). An American pioneer and scout.

brig'an·tine (brĭg'ăn·tēn), *n.* A ship like a brig but not carrying a square mainsail.

broad'side' (brôd'sīd'), *n.* A discharge at the same time of all the guns that can be fired from one side of a ship.

Broad'way' (brôd'wā'). An important street in New York City. There are many theaters in the district.

brunt (brŭnt), *n.* The force of a blow or the shock of an attack; the chief stress or strain in any contention.

brush (brŭsh), *n.* A tap-dance step in which the sole of the foot is moved lightly, or brushed, across the floor.

Bu·chan'an, James. (bū·kăn'ăn). A statesman who served in U. S. Congress and as President during the years preceding the Civil War.

buck'et (bŭk'ĕt) **seat,** *n.* A seat in an aircraft designed to fit the contours of a seat-pack parachute.

bull-pine (bōōl pīn), *n.* A very large pine of the western United States.

Bunk'er Hill (bŭngk'ẽr hĭl). A hill, near Boston, Massachusetts, near which a battle was fought, on June 17, 1775.

Bur·goyne', John. (bûr'goin'). A British army officer during the Revolutionary War; commander, for a time, at Fort Ticonderoga.

Burr, Aar'on (bûr, âr'ŭn). An American Revolutionary officer and political leader; he served as Vice-President of the United States under Thomas Jefferson.

Cad'il·lac, An'toine (kăd'ĭ·lăk, ăn'twäN). A French explorer, founder of the city of Detroit.

Ca·ho'ki·a (kȧ·hō'kĭ·ȧ). A village settled by the French in the area that is now the state of Illinois.

Cai'ro (kâr'ō). A city in Illinois at the point where the Ohio joins the Mississippi. During the Civil War it was an important military depot.

cal'cu·la'tion (kăl'kū·lā'shŭn), *n.* That which has been estimated or planned.

Cal'ga·ry (kăl'gȧ·rĭ). A city in Alberta, Canada.

camp meet'ing (kămp mēt'ĭng), *n.* A gathering held, usually by Methodists, for conducting a series of religious services in the open air or in a tent.

Cap'i·tol (kăp'ĭ·tŏl) **Hill.** A slight incline or hill upon which stands the United States Capitol, or building in which Congress meets, at Washington, D. C.

Car'son (kär's'n), **Kit.** An American trapper, scout, and Indian agent.

chal'lenge (chăl'ĕnj), *n.* An invitation to engage in a contest.

Chal·mette' (shäl·mĕt'). A plain outside the city of New Orleans. It is now a national monument.

chasm (kăz"m), *n.* A deep opening or gap in the earth; an abyss.

Chat·ter·a'wha (chăt·ẽr·ä'wä). A river in Kentucky, often called Sandy River.

Cher'o·kee' (chĕr'ô·kē'). A member of a tribe of Indians, one of the Five Civilized Tribes, who were forced to leave their lands and settle in country that is now Oklahoma.

Chey·enne' (shī·ĕn') *n.* 1. The capital of Wyoming. 2. A member of a warlike Indian tribe of the West.

Chick'a·saw (chĭk'ȧ·sô). An Indian of a powerful tribe, one of the Five Civilized Tribes, formerly living in northern Mississippi and Alabama. They were forced to leave their lands and settle in country that is now Oklahoma.

Chis'holm (chĭz'ŭm) **Trail.** The great cattle trail northward from Texas.

Choc'taw (chŏk'tô). An Indian of an important tribe, one of the Five Civilized Tribes, formerly living in Mississippi and Alabama. They were forced to leave their lands and settle in country that is now Oklahoma.

chlo'ro·form (klō'rô·fôrm) *n.* A colorless, sweetish-tasting liquid used to make senseless or to numb pain.

chol'er·a (kŏl'ẽr·ȧ) *n.* Acute inflammation of the stomach causing pain and extreme weakness.

cir'ca (sûr'kȧ) *prep.* About; around; as *circa* '20, meaning about 1920.

Clark (klärk), **George Rogers.** An American Revolutionary frontier leader.

---

lāte, alwãys, ăm, ȧppear, ärm, ȧsk, câre, hē, ênough, nĕt, silĕnt, makẽr, hẽre, rĭde, ĭn, possĭble, ōld, ôbey, nŏt, cŏnnect, sôft, hôrse, ūse, ûnite, ŭs, circŭs, bûrn, mōōn, tŏŏk, oil, out, ~~that~~, thin, natŭre, verdŭre, boN.

Clay (klā), **Henry.** An American statesman who devoted his efforts to prevent armed conflict between the North and the South.

clay pigeon, *n.* A saucer of baked clay or other material to be thrown from the trap, for a target in trap shooting.

code (kōd), *n.* 1. Any systematic body of law. 2. Any system of principles or rules. 3. A system of signals for communication by telegraph, flags, etc.

Co·dy (kō′dĭ), **William Frederick.** An American Indian fighter, known as *Buffalo Bill.* He later produced the *Wild West Show,* which traveled widely in America and Europe.

co·ma (kō′mȧ), *n.* A kind of deep sleep into which a dying or very ill person falls.

Co·man′che (kȯ·măn′chĕ). An Indian of a tribe living in western Wyoming, later ranging widely between Kansas and northern Mexico.

com′man·dant′ (kŏm′ȧn·dänt′), *n.* A commanding officer.

com′mon·wealth (kŏm′ŭn·wĕlth), *n.* A state or nation, or the people living in it. Three of the states, Massachusetts, Pennsylvania, and Virginia, are officially called *commonwealths.*

Com′stock Lode (kŏm′stŏk lōd). A gold and silver deposit, famous for its size. *See* Virginia City.

con·ceive′ (kȯn·sēv′), *v.* To grasp something as a notion or an idea; to begin something new in one's mind.

con′cer·ti′na (kŏn′sēr·tē′nȧ), *n.* A small musical wind instrument played much like an accordion.

con·cus′sion (kȯn·kŭsh′ŭn), *n.* A shock or injury, caused by collision of bodies.

Con·es·to′ga (kŏn′ĕs·tō′gȧ) **wagon.** A style of large wagon, usually covered, with broad wheels for traveling over soft soil and on prairies. First made at Conestoga, Pennsylvania.

Con·quis′ta·dor·a (kŏn·kwĭs′tȧ·dôr·ȧ), **La.** A Spanish expression meaning *She who conquers,* thus, Our Lady of the Conquest.

con′ser·va′tion (kŏn′sēr·vā′shŭn), *n.* The protection or preservation of something; official supervision of rivers, forests, etc.

con·sid′er·a′tion (kŏn·sĭd′ēr·ā′shŭn), *n.* Sympathetic or thoughtful regard or notice.

con·sign′ (kȯn·sīn′), *v.* To put in a prepared place; as, to *consign* to the grave.

Con′ti·nen′tal (kŏn′tĭ·nĕn′tȧl), *n.* A soldier of the united American colonies at the time of the American Revolution.

Con′ti·nen′tal Di·vide′ (kŏn′tĭ·nĕn′tȧl dĭ·vīd′). The line of highest points of land of the North American continent separating the waters flowing west from those flowing north or east. Known also as the *Great Divide.*

con′voy (kŏn′voi), *n.* A train, a fleet, or a vessel, or train of wagons or trucks, employed in transporting merchandise, money, etc., and having an armed escort.

cop′ra (kŏp′rȧ), *n.* The dried meat of coconuts, from which coconut oil is obtained.

corn dodg′er (kôrn dŏj′ēr), *n.* Corn bread baked in small shapes.

Corn·wal′lis (kôrn·wŏl′ĭs), **Charles.** A British general in the Revolutionary War; defeated at Yorktown and surrendered to General Washington.

coun′ter·charge′ (koun′tēr chärj′), *n.* A charge, or rushing attack, made in return.

course (kōrs), *n.* Progress from point to point without change of direction.

Creek (krēk). An Indian of a tribe, one of the Five Civilized Tribes, formerly living in Alabama, Georgia, and northern Florida. They were forced to leave their lands and settle in country that is now Oklahoma.

cre·scen′do (krĕ·shĕn′dō), *n.* A gradual increase in the quantity of sound.

cres′cent (krĕs′ĕnt) **moon,** *n.* A new moon, shaped like a crescent.

crow's′-nest (krōz′nĕst), *n.* A partly inclosed platform high on a ship's mast for a lookout.

cru′cial (krōō′shȧl), *adj.* Concerning a final test or decision; decisive, as a *crucial* battle.

Cur′ri·er (kûr′ĭ·ēr) **& Ives** (īvz). A series of prints, brought out in the last half of the nineteenth century by the firm of the same name. The prints vividly depicted the customs and people of the era, and are much prized today by collectors.

Cus′ter (kŭs′tēr), **George.** An American Army officer who was killed by Indians in the battle of Little Big Horn.

cus·to′di·an (kŭs·tō′dĭ·ȧn), *n.* A person who has charge, or the care of, something.

Da·kar′ (dȧ·kär′). The capital of French West Africa.

Dan′te (dän′tĕ), **Professor.**

Da′vis (dā′vĭs), **Jefferson.** President of the Confederate States of America.

Daw′son (dô′s'n). The capital of Yukon Territory, Canada.

dead reck′on·ing (dĕd rĕk′ŭn·ĭng), *n.* The method of finding the position of a ship without celestial observation, from a record of the courses sailed.

Dead′wood′ (dĕd′wŏŏd′). A city in South Dakota, formerly a famous mining camp.

de·bris′ (dĕ·brē′), *n.* Rubbish; litter; ruins.

de Chan′tal′ (dē shäɴ′tȧl′), **Mother Mary.** An Ursuline nun whose Community formed in New Orleans the first Catholic school for girls in what is now the United States.

de·fend'ant (dē·fĕn'dănt), *n.* A person who is required to make answer in a legal action.

del'i·ca·cies (dĕl'ĭ·kȧ·sĭz), *n. pl.* Choice kinds of foods, such as candies and nuts.

Del'phine' (dĕl'fēn').

del'uge (dĕl'ûj), *n.* An overpowering amount of water.

dem'o·crat (dĕm'ŏ·krăt) wagon, *n.* A light uncovered wagon with two or more seats.

de Sales (dē sälz), Mother Mary. A Sister of the Order of Mercy, known during the Civil War as "the Sisters of Mercy." A hospital at Vicksburg is still maintained by the Community.

De Smet', Pierre-Jean (dē smĕt', pyâr zhäN). A Belgian Jesuit priest who did missionary work among American Indians.

des'per·a'do (dĕs'pēr·ā'dō), *n.* A desperate criminal or lawbreaker; a reckless ruffian.

de·tract' (dē·trăkt'), *v.* To take away; to lessen.

din'ghy (dĭng' gĭ), *n.* A small, light boat; especially, a kind of rowboat.

din'na ken (dĭn'ȧ kĕn). Scottish dialect for the expression *don't know.*

di'o·ra'ma (dī'ŏ·rä'mȧ), *n.* A method of scenic representation in which a painting is seen from a distance through an opening. Vivid and realistic effects are often obtained.

dis·band' (dĭs·bănd'), *v.* To break up an organized body of men and dismiss its members.

dis·em·bark' (dĭs'ĕm·bärk'), *v.* To land from a ship.

dis·man'tle (dĭs·măn't'l), *v.* 1. To strip of covering. 2. To strip of furniture and equipment.

dis·pir'it·ed (dĭs·pĭr'ĭt·ĕd), *adj.* Discouraged.

dis·posed' (dĭs·pōzd'), *adj.* Having an inclination or willingness to do something.

dis'trict at·tor'ney (dĭs'trĭkt ă·tûr'nĭ), *n.* The lawyer of a given district whose duty it is to carry on legal action against an accused person to prove his guilt.

doc'trine (dŏk'trĭn), *n.* A statement of belief on any subject.

Don Di·e'go (dŏn dē·ā'gō). Son of Christopher Columbus.

Do'ver (dō'vēr). A reference to a song, "Put on Your Old Gray Bonnet," in which two people celebrate their golden-wedding anniversary by riding to Dover.

down'wind' (doun'wĭnd'), *adv.* With the wind against one's back.

dry dock (dŏk), *n.* A dock from which the water may be pumped out, used in building and repairing ships.

Du·bourg' (dü·boor'), Father William Louis. A French Sulpician priest and educator who later became bishop of New Orleans.

dum'found' (dŭm'found'), *v.* To confuse; to amaze.

Ed'mon·ton (ĕd'mŭn·tŭn). The capital of the Province of Alberta, Canada.

el'o·quent (ĕl'ŏ·kwĕnt), *adj.* Vividly or movingly expressive or revealing.

Em'er·son (ĕm'ēr·s'n), Ralph Waldo. An American essayist and poet, living in Boston at the time of the Civil War.

Em'mits·burg (ĕm'ĭts·bûrg). The Maryland Motherhouse of The Sisters of Charity of Cincinnati, founded by Mother Elizabeth Seton in 1809.

en·gross' (ĕn·grōs'), *v.* To absorb; to occupy fully.

En·ri'co (än·rē'kŏ).

e·ques'tri·an (ê·kwĕs'trĭ·ăn), *adj.* Of or relating to horses or horsemanship.

er'mine (ĕr'mĭn), *n.* A pure white fur. It is used to trim or line the robes of royalty or of judges as a symbol of purity.

es'ca·pade' (ĕs'kȧ·pād'), *n.* A mischievous adventure.

e·vac'u·ate (ê·văk'û·āt), *v.* To clear a city or a place by withdrawing the soldiers or civilians in it to a safer area.

e·vic'tion (ê·vĭk'shŭn), *n.* The act of putting out, as from a house, by lawful means.

ex'e·unt om'nes (ĕk'sê·ŭnt ŏm'nēz). A Latin phrase, meaning *all go out or retire.*

fa·cil'i·tate (fȧ·sĭl'ĭ·tāt), *v.* To make easy or less difficult.

fac'tor (făk'tēr), *n.* 1. A person who does business for someone else; an agent. 2. An influence or circumstance that helps to produce a result.

fade in, *v.* In broadcasting, to cause a sound to grow gradually louder.

fade out, *v.* In broadcasting, to lower the volume of sound gradually.

Fair'banks (fâr'băngks). The chief town in central Alaska. It is located at the end of the Alaska Highway.

Fia'cre (fyȧ'k'r), Saint. The patron saint of gardeners.

fight'ing cock (fīt'ĭng kŏk), *n.* A domestic fowl bred largely for fighting. They are noted for the ferocity of their attack.

fil'i·al (fĭl'ĭ·ȧl), *adj.* Relating to a son or daughter.

fi·na'le (fê·nä'lȧ), *n.* The closing part, piece, scene, or number in any public performance.

Fink (fĭngk), Mike. An American frontier hero. Many colorful "tall tales" have been told of his exploits as a Mississippi river boatman and as a marksman.

---

lāte, alwāys, ăm, ȧppear, ärm, ȧsk, câre, hē, ênough, nĕt, silĕnt, makēr, hẽre, rīde, ĭn, possĭble, ōld, ôbey, nŏt, cŏnnect, sŏft, hôrse, ūse, ûnite, ŭs, circŭs, bûrn, mōōn, tŏŏk, oil, out, ~~that~~, thin, natūre, verdūre, boN.

Five Civilized Tribes. The Cherokee, Chickasaw, Choctaw, Creek, and Seminole nations of Oklahoma. *See* individual tribes.

flight bub'ble (flīt bŭb''l), *n.* A bubble sextant, one of the instruments used by pilots to determine the position of the plane.

Flor'ence (flŏr'ĕns). A city in Italy, famous for its art treasures. Among the most priceless are the bronze doors, covered with gold, of the Baptistery.

fore·run'ner (fōr·rŭn'ẽr), *n.* That which goes ahead to tell of the approach of others.

fore'sail (fōr's'l), *n.* A sail on the foremast, the mast nearest the bow of a vessel.

Fort Bridg'er (brĭj'ẽr). A village in southwestern Wyoming; formerly an important fort on the Oregon Trail. *See* Jim Bridger.

Fort Du·quesne' (dōō·kān'). A fort built by the French at the point where the Allegheny and the Monongahela rivers join to form the Ohio. When captured by the British it was renamed Fort Pitt.

Fort Gage (gāj). The British post at Kaskaskia, a French village in what is now Illinois.

Fort Lar'a·mie (lăr'à·mĭ). A former fort, in Wyoming, built for the protection of travelers on the Oregon Trail.

Fort Lin'coln (lĭng'kŭn). A fort in what is now North Dakota, headquarters for troops engaged in the war with Sitting Bull.

Fort Mas'sac (măs'ăk). A former fort in Illinois.

Fort Pitt. *See* Fort Duquesne.

Fort Sum'ter (sŭm'tẽr). A fort in Charleston harbor, South Carolina. The attack on Sumter by Confederates began the Civil War.

Fort Van·cou'ver (văn·kōō'vẽr). A trading post, founded by Hudson's Bay Company. The city of Vancouver, Washington, now occupies the same site.

for'ty-nin'er (fôr'tĭ-nīn'ẽr), *n.* One who went to California in the rush for gold in 1849.

four'square' (fōr'skwâr'), *adj.* Square in shape.

Fox (fŏx). An Indian of a tribe formerly living in Wisconsin.

Frank'lin (frăngk'lĭn), **Benjamin.** A statesman, patriot, scientist, and philosopher; signer of the Declaration of Independence. His home was in Philadelphia.

Fred'er·ick (frĕd'rĭk). A city in northern Maryland, about twenty-four miles southeast of Hagerstown.

French cal'i·co (kăl'ĭ·kō), *n.* Cotton cloth, especially with a colored pattern printed on one side.

French horn, *n.* A musical wind instrument of brass. It is a long, bent, cone-shaped tube.

fruit'less (frōōt'lĕs), *adj.* Useless; without results.

gal·van'ic (găl·văn'ĭk), *adj.* Acting as if affected by an electric shock.

Gar'ri·son (găr'ĭ·s'n), **William Lloyd.** A leader of fanatical abolitionists, living in Boston.

gaunt (gônt), *adj.* Very thin, as with suffering or privation.

gav'el (găv'ĕl), *n.* A small mallet, usually of wood, with which the person presiding over a meeting calls it to order.

Gen'o·a (jĕn'ō·à). A seaport of northwestern Italy.

ge·ol'o·gist (jê·ŏl'ō·jĭst) *n.* One versed in the science of the history of the earth.

Ger'man·town (jûr'măn·toun). The site of a battle during the Revolutionary War. It is now a section of Philadelphia.

Gi·bault', Pierre (zhê·bō', pyâr). A French priest and missionary.

gib'ber·ing (jĭb'ẽr·ĭng), *v.* Talking rapidly and confusedly; also, talking fluently and foolishly.

Gi·bral'tar (jĭ·brôl'tẽr). A town and fortress on the Rock of Gibraltar, a headland at the southwestern tip of Europe. It is a British colony.

Gla'cier (glā'shẽr) **Park.** A national park, located in northwest Montana; famed for its scenic beauty.

Gol'den Gate. The entrance to San Francisco Bay.

Go'shen·hop'pen (gō'shĕn·hŏp'ĕn). An early settlement in Pennsylvania.

grass roots, *n.* A figurative expression meaning the very foundation, or source.

grease'wood' (grēs'wōōd'), *n.* A low, stiff shrub common in western United States. It flames quickly with a bright blaze when set afire.

Great American Desert. Formerly, a name given to the area between the Coast ranges of California and the Rocky Mountains.

Green Mountain Boys. A group of Vermont soldiers, during the Revolutionary War, who fought under the leadership of Ethan Allen.

Green'wich (grĕn'ĭch) **Village.** A part of New York City. Many authors, artists, and students make their homes in the area.

grilled, (grĭld), *adj.* Having a grating of iron, bronze, etc., which forms an openwork screen.

gris'ly (grĭz'lĭ), *adj.* Horrible; ghastly; shocking.

gro·tesque' (grō·tĕsk'), *adj.* Strange and fantastic.

gun'ny (gŭn'ĭ) **sack,** *n.* A bag, or sack, made of a coarse, rough material.

Ha'gers·town (hā'gẽrz·toun). A city in Maryland.

Ham'il·ton (hăm'ĭl·tŭn), **Henry.** British governor at Detroit during the Revolutionary War. He earned the hatred of the frontier people because of his activity in stirring the Indians to attack American settlements.

Hamp'shire Grants (hăm'shẽr grănts). A large area of land open to settlers in what is now New Hampshire and Vermont.

Han'del (hăn'd'l), **George Frederic.** A famous German composer.

Han'ni·bal (hăn'ĭ·băl). A town in Missouri; the boyhood home of Samuel L. Clemens (Mark Twain).

har'py (här'pĭ), *n.* A person who fastens upon and torments another person.

har'row (hăr'ō), *v.* 1. To cultivate with a harrow, a farm implement designed to break up clods of earth. 2. To break as with a harrow; to wound; to distress.

Haugh'ery (hô'rĭ), **Margaret.**

Ha·van'a (há·văn'á). The capital of Cuba.

Haw'thorne (hô'thôrn), **Nathaniel.** A famed American novelist.

heave (hēv) **to,** *v.* To bring a vessel to a standstill by heading into the wind.

Hen'ry, Pat'rick. An American Revolutionary patriot, orator, and leader.

Her'e·ford (hĕr'ê·fêrd). An animal of an important breed of hardy beef cattle. They are red with white faces and markings.

heif'er (hĕf'ēr), *n.* A young cow.

Hi'ro·shi'ma (hē'rô·shē'má). A city in Japan, almost completely destroyed by the explosion of the first atomic bomb used in warfare.

hock (hŏk), *n.* The joint about midway in the hind leg of horses and cattle, corresponding to the ankle of man.

home'stead·er (hōm'stĕd·ēr), *n.* One who has settled upon a tract of public land under certain conditions established by law.

Hous'ton (hūs'tŭn), **Sam.** An American soldier and political leader.

Hud'son's (hŭd's'nz) **Bay Company.** A company formed in England with exclusive trade rights throughout what is now Canada. Its chain of forts and trading posts stretched from the Atlantic to the Pacific. It is still active today.

Hy·pe'ri·on (hī·pēr'ĭ·ŏn). A mythological character. Such names were often used for sailing vessels.

im'pact (ĭm'păkt), *n.* The forcible striking of one thing against another.

im·pov'er·ished (ĭm·pŏv'ēr·ĭshed), *adj.* Poor; without means of support.

in'ci·den'tal (ĭn'sĭ·dĕn'tăl), *adj.* Likely to happen along with something else; as, the music was *incidental* to the action of the play.

in·cite' (ĭn·sīt'). *v.* To arouse to action; to spur or urge on.

In'di·an Ter'ri·to'ry. Formerly a United States territory to which many Indian tribes were removed. It is now a part of Oklahoma.

in·fir'ma·ry (ĭn·fûr'má·rĭ), *n.* A place where the sick or wounded are nursed.

in·i'ti·a'tive (ĭ·nish'ĭ·á'tĭv), *n.* 1. An introductory step. 2. Energy in taking action; also self-reliant enterprise.

in·tel'li·gence serv'ice, *n.* The branch of government work which has to do with obtaining secret information; secret service.

in'ter·vene' (ĭn'tēr·vēn'), *v.* 1. To happen between events. 2. To come between to settle a dispute.

in·vi'o·late (ĭn·vī'ô·lāt), *adj.* Untouched or unharmed.

jas'mine (jăs'mĭn), *n.* A vine or bush with shiny leaves and sweet-smelling flowers.

Jef'fer·son (jĕf'ēr·s'n), **Thomas.** A patriot and leader during the Revolutionary War; signer of the Declaration of Independence; third President of the United States.

jib (jĭb), *n.* A triangular sail extending from the head of the foremast to the bowsprit.

Jogues (zhôg), **Saint Isaac.** French Jesuit missionary in America, martyred by the Indians.

Jo'li·et' (jō'lĭ·ĕt'), **Louis.** Companion of Father Marquette on the journey which led to the discovery of the Mississippi.

Josh'u·a (jŏsh'û·á) **tree.** One of a family of trees found in southwestern United States. It is large and ragged in appearance, with leaves clustered at the ends of its branches.

Ju'neau (jōō'nō). The state capital of Alaska.

Kas·kas'ki·a (kăs·kăs'kĭ·á). An early French settlement in what is now Illinois.

keel (kēl), *n.* A timber, plate, or the like running lengthwise along the bottom of a vessel. In poetry, the word often means the entire ship.

Ken'ton (kĕn't'n), **Simon.** An American pioneer and Indian fighter; friend of Daniel Boone.

Kings Mountain. A ridge in South Carolina, the scene of an American victory over the British during the Revolutionary War.

Klon'dike (klŏn'dīk). A region of the Yukon Territory in northwest Canada, the site of many valuable gold deposits.

knee'-high' (nē'hī'), *adv.* Rising or reaching upward to the knees; thus, not very tall.

L, The. The name, commonly used in New York City, for the elevated railway.

Laf·font', Jean (lá·fôN', zhäN). One of the early settlers at Kaskaskia.

La'fitte', Jean (lá'fēt', zhäN). A French adventurer of the Gulf of Mexico islands, who, with his brother **Pierre** (pyâr), engaged in privateering.

---

lāte, alwăys, ăm, ăppear, ärm, àsk, câre, hē, ênough, nĕt, silĕnt, makēr, hēre, rīde, ĭn, possĭble, ōld, ôbey, nŏt, cŏnnect, sŏft, hôrse, ūse, ûnite, ŭs, circŭs, bûrn, mōōn, tŏŏk, oil, out, that, thin, natŭre, verdŭre, boN.

lam′en·ta·bly (lăm′ĕn·tȧ·blĭ), *adv.* In a mournful manner.

La Ra′bi·da (lä rä′bē·dä). A Franciscan convent in Palos, Spain.

La Salle′ (là săl′). A French explorer in America.

Le′gion (lē′jŭn) **Post.** The local members of the American Legion, an organization of war veterans.

le·vi′a·than (lê·vī′ȧ·thȧn), *n.* A huge water animal mentioned several times in the Bible; therefore, something huge.

Lew′is (lū′ĭs), **Meriwether, and Clark** (klärk), **William.** Leaders of the exploring expedition to find a route to the Pacific Ocean. The expedition (1804–1806) went up the Missouri River, crossed the Great Divide, and descended the Columbia River to the Pacific.

Li′ma (lē′mà). The capital of Peru.

log (lŏg), *n.* The record of a ship's progress. *v.* To sail or move a specified distance, as shown by a ship's log.

Long′fel′low (lŏng′fĕl′ō), **Henry Wadsworth.** A famous New England poet.

Long Knife. A white man; formerly so-called by American Indians.

long-nine (lŏng nīn), *n.* A variety of cigar smoked about the middle of the nineteenth century; also, a clay pipe.

Los Al′a·mos (lŏs ăl′ȧ·mōs). A town in New Mexico, the site of an important atomic-bomb plant.

Low′ell (lō′ĕl), **James Russell.** A famous American poet and writer.

Loy·o′la (loi·ō′là), **Saint Ignatius of.** A Spanish priest; founder of the Society of Jesus.

lu′ci·fer (lū′sĭ·fẽr) **match,** *n.* The name applied to one of the earliest of the friction matches.

Mack′i·nac (măk′ĭ·nô), **Straits of.** A narrow body of water connecting Lake Michigan and Lake Huron. Father Marquette founded the Mission of St. Ignace on the northern shore of the Straits.

McLough′lin (măk·lŏf′lĭn), **John.** A Scotsman, factor of the Hudson's Bay Company territory in the Northwest.

Mad′i·son (măd′ĭ·sŭn), **James.** Patriot, statesman, and fourth President of the United States.

Man′i·tou (măn′ĭ·tōō). Among the pagan Indians, a spirit that rules nature; the Christian Indians used the same name for God.

ma·raud′er (mȧ·rôd′ẽr), *n.* A person seeking plunder; a pillager.

Mar′i·on (măr′ĭ·ŭn), **Francis.** An American Revolutionary commander in the South. Sometimes called "the Swamp Fox."

Mar′quette′, Jacques (mär′kĕt′, zhäk). A French Jesuit priest and missionary who explored the Mississippi River.

Mas·cou′ten (màs·kōō′tĕn). An Indian of a tribe that formerly lived in southern Michigan and Illinois.

Ma′son, George. A Revolutionary War statesman; prepared the Declaration of Rights.

Mem′phis (mĕm′fĭs). A city in Tennessee, the center of much fighting during the Civil War.

Me·nard′, Re·né′ (mĕ·närd′, rē·nā′). A French Jesuit missionary priest, martyred by the Indians in northern Michigan.

men-at-arms (mĕn ăt ärmz), *n.* Armed soldiers.

Merrimac. *See* Monitor and Merrimac.

mes·quite′ (mĕs·kēt′), *n.* A thorny deep-rooted tree or bush that grows in the southwestern United States and Mexico.

Mes·si′ah (mĕ·sī′ȧ). The title of a famous music composition by Handel.

Mi·am′i (mī·ăm′ĭ). An Indian of a tribe formerly living in the region about Indiana.

Mi′chel′ (mē′shĕl′).

"mid′dy" (mĭd′ĭ), *n.* A popular name for a midshipman.

Mi·lan′ (mĭ·lăn′). A large city of northern Italy. Its Gothic cathedral is one of the most beautiful in the world.

milk′sop′ (mĭlk′sŏp′), *n.* A person, especially a boy or man, who is used to being petted or pampered.

mi·rage′ (mĭ·räzh′), *n.* A reflection visible at sea, in the desert, etc., of a distant and, often, unseen object.

mis′rep·re·sen·ta′tion (mĭs′rĕp·rē·sĕn·tā′shŭn) *n.* Anything said or done that gives a false impression, especially when the thing is meant to give a wrong idea.

mode (mōd), *n.* A popular style or custom. 2. A manner of doing something; a method.

mol′li·fy (mŏl′ĭ·fī), *v.* To soften; to calm.

Mon′i·tor (mŏn′ĭ·tẽr) **and Mer′ri·mac** (mĕr′ĭ·măk). The *Monitor*, a Union ship, and the *Merrimac* (renamed the *Virginia* by the Confederates) were the first ironclad vessels to engage in combat.

Mon′mouth (mŏn′mŭth) **Court House.** Now Freehold, N. J., the scene of a battle during the Revolutionary War.

mon′o·logue (mŏn′ō·lŏg), *n.* A long speech by one person.

mon·sieur′ (mē·syû′), *n.* A French title of respect, meaning literally, *my lord.* It corresponds to English *Mr.*

Mor′mon (môr′mŭn). A member of the Mormon Church, so-called because its people profess belief in *The Book of Mormon,* which, according to them, is a sacred history of the early inhabitants of America.

Mount′ie (moun′tĭ), *n.* A member of the Royal Canadian Mounted Police, originally the Northwest Mounted Police.

mule'-skin'ner (mūl'skĭn'ẽr), *n.* A mule-driver.

mul'ti·na'tion·al (mŭl'tĭ·năsh'ŭn·ăl), *n.* A citizen or subject of several countries in turn. A term of contempt for a person who changes his allegiance as often as it is profitable for him to do so.

Mu'nich (mū'nĭk). A city in Germany, famed for its skilled craftsmen.

Mus'co·vy (mŭs'kō·vĭ). An old name of Russia.

Mus·ko'gee (mŭs·kō'gē). A city in Oklahoma.

mys'tic (mĭs'tĭk), *adj.* Mysterious; having a deeper meaning.

Na'ga·sa'ki (nä'gȧ·sä'kè). An important city in Japan, nearly half of which was destroyed by atomic bomb in World War II.

Na'mur' (nȧ·mür'). A province of southeastern Belgium.

Na'pi·er (nā'pĭ·ẽr). A British manufacturing concern whose name is used in identifying certain aircraft.

Nas'by, Pe·tro'le·um (năz'bĭ, pê·trō'lê·ŭm). The pen name of an American humorist, David R. Locke.

Natch'ez (năch'ĕz) **under-the-Hill.** The riverfront section of Natchez, Mississippi.

Naz'a·reth (năz'ȧ·rĕth). The Kentucky Motherhouse of the Sisters of Charity of Nazareth, established near Bardstown in 1812.

nick'er (nĭk'ẽr), *v.* To neigh.

Nix'on (nĭk's'n), **John.** An American Revolutionary leader.

No'tre Dame' (nō'tr' dȧm'). French words meaning *Our Lady*; the Virgin Mary; Our Blessed Mother.

No'va Sco'tia (nō'vȧ skō'shȧ), *n.* One of the maritime provinces of eastern Canada.

ob·lit'er·ate (ŏb·lĭt'ẽr·āt), *v.* 1. To erase or blot out. 2. To destroy completely.

off mike. In broadcasting, at a distance from the microphone.

O'kla·ho'ma Ter'ri·to'ry (ō'klȧ·hō'mȧ tĕr'ĭ·tō'rĭ). An area, originally part of the lands assigned to the Indians in what is now Oklahoma, later opened up to settlement by the white men.

Old Hickory. A nickname for President Andrew Jackson.

O·li'vi·er' (ô·lē'vyā'), **Mother Marie.** Mother Superior at the Ursuline Convent of New Orleans in 1815.

Ot'ta·wa (ŏt'ȧ·wȧ). One of a tribe of Indians who lived on the shores of Lake Superior and Lake Michigan.

pal'let (păl'ĕt), *n.* A small, poor bed, often of straw.

pan'a·ce'a (păn'ȧ·sē'ȧ), *n.* A remedy for all diseases.

Pa'pal Nun'ci·o (pā'păl nŭn'shĭ·ō). The permanent official representative of the Pope at a foreign court or seat of government.

pa·rade' (pȧ·rād') **ground,** *n.* The area upon which troops regularly assemble for inspection, review, etc.

Pat'a·go'ni·a (păt'ȧ·gō'nĭ·ȧ). A region of southern America.

Paw·nee' (pô·nē'). An Indian of a tribe that ranged the plains south of the Platte River.

pawn'shop' (pôn'shŏp'), *n.* A shop where one may leave personal property such as jewelry, musical instruments, etc., as security in return for a loan of money.

paw'paw' (pô'pô'), *n.* A yellowish fruit of a tree that grows in southern United States.

Pearl (pûrl) **Harbor.** A land-locked harbor on the island of Oahu, Hawaii, used by the United States as a naval base.

Pec'ci, Jo'a·chim Vin'cent (pā'chē, jō'ȧ·kĭm vĭn'sĕnt). An Italian cardinal who became Pope Leo XIII.

Pe'cos (pā'kŭs). A river in Texas.

Pen'ta·gon (pĕn'tȧ·gŏn), **The.** Headquarters of the U. S. Department of Defense. It is a five-story, five-sided structure, hence the name, *Pentagon.*

pent'house' (pĕnt'hous'), *n.* 1. A shed or roof attached to a building. 2. An apartment built on a roof.

Per'rin', Jacques (pĕ'răɴ', zhäk).

per'son·nel' (pûr'sŏ·nĕl'), *n.* The body of persons employed in some service.

pert (pûrt), *adj.* Saucy, bold. *In a meaning rarely used,* clever, keen.

phi·los'o·phy (fĭ·lŏs'ō·fĭ), *n.* A consistent personal attitude toward life, especially if this attitude is expressed in principles of conduct.

phos'phate (fŏs'fāt), *n.* A chemical salt much used in fertilizers.

Phyfe (fif), **Duncan.** A Scottish furniture maker who immigrated to the United States soon after the Revolutionary War. He is famous for the beauty of the furniture he made.

pi'noch'le (pē'nŭk''l), *n.* A card game.

pit'tance (pĭt'ăns), *n.* A small amount of money.

Platte (plăt). A river in Nebraska, formed by the joining of the North Platte and the South Platte. It flows east into the Missouri River.

Point Bar'row (point băr'ō). The most northerly point of Alaska. The village of Barrow is a government station with post office and radio and weather-bureau stations.

---

lāte, alwȧys, ăm, ȧppear, ärm, ȧsk, câre, hē, ênough, nĕt, silĕnt, makẽr, hẽre, rīde, ĭn, possĭble, ōld, ôbey, nŏt, cŏnnect, sŏft, hôrse, ūse, ûnite, ŭs, circŭs, bûrn, mōon, took, oil, out, that, thin, natṳre, verdṳre, boɴ.

Pol′y·ne′sian (pŏl′ĭ·nē′shăn). 1. Of or pertaining to Polynesia, the islands of the central Pacific Ocean. 2. A member of any of the brown races of those islands. 3. The language of Polynesia.

Pom·pe′ii (pŏm·pā′yē).

port′age (pōr′tĭj), *n.* 1. The act or cost of carrying something. 2. The carrying of boats and goods overland between navigable waters.

Port′ E·tienne′ (pôr′ tă·tyĕn′).

post (pōst), *n.* 1. The place at which a soldier is stationed; also, the place where a body of troops is stationed. 2. A trading settlement.

Post, Wi′ley (pōst, wī′lĭ). An American aviator who twice flew around the world.

post′haste′ (pōst′hāst′), *adv.* With great speed; hastily.

Po·to′mac (pŏ·tō′măk). A river in eastern United States. Washington, D. C., is situated on its shores.

pow′der mag′a·zine′ (pou′dĕr măg′a·zēn′), *n.* A place where ammunition and gunpowder may be stored.

prai′rie-dog town (prâr′ĭ dŏg toun), *n.* A great number of prairie dogs living, according to their habit, in a colony, or "town."

prai′rie schoon′er (prâr′ĭ skōōn′ēr), *n.* A wagon with a rounded top, usually of heavy canvas.

pre·car′i·ous·ly (prē·kâr′ĭ·ŭs·lĭ), *adv.* In a hazardous manner; insecurely.

pre′mi·um (prē′mĭ·ŭm), *n.* A reward; a prize in a competition.

pre·rog′a·tive (prē·rŏg′a·tĭv), *n.* A right to special powers or privileges.

Pres′cott (prĕs′kŭt), **William.** An American Revolutionary soldier; commanded a regiment in battle known as the Battle of Bunker Hill.

pre·ten′tious (prē·tĕn′shŭs), *adj.* Showy.

prie′-dieu′ (prē′dyû′), *n.* A small desk, or table, suitable for a person kneeling at prayer.

prize (prīz), *n.* Something won in competition; also, a person or thing taken by superior force; as "The boat became the *prize* of the enemy vessel." A **prize crew** is a group of men put in charge of a captured ship to sail it to port.

pro·found′ (prŏ·found′), *adj.* 1. Very deep; as, *profound* sorrow. 2. Intellectually deep; as, *profound* thought.

pros′e·cute (prŏs′ê·kūt), *v.* To carry on a legal action against an accused person to prove his guilt.

pro′vost mar′shal (prō′vō mär′shăl), *n.* A military officer appointed to serve as head of the military police. His duties include the care of prisoners of war.

Pry·tan′i·a (prĭ·tăn′ĭ·ä). A famed street in New Orleans.

pun′dit (pŭn′dĭt), *n.* A learned man.

Put′nam (pŭt′năm), **Israel.** An American general during the Revolutionary War.

qua′ver (kwā′vēr), *v.* To speak in trembling, uncertain tones.

que′ry (kwēr′ĭ), *n.* Question.

quirt (kwûrt), *n.* A riding whip with a short handle and a lash of rawhide.

rack (răk), *n.* A wind-driven mass of high, often broken, clouds; a driving mist or fog.

rau′cous (rô′kŭs), *adj.* Disagreeably harsh.

Red′coat′ (rĕd′kōt′), *n.* A British soldier.

re·fec′to·ry (rê·fĕk′tô·rĭ), *n.* A dining hall, especially in a monastery or a convent; formerly dining halls in convent boarding schools were so called.

re·sign′ed·ly (rê·zīn′ĕd·lĭ), *adv.* Submissively, uncomplainingly.

Ri·chard′, Ga′bri·el′ (rē·shàr′, gä′brĭ·ĕl′). A French Sulpician priest, missionary, and educator.

Ri′gaud′, E′lise′ (rē′gō′, ä′lēz′).

Ri′gaud′, Lou′is (rē′go′, lōō′ĭ).

Ri′o de Ja·nei′ro (rē′ō dä zha·nā′rō). A seaport, the capital of Brazil.

road run′ner (rōd rŭn′ēr), *n.* A swift-running bird, with a long tail, found mainly in southwestern United States.

Roche′blave′, Che·va′lier′ de (rôsh′blàv′, shē·vä′lyä′dĕ). French commander at Fort Kaskaskia.

Ro·me′ro, Lu′pe (rô·mā′rô, lōō′pā).

Ro·sa′rio (rô·sä′ryŏ).

Rose of Li′ma (lē′mà), **Saint.** The first American to be canonized.

Ross Bar′ri·er (rŏs băr′ĭ·ēr). A large ice wall and the ice shelf back of it, bordering Ross Sea in Antarctica.

sa′chem (sā′chĕm), *n.* Any North American Indian chief.

sad′dle horn (săd′l hôrn), *n.* The high pommel of a saddle.

sa′ga (sà′gà), *n.* Any story of heroic deeds.

Sainte′ Anne′ (săNt′ ăn′); *Eng.* Saint Ann. An early parish in Detroit, Michigan.

Sa·ka′ja·we′a (sä·kä′jä·wā′ä). An Indian squaw, the Bird Woman, who guided Lewis and Clark across the Rockies to the West Coast.

Sal′a·man′ca (săl′a·măng′ka) **Royal Council of.** A special committee, appointed by Ferdinand and Isabella, to hear Columbus present his plans for sailing west to Asia. The Council met at the University of Salamanca, one of the famous universities of Spain.

San Joa·quin′ (săn wŏ·kēn′). A river in California; also, the valley through which it flows.

San′ta Fe′ (săn′ta fā′). The capital of New Mexico. Founded in 1605, it was long an important center in the Southwest.

378

San'ta Fe' (săn'tᴀ fā') **Trail.** A route to the West, starting in western Missouri and running to Santa Fe. It was used especially from 1821–1880.

Sault Sainte Ma·rie' (sōō sȧnt mᴀ·rē'). The rapids of the St. Mary's River between northern Michigan and Ontario, Canada.

scep'ti·cal (skĕp'tĭ·kăl), *adj*. Inclined to show disbelief.

Schnei'der (shnī'dĕr), **Father.** A priest from Germany who established, at Goshenhoppen, a school for children of all creeds.

Schu'bert (shōō'bĕrt), **Franz.** A famous Austrian composer.

Sem'i·nole (sĕm'ĭ·nōl). An Indian of a tribe, originally a part of the Creeks. *See* Creek.

se·ra'pe (sĕ·rä'pā), *n*. A blanket or shawl worn as an outer garment by South Americans.

Se'ton (sē't'n), **Mother.** Foundress of the Sisters of Charity.

Sev'ern (sĕv'ĕrn). A river in Maryland. The United States Naval Academy is situated on its banks.

sham'bles (shăm'b'lz), *n*. A place or scene of slaughter.

Shaw·nee' (shô·nē'). At one time, a warlike Indian tribe, living in the area of Tennessee and South Carolina.

Shi'loh (shī'lō). The site of the second major engagement of the Civil War.

ship of the line, *n*. In old times, a ship of war large enough to be in the line of battle.

Short' horn' (shôrt' hôrn'). An animal of a red, white, and roan breed of cattle.

Sic'i·ly (sĭs'ĭ·lĭ). An Italian island, southwest of Italy. Many people from Sicily have immigrated to the United States.

Si·er'ras (sĭ·ĕr'ȧz). A mountain range in eastern California. The complete name is Sierra Nevada.

Sioux (sōō). A member of one of the most important tribes of North American Indians.

Si'wash (sī'wŏsh). An Indian of the northern Pacific coast.

Skag'way (skăg'wā). A city in Alaska, founded during the gold rush.

skulk'ing (skŭlk'ĭng), *v*. 1. To hide in a sneaking manner. 2. To shirk.

snare (snâr) **drum,** *n*. A small drum with strings of catgut stretched over its end.

sod house, *n*. A shelter with walls built of sod or turf. Pioneers often used this type of shelter until a better home could be built.

so·lic'i·tude (sŏ·lĭs'ĭ·tūd), *n*. Worry; concern.

som·bre'ro (sŏm·brā'rō), *n*. A broad-brimmed hat, originally worn in Spanish countries.

Sons of Liberty. A patriotic society formed in the years before the Revolutionary War. It was active in working for American independence.

so·phis'ti·cat'ed (sŏ·fĭs'tĭ·kāt'ĕd), *adj*. No longer simple.

spec'u·la'tive·ly (spĕk'ū·là'tĭv·lĭ), *adv*. In a thoughtful manner.

sphe'roid (sfē̞r'oid), *n*. Something shaped like a sphere or a globe.

spin'et (spĭn'ĕt), *n*. A small piano-like instrument, no longer in use.

spleen (splēn), *n*. Anger; spite; malice.

spliced (splīst), *v*. 1. Joined together, as two ropes, by weaving the strands together. 2. Joined as two timbers, by lapping the two ends.

split (splĭt), *n*. In fancy dancing, a movement by which the body is lowered to the floor with legs extended sideways.

Spring'field (sprĭng'fēld). Capital of Illinois; home of Abraham Lincoln.

stage sta'tion, *n*. A stopping-place along the route of a stagecoach where fresh horses, supplies, etc., could be obtained.

stam'i·na (stăm'ĭ·nᴀ), *n*. Endurance or capacity for endurance.

Stark (stärk), **John.** An American Revolutionary officer.

Stars and Bars. The first flag adopted by the Confederate States. It had three bars, of red, white, and red, and a blue field with white stars.

states'man·ship (stāts'măn·shĭp, *n*. The quality of showing unusual wisdom in treating or directing great public affairs.

staunch (stônch), *adj*. Firm; strong; steadfast.

stay'sail (stā's'l), *n*. Any sail on a stay; a strong rope or wire used to support a mast.

ste've·dore' (stē'vĕ·dōr'), *n*. A person whose work it is to load or unload vessels.

stint (stĭnt), *n*. A quantity or task assigned.

stow (stō) **away,** *v*. To conceal onself on a vessel, train, aircraft, etc., during a passage.

sub·due' (sŭb·dū'), *v*. To conquer; to vanquish. 2. To reduce or soften in intensity.

Sul·pi'cian (sŭl·pĭsh'ᴀn). One of an Order of priests established in France to teach men for the priesthood.

Sum'ner (sŭm'nĕr), **Charles.** One of the leaders of the anti-slavery group in Congress.

sup'pli·cate (sŭp'lĭ·kāt), *v*. To make a humble entreaty; to pray.

Ta·hi'ti (tä·hē'tê). One of the Society Islands of the South Pacific Ocean.

Ta'ney (tô'nĭ), **Roger Brooke.** A lawyer from Maryland who later became a Chief Justice of the Supreme Court of the United States.

---

lāte, alwăys, ăm, ăppear, ärm, ȧsk, câre, hē, ênough, nĕt, silĕnt, makĕr, hȩre, ride, ĭn, possĭble, ōld, ôbey, nŏt, cŏnnect, sŏft, hôrse, ūse, ûnite, ŭs, circŭs, bûrn, mōōn, tŏŏk, oil, out, ~~that~~, thin, natų̄re, verdų̄re, boɴ.

Ta'os (tä'ōs). A village in New Mexico, formerly an important trading center on the Santa Fe Trail.

tar·pau'lin (tär·pô'lĭn), *n.* Canvas covered with waterproof material, and used as a protective covering.

Te·cum'seh (tê·kŭm'sĕ). A chief of the Shawnee Indians. A statue of Tecumseh stands on the grounds of the United States Naval Academy. It is a tradition for midshipmen to toss pennies at the statue to insure passing their exams.

tem'po (tĕm'pō), *n.* Rate of activity in general.

ten'der (tĕn'dēr), *v.* To offer.

ten'ta·cle (tĕn'tá·k'l), *n.* One of the long, thin, flexible projections from the head or mouth of some insects and sea creatures.

Te·re'sa (tĕ·rē'sá) **of A'vi·la** (ä'vĕ·lä), **Saint.** A Carmelite nun; founded reformed order of Carmelites.

Thé'rèse' (tā'râz'), **Mother.** Mother Superior of the Ursulines in New Orleans in 1804.

Ti'con·der·o'ga (tī'kŏn·dēr·ō'gá). A fort at the head of Lake Champlain. During the Revolutionary War it was the scene of much action. *See* Ethan Allen, John Burgoyne.

tide'wa'ter (tīd'wô'tēr), *n.* Water flowing onto the land at high tide. Thus, the country bordering the coast is sometimes referred to as "tidewater country."

To·le'do (tô·lē'dō). A city in Spain. Its great Gothic cathedral dates from the 13th century.

top'sail (tŏp's'l), *n.* The sail above the lowermost sail on a mast.

tour (tŏŏr), *n.* One's turn in an orderly schedule.

trans·fig'ure (trăns·fĭg'ûr), *v.* To change in appearance or form; to transform.

trap (trăp), *n.* A device for throwing balls or other objects into the air to be targets for shooters.

Treas'ur·y (trĕzh'ēr·ĭ). The building housing the governmental department that has charge of government funds. The Treasury is next door to the White House, just across a narrow drive.

Tren'ton (trĕn't'n). The scene of an important battle during the Revolutionary War, where Washington crossed the Delaware for a surprise attack against the enemy.

troup'er (trŏŏp'ēr), *n.* A member of a group of actors, singers, performers.

truce (trŏŏs), *n.* A cessation of fighting. A **flag of truce** is a white flag, which, when displayed to an enemy signifies the desire to make some communication, not hostile.

two bits, *n.* Twenty-five cents, or a quarter dollar. A term frequently used in the West.

un·al'ien·a·ble (ŭn·āl'yĕn·á·b'l), *adj.* Not capable of being given up or transferred. Usually spelled *inalienable*.

un·de·filed' (ŭn·dê·fīld'), *adj.* Pure, stainless.

under and out. In broadcasting, to play music as background of conversation for several measures.

un·kempt' (ŭn·kĕmpt'), *adj.* 1. Not combed; tousled. 2. Not refined; rough and uncouth.

un·reck'oned (ŭn·rĕk'ŭnd), *adj.* Not counted upon; unexpected.

up and out. In broadcasting, to play the music alone for several measures.

up and under. In broadcasting, to begin music alone and then continue as background for conversation.

up'draft' (ŭp'drȧft'), *n.* An upward movement of gas, air, or the like.

up'wind' (ŭp'wĭnd'), *adv.* With face or course against the wind.

u·ra'ni·um (û·rā'nĭ·ŭm), *n.* A valuable metal used in the manufacture of atomic energy.

Ur'su·line (ûr'sû·lĭn). An Order of nuns, originally established in France. The Ursulines founded the first convent of nuns in what is now the United States in New Orleans in 1727.

Val'la·do·lid' (väl'yä·~~thō·lēth~~'). A city in Spain.

Val·ley Forge (fôrj). A small locality in Pennsylvania, where Washington and his army camped during the winter of 1777–78.

Val'pa·rai'so (văl'pá·rā'zō). A seaport in Chile.

van'dal·ism (văn'dȧl·ĭz'm), *n.* The spirit or acts of vandals; reckless destructiveness.

va·que'ro (vä·kā'rō), *n.* A Spanish word, meaning *cowboy*. The term is frequently heard in Southwestern United States.

ven'er·a·ble (vĕn'ēr·á·b'l), *adj.* Worthy of respect and reverence; generally implying an advanced age.

Vicks'burg (vĭks'bûrg). A city in Tennessee, the object of siege by Union troops during the Civil War.

Vin·cennes' (vĭn·sĕnz'). A French settlement in what is now the state of Indiana.

vin'tage (vĭn'tĭj), *n.* 1. A season's harvest of the vine. 2. The act of gathering grapes for harvest.

Vir·gin'ia (vēr·jĭn'yá) **City.** A settlement in Montana; the site of the Comstock Lode.

vis'i·bil'i·ty (vĭz'ĭ·bĭl'ĭ·tĭ), *n.* The range of clearness in the air through which one sees.

vis'age (vĭs'ĭj), *n.* The face or appearance of a person.

Vive le Con'gress (vēv lē kŏng'grĕs). A French expression meaning *long live Congress*.

vo'ya·geur' (vwȧ'yȧ·zhûr'), *n.* A French word meaning *traveler*. 1. A man hired by fur companies to transport men and goods to and from distant stations. 2. Any boatman or trapper of the Great Lakes region.

Ward, Ar'te·mus (wôrd, är'tê·mŭs). The pen name of an American humorist, Charles F. Browne.

ward'room' (wôrd'rōōm'), *n.* The space in a war vessel, allotted for living quarters, to officers above the rank of ensign.

war'rant (wŏr'ănt), *n.* A written order, issued by lawful authority, directing an officer of the law to make an arrest, a search, or the like.

watch fire, *n.* A fire lighted at night, as a signal, or for the use of a watch or guard.

Web'ster (wĕb'stēr), **Daniel.** An American statesman, famous for his skill as an orator.

Whit'man (hwĭt'măn), **Marcus.** An American missionary and pioneer. He worked chiefly in Oregon where he, his wife, and twelve other persons were massacred by Indians.

Wich'i·ta (wĭch'ĭ·tô). An American Indian tribe, formerly living in the Middle West and Southwest.

Wig'wam (wĭg'wŏm), *n.* A large temporary building used for a political convention.

Wil'der·ness (wĭl'dēr·nĕs) **Road.** A road from eastern Virginia, through the Cumberland Gap and central Kentucky to the Ohio River. The trail was blazed and cleared by Daniel Boone; later used by pioneers to the West.

Wil·lam'ette (wĭ·lăm'ĕt) **River.** A river in Oregon, flowing north into the Columbia River near Portland.

Wil'liams·burg (wĭl'yămz·bûrg). A city in Virginia; during the Revolutionary War, the capital and political, educational, and social center of Virginia.

winch (wĭnch), *n.* A machine having a roller or rollers on which rope is coiled for hauling or hoisting. It is operated by a crank.

Win'ches'ter ri'fle (wĭn'chĕs'tēr rī'fl'). A widely used rifle.

wing and rifle shot, *n.* One skilled in shooting, with a rifle, birds on the wing.

wran'gler (răng'glēr) *n.* A cowboy, especially one who works on the range, rounding up livestock, etc.

Yel'low·stone' (yĕl'ô·stōn'). A river in Wyoming and Montana.

York'town (yôrk'toun). A town in Virginia, the scene of Cornwallis's surrender to George Washington.

Young (yŭng), **Brigham.** Leader of the Mormon colonists in Utah.

Zieg'feld (zĭg'fĕld) **Follies.** A theatrical "revue," popular during the first quarter of the 20th century; produced by Florenz Ziegfeld. The productions were lavish and featured the top stars of the day.

Zeus (zūs). The chief of the Greek gods.

Zu'lu·land' (zōō'lōō·lănd'). A territory in the Union of South Africa.

---

lāte, alwăys, ăm, ăppear, ärm, ȧsk, câre, hē, ĕnough, nĕt, silĕnt, makēr, hẹre, rīde, ĭn, possĭble, ōld, ȯbey, nŏt, cŏnnect, sŏft, hôrse, ūse, ûnite, ŭs, circŭs, bûrn, mōōn, tŏŏk, oil, out, ~~that~~, thin, natụre, verdụre, boN.